The Man Who Killed Martin Luther King

The Man Who Killed Martin Luther King

The Life and Crimes of James Earl Ray

Mel Ayton

FRONTLINE
BOOKS

An imprint of
Pen & Sword Books Ltd
Yorkshire – Philadelphia

FRONTLINE
BOOKS

First published in Great Britain in 2023 by

Frontline Books
an imprint of Pen & Sword Books Ltd,
47 Church Street, Barnsley, S. Yorkshire, S70 2AS

ISBN 978 1 39908 138 2

Typeset in Chennai, India
by Lapiz Digital Services.

Printed and bound by CPI Group (UK) Ltd, Croydon, CR0 4YY

Pen & Sword Books Ltd incorporates the imprints of Pen & Sword Archaeology, Atlas, Aviation, Battleground, Discovery, Family History, History, Maritime, Military, Naval, Politics, Social History, Transport, True Crime, Claymore Press, Frontline Books, Praetorian Press, Seaforth Publishing and White Owl

For a complete list of Pen & Sword titles please contact

PEN & SWORD BOOKS LTD
47 Church Street, Barnsley, South Yorkshire, S70 2AS, England
E-mail: enquiries@pen-and-sword.co.uk
Website: www.pen-and-sword.co.uk

Or

PEN AND SWORD BOOKS
1950 Lawrence Rd, Havertown, PA 19083, USA
E-mail: Uspen-and-sword@casematepublishers.com
Website: www.penandswordbooks.com

Contents

Timeline

23 April 1967
James Earl Ray escapes from Missouri State Penitentiary. His brother John is supposed to meet up with him, but communications become tangled. James spends five days walking at night and sleeping by day, eventually arriving in St Louis. John and James Ray take a Greyhound bus to Chicago to meet their younger brother Jerry at the Fairview Hotel.

3 May 1967
Ray answers an ad for a dishwashing job at the Indian Trails Restaurant, North Sheffield Avenue, Chicago. After three weeks he buys a 1959 Chrysler.

13 July 1967
Ray and his brothers rob a bank of $27,000 in Alton, Illinois.

14 July 1967
Ray sells his Chrysler for $45.

'Early July' 1967
Ray and his brother Jerry rob a 'gambling joint' in Chicago.

17 July 1967
Ray leaves his dishwashing job and, after buying a 1962 Plymouth, drives to Montreal, Canada.

25 August 1967
Ray returns to Chicago and transfers ownership of his car to his brother Jerry.

26 August 1967
Ray is in Birmingham, Alabama, and purchases a Mustang car. He spends seven weeks in Birmingham.

7 October 1967
Ray drives to Mexico where he hopes to start a porn business by hiring local prostitutes in Puerto Vallarta. He spends the next five weeks there.

18 November 1967
Ray arrives in Los Angeles.

15 December 1967
Ray drives to New Orleans as a favour to a woman he met in Los Angeles. He is in the city from 17–19 December.

19 December 1967
Ray returns to Los Angeles and is there until 17 March 1968 when he returns east to stalk Martin Luther King.

February 1968
Jerry Ray arranges a meeting with his brother James in New Orleans for March 1968.

20 March 1968
Ray arrives in New Orleans. Sometime between 2 and 19 March he tells a fellow student at the dance school he attends he was going to meet 'his brother' in Birmingham.

22 March 1968
Ray is in Selma, Alabama, after dropping off a package for his friend's daughters in New Orleans. King is scheduled to visit Selma, but the Civil Rights leader changes his plans.

24 March 1968
Ray drives to Atlanta, Georgia, where he rents a room.

29 March 1968
James and Jerry drive to Birmingham where James purchases a .243 calibre Remington rifle at the Aeromarine Supply Company.

31 March 1968
Ray returns to Atlanta, Georgia, and marks places on a map where King works and lives.

3 April 1968
John Ray meets with his brother James the night before the assassination in West Memphis, Arkansas, across the Mississippi River from Memphis, Tennessee.

4 April 1968

From Memphis television news broadcasts and a morning newspaper – the *Commercial Appeal* – James Earl Ray discovers that Martin Luther King is staying at the Lorraine Motel, Room 306. Ray is staying at the New Rebel Motel, Memphis. He discovers that Bessie Brewer's Rooming House is across the street from the Lorraine Motel and checks in using the name John Willard.

3.30pm Ray is offered Room 8 but asks for Room 5b because it affords him a view of the Lorraine Motel.

4pm Ray purchases a pair of binoculars at the York Arms Company for $41.55, and returns to his room at Bessie Brewer's. Ray keeps watch on Martin Luther King's Lorraine Motel room by leaning out of his window using the binoculars. Ray discovers that the bathroom window, a few short steps from his room, has the better line of sight to King's motel room.

5.55pm Martin Luther King and Revd Ralph Abernathy exit their hotel rooms after changing for dinner. Emerging from his room, King lingers on the balcony to talk to his driver Solomon Jones and his young aide Jesse Jackson in the courtyard below.

6.01pm King is shot in the head and wounded badly. Ray leaves the bathroom, throws his rifle in a rifle box, bundles up his possessions in a green blanket then departs his room. Exiting the Main Street door of the rooming house he spots a police car and drops his bundle in the doorway of Canipe's Amusement Store. He is spotted by two patrons of Canipe's who observe one man in a white Mustang, tyres screeching, drive away.

6.03pm The shooting is radioed to police headquarters.

6.09pm Barely alive, King is rushed to St Joseph's Hospital, accompanied by Abernathy and escorted by several police on motorcycles. At 7.05pm he is pronounced dead.

8.15pm By this time, Ray has travelled into Alabama where he will empty the Mustang of his belongings, dumping his expensive film equipment in a ditch by the side of the road.

Race riots break out in major black neighbourhoods in more than 110 US cities.

5 April 1968

Ray arrives in Atlanta after travelling on back roads. He abandons his white Mustang after wiping it clean of fingerprints. After retrieving a few things from his room, Ray boards a Greyhound bus to Detroit. The FBI traces the rifle to the Aeromarine Supply Company in Birmingham and finds the receipt signed by a Harvey Lowmeyer.

6 April 1968

From Detroit, Ray takes a taxi across the Canadian border.

8 April 1968

Ray rents a room in a Toronto boarding house and attempts to get a Canadian passport. His goal is to fly to Rhodesia, a segregated country he sees as a place of refuge where he will be protected and celebrated for his deed. Arrangements for his passport are made by a travel agency.

6–10 April 1968

The FBI traces laundry tags on Ray's shirt and shorts to Home Service Laundry in Los Angeles, who tells them the name on the receipt is Eric S. Galt. They also trace a pair of pliers to a hardware store, two blocks from Home Service Laundry.

11 April 1968

The FBI finds a white Ford Mustang registered to Eric Galt in an Atlanta parking lot. Through a sticker on the Mustang's window, the FBI realize the car was serviced in Los Angeles the previous February. The garage's records give the address for Ray's Serrano apartment in Los Angeles.

Further investigation into Eric S. Galt reveals that Galt took dancing lessons. This information, when coupled with the fact that Galt's Mustang was traced to Los Angeles, led investigators to a photograph of Eric Starvo Galt at a dance studio in Los Angeles.

Finding Ray's old boarding house in Birmingham, the FBI gets more information on the Mustang. They locate and contact the car's previous owner.

Los Angeles post-office records reveal that Galt moved from the Serrano apartment to St Francis, and that he put in a change of address on 17 March for Atlanta.

12–16 April 1968
The FBI obtains a photo of Eric Galt from the International School of Bartending. Investigators examine all money orders recently purchased in Los Angeles, and find one from Galt to the Locksmithing Institute. The FBI discovers that Ray completed his first locksmithing lesson in Montreal, and a later lesson in Atlanta, where a local address is listed.

Searching Galt's room in Atlanta, the FBI finds a map of Atlanta with pencil markings showing he stalked King's movements. Four places are circled on the map – Ebenezer Baptist Church, SCLC headquarters, King's home and the Capitol Homes housing projects. The map also provides detectives with a clear left thumbprint.

17 April 1968
Investigators have begun to believe that one man using various aliases committed the murder, as all the prints left behind belonged to a single man. Hoover orders fingerprint comparisons with all known fugitives in the country – a collection of over 53,000 prints. At around the 700th fingerprint detectives find a match – James Earl Ray. The FBI immediately distributes Ray's name and mugshot on posters around the country, announcing that Eric Starvo Galt is in fact Ray.

19 April 1968
Investigators include both Mexican and Canadian authorities in the case, as the FBI has proof that Ray visited both countries after his escape from Missouri State Penitentiary in April 1967.

24 April 1968
Ray obtains a passport from Canada under the name of Ramon George Sneyd and purchases a roundtrip ticket from Toronto to London.

6 May 1968
Ray flies to London and then exchanges his return ticket to Canada for a new ticket to Lisbon, Portugal. His ultimate destination is Rhodesia, Africa, where he wants to become a mercenary. Rhodesia, which will become Zimbabwe in 1980, observes no extradition treaty with the United States.

7 May 1968
Ray arrives in Portugal and learns he had missed a boat to Africa by just two days. Despite running out of money, Ray decides against robbing a bank

in Portugal because he is not conversant with the language. He decides to return to London where he believes robbing a bank will be easier.

17 May 1968

Ray arrives in London, looking for another way into Rhodesia. With money running low, Ray decides to carry out an armed robbery using his pistol.

27 May 1968

Ray attempts to rob a Paddington jewellery store owned by Maurice and Billie Isaacs. After encountering unexpected resistance from the Isaacs, Ray takes off down the street, empty handed.

1 June 1968

The Royal Canadian Mounted Police find a match between the photograph of Eric Galt and a passport application for a 'Ramon George Sneyd'. Investigators track the information on the passport to 962 Dundas Street, where Ray had used the alias Paul Bridgman before he left the country. Sneyd's passport enables investigators to then track Ray's trail from Toronto to London to Portugal and back to London. The FBI releases Ray's name and an updated list of aliases to airports around the world for the 'Watch and Detain' list.

4 June 1968

Ray attempts to rob the Trustee Savings Bank in Fulham, England, but is startled when the teller accidentally kicks a metal box, producing a sound similar to a gunshot. Ray runs from the bank with £95, the equivalent of $240.

8 June 1968

At Heathrow Airport Ray attempts to buy a ticket on European Airways Flight 466 to Brussels, Belgium, where he hopes to meet up with mercenary soldiers operating out of the city. An immigration officer spots Ray's two passports and, concerned, finds 'Ramon George Sneyd' on the 'Watch for and Detain' list. Ray is quickly arrested and the FBI immediately begins the process for extradition.

19 July 1968

James Earl Ray is extradited to Memphis.

10 November 1968

After Ray learns that his lawyer Arthur Hanes believes he faces no chance of acquittal, he fires him. Two days later, in an interview for *Look* magazine, Ray alleges that a fellow criminal named Raoul was the perpetrator and actual assassin of King. Ray argues he was simply the getaway driver.

11 February 1969

Ray hires Percy Foreman as his new attorney, a Texas lawyer who was famous for defending 778 accused murders and successfully acquitting 705 of them. However, after listening to his client for over 30 hours, Foreman tells Ray that his case is hopeless. Ray finally agrees to plead guilty.

10 March 1969

James Earl Ray pleads guilty to killing Martin Luther King Jr and is sentenced to ninety-nine years in Brushy Mountain State Penitentiary in Tennessee.

13 March 1969

Ray recants his plea, claiming he was coerced into giving a guilty plea. Ray will maintain his innocence for the rest of his life and will come up with various conspiracy theories explaining King's assassination.

23 April 1998

James Earl Ray dies in prison from kidney and liver disease at age 70. His liver failure is caused by the hepatitis C he contracted from blood transfusions received after being stabbed in prison.

Introduction

James Earl Ray's most successful crime was not his murder of Martin Luther King Jr., because for that crime he was imprisoned for life. No, Ray's most successful crime was the huge and grotesque historical scam that he triumphantly perpetrated upon the King family during the last year of his life. Having destroyed, irretrievably, the surviving family members' credibility, it remains to be seen whether King's own long-term legacy has also been harmed and diminished by the foolishness of his widow and children.

Professor David J. Garrow,
University of Pittsburgh School of Law[1]

Martin Luther King's assassination is a subject that remains contemporary and the circumstances of his death mirror the racial preoccupations of US society. Even today as African Americans take to the streets protesting that King's dream of racial justice has not been fulfilled the fatal shot that killed King still echoes across a racially divided nation he dreamed of uniting.

The case also remains contemporary with many Americans who continue to ask questions about the manner of King's death. In 2019 a group of 'concerned citizens' was formed, the Truth and Reconciliation Committee (TRC). The TRC membership includes numerous Hollywood celebrities such as Oliver Stone, Alec Baldwin and Martin Sheen, and RFK and MLK family members Robert F. Kennedy Jr and MLK's nephew Isaac Newton Farris Jr who believe the assassinations of Martin Luther King, John F. Kennedy, Robert F. Kennedy and Malcolm X were the result of conspiracies and covered up by the government.[2]

In 2018 Bernice King, the youngest of Martin Luther King's four children and the executive director of the King Centre in Atlanta, said, 'It pains my heart that James Earl Ray had to spend his life in prison paying for things he didn't do.'[3] King's two other surviving children Dexter and Martin III concurred with their sister that Ray was innocent. Even today, many black leaders hold that view. 'I think there was a major conspiracy to remove Doctor King from the American scene,' Congressman John Lewis said shortly before his death. 'I don't know what happened, but the truth of what happened to Dr. King should be made available for history's sake.'[4]

From the start, King's aides voiced suspicions that a conspiracy was responsible for their leader's death and following convicted assassin James Earl Ray's plea, in which he accepted a ninety-nine-year prison sentence to avoid execution, there was a feeling that the American people had been robbed of a proper trial in which all issues surrounding the tragedy had not been thoroughly examined. King's widow Coretta Scott King voiced her suspicions about a conspiracy shortly after her husband was murdered and continued to do so long after. 'There is abundant evidence,' Coretta King said in 1999, 'of a major, high-level conspiracy in the assassination of my husband . . .'.[5]

The fact that no one had actually seen Ray shoot King was a problem. Some witnesses were not consistent with their stories and the circumstantial and ballistics evidence in the case provided opportunities for Ray's defenders to claim that there was 'reasonable doubt' as to the assassin's guilt.

Conspiracists, who never accepted the conclusion that a 'lone assassin' killed JFK, refused to accept the official version by the FBI and Memphis authorities that Ray was the assassin and had not been part of any type of conspiracy.

As the 1970s progressed purported conspiracy theories involving the US government, and other similar theories about the JFK assassination became accepted by many Americans especially after government investigations into the illegal activities of the FBI disclosed that FBI Director J. Edgar Hoover had carried out a vendetta against King during the 1960s.

Accordingly, pressure built which persuaded the US Congress that the assassinations should be re-investigated. The House Select Committee on Assassinations (HSCA) was formed and spent three years investigating the King and Kennedy assassinations between 1976 and 1979. The 1979 report concluded that James Earl Ray had been the assassin but there was a possibility that he had been part of a conspiracy organized by racists. However, Justice Department officials, responding to the HSCA's report, could find no solid evidence with which to charge anyone with conspiring with Ray to kill King. Suspects were named, two wealthy and racially inspired St Louis businessmen, and evidence was provided which concluded they had offered a 'bounty' on King's head. However, both men had died years before the inquiry began.

Conspiracists criticized the HSCA report calling it biased and heavily reliant on the word of government agencies like the FBI and CIA. They insisted that the evidence in the case did not prove Ray's guilt and most conspiracy writers, including Ray's lawyer William Pepper, insisted that Ray had been set up to take the fall. The plot had been organized, Pepper said, by the FBI/CIA/Military/Mafia or any combination of these groups. Some authors go so far as to accuse President Johnson of complicity in the crime.

In the mid to late 1990s, a number of other events helped to keep the King assassination in the public eye. In 1997 ballistics tests on the rifle used in the shooting proved inconclusive. And, in the same year, the youngest son of Martin Luther King sat face to face with James Earl Ray to hear his explanation of what happened to his father. With the blessings of King's widow Coretta Scott King and the other King children, Dexter King shook James Earl Ray's hand and professed belief in his innocence. 'I just want to ask you for the record,' Dexter King said, 'did you kill my father?' Ray replied, 'No, I didn't, no.' Then Ray added, 'But, like I say, sometimes these questions are difficult to answer … sometimes you have to make your own evaluation and maybe come to the conclusion. I think that could be done today, but not 30 years ago …'. Dexter King declared, 'As awkward as it may seem, I believe you, and my family believes you … and we will do everything in our power to see you prevail'.[6]

After the two men had spoken for about 20 minutes, the room was cleared and they spoke privately. Dexter King later made the stunning claim that James Earl Ray's lawyer William Pepper had been correct in claiming the federal government had plotted his father's slaying to silence the Civil Rights leader's opposition to the Vietnam War. Dexter King also said that President Johnson was part of the plot.

The conspiracists' hysteria peaked in 1999 when Loyd Jowers, the owner of 'Jim's Grill' situated below Ray's Memphis rooming house from which the shot that killed King was fired, was tried in a civil court for his alleged participation in the plot. This was the most disturbing event in the whole conspiracy saga.

Jowers had claimed he was paid $100,000 to hire an assassin - and the man hired was not Ray but a Memphis Police Department officer. Jowers had refused to name the person he believed had murdered King but insisted it was not Ray. He told of how the fatal shot had been fired from the bushes behind his restaurant and across the street from the balcony of the Lorraine

Motel where King was standing when he was shot. The killer, he said, handed him the rifle moments after the assassination. Jowers said he gave the weapon to another unidentified conspirator the next day.

Although author Gerald Posner had debunked much of the speculative accounts of the assassination in his ground-breaking 1998 book *Killing the Dream*, the conspiracy hysteria continued unabated and peaked in 1999 when Jowers was enlisted by Pepper and tried in a civil court for his alleged participation in the plot. William Pepper was quick to enlist Jowers in the idea that Ray was innocent and began to make elaborate plans to put him on trial. In 1999 Pepper persuaded the King family to sue Jowers in a wrongful death lawsuit. The fact that Jowers had confessed to the killing on national television bolstered their case. (In civil trials the suit is brought by an individual plaintiff or group of plaintiffs instead of the state. The plaintiffs must merely show 'a preponderance of evidence' against the defendant, rather than prove 'beyond a reasonable doubt' that a crime was committed, as in a criminal trial.)

During the 'trial' many witnesses called by Pepper experienced a remarkable improvement in memory and gave different testimonies from the ones they had originally provided to the Shelby County prosecutors and the FBI. The witnesses gave succour to Pepper's thesis that the order to kill King was issued by the Mafia who enlisted Jowers to hire an assassin then hide the murder weapon after the assassination. The Memphis Police would assist them in the commission of the crime with the assistance of a US Army sniper team put in place near the Lorraine Motel to shoot King if the Mafia hit failed. Pepper called witnesses who claimed that King's police protection was pulled back moments before the shooting; that army agents had him under surveillance and that the real assassin, a mysterious killer called Raoul, was allowed to flee the scene of the crime. Pepper maintained that James Earl Ray had been an innocent 'patsy'.

Incredibly, Jowers' lawyer Lewis Garrison gave a half-hearted defence of his client and told the jury that while they could reasonably conclude King was the victim of a conspiracy, his client's role was minor at best. Garrison agreed with the plaintiffs on numerous claims made by Pepper and agreed with him there had been a conspiracy involving the US government, the Memphis police and the State of Tennessee. The 73-year-old Jowers, who had never repeated his 1993 claim but had never recanted it either, was ill for much of the trial and did not testify.

In December 1999, the jury, which consisted of six black and six white jurors, took 3 hours to reach their verdict of a conspiracy involving Jowers. This was hardly surprising, considering that Jowers' lawyer never disputed most of the evidence presented by King's lawyers. As the jury heard no evidence to rebut the conspiracy theory, it was inevitable they would return a verdict favourable to Pepper and the King family.

The Kings, who had sought unspecified damages, were awarded a token $100. They had merely wanted the verdict to lend support to their call for a fresh investigation. There was no demand that Jowers receive a prison sentence and he continued to be a free man.

Following the trial, the King family persuaded President Clinton to reopen the investigation. In announcing a new inquiry, in August 1998, Attorney General Janet Reno said, 'We hope this review will provide answers to new questions that have been raised about a tragedy that still haunts our nation.'[7]

The 'limited investigation' was completed in 2000 and the Justice Department issued its report on the King slaying. The report stated that the recent allegations about a government-led conspiracy to kill King, which had arisen during the Jowers trial, were baseless. Conspiracists responded accordingly and reiterated their demand for a fully-fledged commission, independent of government, to investigate the assassination.

The conclusions of the new investigation were rejected by the King family. They insisted Ray was innocent and he should be given the proper trial he never had. Their support for Ray continued into the new millennium even after Ray's death in 1998 from complications caused by hepatitis C. Their support for William Pepper and James Earl Ray was met with incredulity by many historians including King Pulitzer Prize-winning biographer David Garrow. 'Martin Luther King Jr. often preached that "No lie can live forever,"' Garrow wrote, 'but if his faith is ever to prevail, then all the lies that distort the truth about his death must be not only discredited, but also recanted.'[8]

* * *

Writers who have advocated a government-led conspiracy involving the FBI and other police and government agencies have clearly ignored the lessons of history as the present author argues in this book. In an era when governments have become notoriously prone to leaks and are not capable of faultless operations of mind-boggling complexity the claims of the conspiracy theorists become absurd. It is impossible to put together an obviously illegal operation with hundreds of people and keep it quiet. The risk of a leak and deathbed confessions from credible and reliable sources is omnipresent. In the decades following the end of the Second World War revelations about the Pentagon Papers, the Watergate Scandal, the CIA-Castro scandals and the numerous stories about the ineptitude and financial corruption of government departments and financial institutions place the allegations made by conspiracists into a world of fantasy.

The conspiracy claims about a government-organized plan to rid the country of a bothersome Civil Rights leader are directly contradicted by empirical evidence. Recent government and independent investigations to date have not revealed any smoking gun proof that the FBI and government agencies knew more than they have thus far publicly disclosed about the murder. However, the murder investigations did reveal that the nation's top law-enforcement agency did much to create a climate of suspicion and hate toward the Civil Rights movement that made a sick, demented Ray think it was perfectly right to squeeze off the fatal shot against the movement's greatest symbol.

This was no preposterous 'Deep State' conspiracy to kill the Civil Rights leader. It was, nonetheless, a conspiracy organized by James Earl Ray and others. The definition of 'conspiracy' in Tennessee is, 'a person may be convicted of the crime of Conspiracy if the state prosecutor proves beyond a reasonable doubt that two or more people: Acted for the purpose of promoting or facilitating the commission of an offense; (and) Agreed that one or more of them would engage in conduct that constitutes the offense'.[9] By these standards the men who assisted James Earl Ray in the commission of his crime are clearly guilty of participating in a 'conspiracy'.[10]

John Campbell, who investigated the case for years in the Shelby County, Tennessee, district attorney's office, said, 'I'm not saying James Earl Ray didn't have help. But he didn't have the FBI, the CIA, the Memphis police or the Mafia.'[11]

As the reader will discover, the evidence presented in this book reveals how James Earl Ray was assisted in the commission of his crime and it is the key to an understanding of how and why Martin Luther King was murdered.

Chapter 1

The FBI and Martin Luther King

King is a tomcat with obsessive degenerate sexual urges.

[King is] one of the lowest characters in the country.

[King is] the most notorious liar in America.

Based on King's recent activities and public utterances, it is clear that he is an instrument in the hands of subversive forces seeking to undermine our nation.

I don't like the man. I've said so publicly and I had him up here for forty-five minutes and told him so privately. I don't think he's a good man.

Comments made by FBI Director J. Edgar Hoover

In the years following King's murder on 4 April 1968 in Memphis Tennessee, the mythologizing and reverence for the Civil Rights leader grew. During the 1970s Congressional investigations into the FBI and CIA revealed how the FBI had abused its charter by committing illegal activities in its surveillance of dissident groups across the United States.

One of the FBI's targets was Martin Luther King who J. Edgar Hoover, Director of the FBI, tried to destroy by blackmail, wiretapping and bugging the Civil Rights leader's hotel rooms. It was an act of scandalous proportions and enhanced the image of King as a martyr to his cause. The revelations about the FBI's targeting of King also became central to an understanding of why the agency has been accused by conspiracy authors and defenders of King's assassin of orchestrating his murder. The revelations about the FBI's illegal activities with regard to King promoted the idea that Hoover hated the Civil Rights leader so much he would go to any lengths to rid the United States of a 'Black Messiah'.

The investigations into illegal FBI activities revealed that King's private life was anything but chaste. And during the 1970s and 1980s research by independent writers and authors began to chronicle the true facts behind King's academic career and writings; research that revealed that King had borrowed heavily from other writers for his PhD thesis, speeches and books.[1]

The FBI's excuse for keeping tabs on King was confirmed as justified in 1977. According to the 1977 Justice Department Task Force which examined the activities of the FBI with regard to King:

> ... it was understandable that a security investigation should be initiated into the possible influence of the Communist Party, U.S.A., on Dr. Martin Luther King Jr. Two of King's close advisers, at the outset of the security matter, were reported to be Communist Party members by sources relied upon by the Bureau. The security investigation continued for almost six years until Dr. King's death. It verified, in our view, that one alleged Communist was a very influential adviser to Dr. King (and hence the Southern Christian Leadership Conference) on the strategy and tactics of King's leadership of the black civil rights movement of the early and mid-sixties.[2]

Pulitzer Prize-winning King biographer David J. Garrow also confirmed the true circumstances of the campaign to discredit King in his 1981 book *The FBI and Martin Luther King Jr – From Solo to Memphis.* Until this time many critics had blamed the years of tapping, bugging and smear-mongering on the reaction of the FBI Director to King's criticism of the Bureau, on Hoover's own racism and on agents' willingness to do Hoover's bidding. Few believed the FBI's official statements that King's organization, the Southern Christian Leadership Conference (SCLC), was being infiltrated by communists.

Hoover's ideas were contemporaneous with a culture in Washington and elsewhere in the nation in which loyalty oaths and blacklists were looked on as acceptable means to combat communism. And nowhere was the pathology caused by anti-communism and the fear of communism more marked than in the FBI departments that targeted 'subversive' groups – groups that included not only the American Communist Party but also Civil Rights groups, anti-war groups and even some entertainment-industry celebrities who were judged to have a corrosive influence on US society. For an organization to be targeted it was not necessary for any laws to be broken. It was chosen purely on the discretion of the FBI Director J. Edgar Hoover, in collusion with his top aides working directly under him.

During the 1960s the FBI had established COINTELPRO, a counter-intelligence programme designed to destroy left-wing organizations and individuals who were deemed to be harmful to the country's national security. Counter-intelligence was a misnomer – the programme was action-oriented or action-initiated rather than a response to subversive groups. It was designed to subvert, embarrass, destroy or otherwise render useless those organizations that were classed by the leadership of the FBI to be 'Un-American', 'communist', 'terrorist' or 'subversive' to the interests of the United States. COINTELPRO has been rightly criticized as illegal and unconstitutional. Yet, the programme was very successful in destroying the Ku Klux Klan and other racist organizations. The FBI planted and turned members into informants and created an atmosphere of suspicion within the Klan groups which eventually led to their demise.[3]

Garrow wrote that the claims of communist infiltration of Martin Luther King's organization the SCLC were justified, at least in the beginning. Researching thousands of FBI documents and conducting his own interviews, Garrow discovered that the FBI had received allegations about a communist at the top of the SCLC and that the charges came from the FBI's most authoritative source inside the US Communist Party.[4] The source was identified as brothers Morris and Jack Childs who had worked undercover for more than twenty-five years in an operation code-named 'SOLO'. The Childs brothers also reported that lawyer Stanley Levison, who had become one of King's top advisers, had assisted with the US Communist Party's financial affairs. The FBI kept Levison under surveillance until 1955 when the brothers reported he had ceased to participate in the US Communist Party's affairs. It was during this period that Levison became an important adviser to Martin Luther King. The FBI took an interest in Levison once more when an informant told the Bureau that Levison had written a major speech for the Civil Rights leader in 1961.

President Kennedy and his brother Attorney General Robert Kennedy warned King about Levison, but they were vague as the FBI would not provide any real substantiation. Nevertheless, Robert Kennedy gave Hoover the go-ahead for the FBI to continue surveillance on King and the FBI Director ordered further monitoring of Levison, King, the SCLC offices in New York and Atlanta and numerous hotel rooms where King was staying.

The surveillance never turned up any concrete evidence that Levison was still connected to the US Communist Party or that he was a dangerous influence on King. However, the surveillance did lead to Hoover's comment that King was an immoral man. The surveillance tapes were given to President Johnson and some Congressmen in an attempt to smear King, but the FBI discovered the media were uninterested.

From the early 1960s to the time of King's death, the FBI attempted to 'neutralize' and 'discredit' the Civil Rights leader. Throughout his travels across the United States King was the subject of electronic surveillance – bugs, or 'misurs' (microphone surveillance), were installed in hotels from coast to coast as the Civil Rights leader became the most targeted FBI subject since Teamsters boss Jimmy Hoffa.

Garrow believed that the FBI's actions reflected not so much a desire to 'get King' but reflected Americans' beliefs, fears about communism, immorality and threats to the political status quo. After the results of the FBI's wiretapping surveillance were revealed to Hoover, he became convinced that King's excessive sexual behaviour left him open to communist blackmail. However, these facts did not persuade a number of historians who insisted that the surveillance on King was motivated by Hoover's racism.

According to one of Hoover's aides, Paul Letersky, 'Despite what critics say, the Bureau's surveillance ... didn't begin because Hoover was trying to uncover sexual dirt on the civil rights leader'.[5] However, after agents reported that King had been engaged in promiscuous behaviour Hoover was outraged. To Hoover, King's activities involving drunken parties and extra-marital sex were disgraceful and the worst sort of hypocrisy. Hoover was highly moralistic and was incensed that a man who was named *TIME* magazine's 'Man of the Year' and a recipient of the Nobel Peace Prize could behave in such a way especially as he held a high moral position as a Christian preacher.[6]

Hoover's attitude on discovering a leader who promoted Christian values – celebrating the importance of family, the sanctity of marriage and the biblical prohibition on sex outside marriage – yet acting in direct contradiction to those values was reflective of what most Americans thought. As historian Thomas C. Reeves wrote, 'Certain basic assumptions about character ... a strong moral sense of right and wrong – ... is derived from our Western heritage and deeply imbedded in our culture. Despite shifting lines of tolerance and permissiveness in recent decades, the vast majority of Americans hold fast to certain basic moral imperatives and can and do tell right from wrong.'[7]

Additionally, Hoover's actions were in keeping with what the US public wanted – action with regard to communists and radicals. In the 1960s the United States was beset by sexual promiscuity, drug use, hippies, draft-resisters, black revolutionaries, student radicals who took over university administration buildings and angry feminists. Hoover saw them as an existential threat to the United States. Goaded by politicians, Hoover responded with whatever means necessary to combat the threat. Additionally, Hoover was exhorted by President Johnson to determine if a powerful Civil Rights movement had been infiltrated by agents of a hostile foreign power.

* * *

There is no denying Hoover went over the top in his desire to rid the country of what he called a 'moral degenerate'. Over the years Hoover and the FBI would wage a virtual war against King – engaging in unethical, quasi-legal and illegal methods like bugging his hotel rooms and pressuring universities not to award him honorary degrees. In December 1963 high-level FBI agents held a meeting to discuss various proposals to 'contain' King's influence. The following month the first of fifteen FBI microphones was installed in King's Atlanta 'hideaway' where he took his girlfriends and various hotels where he stayed when he was away from home.

When King visited Washington with his aides, he stayed at the Willard Hotel where agents had previously installed audio listening devices in two lamps. The Willard was a block from the White House. Later the tapes of the King party's sexual activities were transcribed and handed to President Johnson. However, as Johnson had his own indiscretions with women to consider he did not take any action to publicize King's affairs and actually told the FBI not to release them.[8]

J. Edgar Hoover's efforts to 'get King' attained scandalous proportions when aides copied the tape recordings of the Willard Hotel activities and despatched them to King's wife Coretta. The agent responsible was ordered to go to Miami where he was to post the package. It contained an anonymous note and a compilation of the recordings.[9] The FBI, of course, broke not only their own regulations but also the law and violated an FCC regulation prohibiting any government agency from disclosing contents of a taped or bugged conversation to a third party.

Although the tape had been sent anonymously, King and his wife both knew it had been made covertly by the FBI. However, ex-FBI Assistant Director Oliver Revell denied the tape had been sent on the instructions of Hoover. Revell said:

> Having had a personal conversation with Mr Hoover about Dr King,
> I do know that Hoover had little use for Dr King, but I detected no

indication of hatred. Hoover was somewhat of a Victorian figure and had high standards for personal conduct. He believed Dr King had violated those standards, even though he was a clergyman. There is absolutely no evidence that Hoover authorised, or even knew of, the heinous letter that was written by someone in the FBI to Dr King suggesting that he commit suicide.[10]

According to 'FBI insiders" it was King who interpreted the tape as a call to suicide and FBI agents were simply seeking his resignation from the Civil Rights movement.[11]

Another notorious incident involving King and women was discovered by the FBI when the Civil Rights leader visited Norway to collect his 1964 Nobel Peace Prize. Civil Rights leader Bayard Rustin told author John Williams that the King party had been visited at their hotel by a group of prostitutes. Rustin said:

> I was sleeping when they [King's aides] called me from downstairs and said that I had to come down to the [Norwegian hotel's] desk at once. I pulled on my robe and went down. The police were there with a woman later said to be the biggest whore in town. And they had caught her coming out of the hotel with watches and wallets belonging to some of the people in our party. Well, she was there. There had been other women running through the hotel like chickens without their heads looking for Martin. And all the guys were putting it to them that, if the girls gave them some pussy first, they'd see that she got to Martin. The whore? I thought it better to let her go with everything she had rather than embarrass ourselves and our hosts.[12]

Having affairs with women other than his wife was not simply confined to anxiety reducing activities as some of King's supporters allege. King's excesses included affairs with '40–45 women' as well as the singer Joan Baez, according to Garrow. In 2019 Garrow examined a huge archive of documents released by the FBI which exposed in detail King's extra-marital affairs as the Civil Rights leader travelled across the country. Garrow said there could be no doubt of any duplicity or exaggeration as the tapes and transcripts he examined were reviewed by the Justice Department in 1977 and found to be 'genuine'.[13]

In one memo Garrow uncovered, King 'looked on, laughed and offered advice' while his friend Baptist Minister Logan Kearse, the pastor of Baltimore's Cornerstone Baptist Church, had arrived in Washington with 'several women parishioners of his church'. Kearse invited King to meet the women in his hotel room where they 'discussed which women among the parishioners would be suitable for natural and unnatural sex acts'. The FBI document added, 'When one of the women protested that she did not approve, the Baptist minister immediately, and forcibly, raped her' as King watched.[14]

At the same hotel the following evening King and a dozen women 'participated in a sex orgy ... including acts of degeneracy and depravity ... when one of the women shied away from engaging in an unnatural sex act, King and several of the men discussed how she was to be taught and initiated in this respect. King told her that to perform such an act would "help her soul".'[15]

King's excesses included having an illegitimate daughter and consorting with prostitutes. On a visit to Las Vegas King took two women to his room then phoned one of his associates to 'get his damned ass down here because I have a beautiful white broad here'. The prostitute Gail LaRue was paid $100 by King's friend gospel singer Clara Ward. King had sex with the two women and then watched as his friend engaged in sex acts. When LaRue was interviewed by an FBI agent, she said she was 'getting scared as they were pretty drunk and using filthy language. . . . [and it was] the worst orgy I've ever gone through'.[16]

In May 1965 an FBI agent reported that King had gone to the home of one of his female aides and 'torn her clothes off – in an attempt to attack her'.[17]

Another FBI report said Coretta Scott King had complained her husband was 'not fulfilling his marital responsibilities ... if he spent 10 hours a month at home, it would be an exaggeration'. King was alleged to have told his wife she should 'go out and have some sexual affairs of her own'.[18] A 1967 memo revealed that King had been dependent on sleeping pills and 'frequently flew into a rage over relatively insignificant matters'.[19]

In another revealing memo baseball star Don Newcombe contacted President Johnson and told him he had information about King he would like to hear. Newcombe, who was related to one of King's lovers, Dolores Evans, said the Civil Rights leader, in a drunken state, had once threatened to throw himself out of a hotel window unless she said she loved him. Newcombe also said Dolores had fathered a baby girl with King, who had provided financial support for her.[20]

David Garrow said that when he first researched King for his biography of the Civil Rights leader, he 'always thought there were 10–12 other women, not 40 to 45'. He also said that King's indifference to rape 'poses so fundamental a challenge to his historical stature as to require the most complete and extensive historical review possible'.[21]

According to Civil Rights historian Taylor Branch:

> [King] finally confessed to some of his people close around him [about his affairs]. J. Edgar Hoover had been trying to call him a communist. [King said] 'I'm not a communist'. Hoover had been suggesting [King] was corrupt on money. One flaw he never had was wanting to have lots of money around. But he said they are also trying to say that I have mistresses on the side. He said, 'They may have something there'.[22]

Former mistress Georgia Davis Powers had been staying in a Lorraine Motel room when King was shot. After the shooting she ran to his side but was warned by King's aide Andrew Young to remove herself from the scene in case she was photographed. She later said she always feared that King's affairs were going to be revealed, 'because there were so many people who knew about it including his staff members and people around him because they were the ones who would pick me up at the airport and take me to a hotel or wherever I was going, so they knew. And I was really surprised that it didn't come out.'[23]

In an interview released in 2013 Jacqueline Kennedy was quoted as saying she knew about King's adultery. She said Robert Kennedy had told her the FBI had recorded King trying to arrange a sex party on the night before King's famous 'I Have a Dream' speech held on the steps of the Lincoln Memorial in August 1963. 'I can't see a picture of Martin Luther King,' she said, 'without thinking, you know, that man's terrible.' She also said Robert Kennedy had told her that King was 'calling up all those girls and arranging for a party of men and women, I mean, sort of orgy.'[24]

King confirmed the truth of his indiscretions to Civil Rights leader James Farmer, who said, '[King] not only had known of [close friend and aide] Ralph Abernathy's extra-marital affairs in Montgomery but had joined in some of them himself'.[25]

To the consternation of King's followers, Abernathy confirmed the stories of King's womanizing in his autobiography, which was published in 1989. Abernathy said that King indulged in his weakness for women up to the last day of his life. Abernathy said King met with two women at different times on the final evening of his life.[26] Abernathy's allegations are confirmed by an FBI memo which cites King's closest friend as having stated that King spent the last night of his life with two lovers followed by a meeting with a third lover who he physically abused during an argument. Abernathy said King had a 'weakness for women' and 'understood and believed in the Biblical prohibition against sex outside marriage. It was just that he had a particularly difficult time with that temptation.'[27]

Abernathy also revealed that the night before the King assassination he accompanied King and Bernard Lee to the home of one of King's female friends for a late-night dinner. At 1am Abernathy saw King emerging from a bedroom with the woman. King and Abernathy returned to the Lorraine Motel where a 'black female politician' was waiting for them. At 7 or 8am an alarmed King went to see Abernathy to ask him to calm the woman down because she was mad at him for being 'unfaithful'.[28]

King had been aware that many people in the Civil Rights movement knew about his indiscretions and it provoked intense anxiety. One of King's mistresses, Dorothy Cotton, who had been in Room 307 of the Lorraine Motel at the time of Dr King's death, believed his womanizing became a habit when he attended college.[29] King told his friends that his assignations with women reduced tensions in him that resulted from being away from home most of the time.

It is likely King recognized that he had placed his campaign for Civil Rights in jeopardy but writers are split on the issue of whether or not King was disturbed about his own behaviour. On the one hand, through his sermons, he inveighed against sin and on the other, willingly pursued those ends. It is debatable whether or not King was making reference to his transgressions in his speeches. Those who believe he did, cite many comments King made in the latter part of his life. In one speech he spoke about 'a friend':

> Some weeks ago somebody was saying something to me about a person I have great magnificent respect for. And they were trying to say something that didn't sound too good about his character, something he was doing. And I said, number one, I don't believe it. But, number two, even if he is, he's a good man because his heart is right. And, in the final analysis, God isn't going to judge him by that little separate mistake that he's making, because the bent of his life is right.[30]

* * *

The King family have promoted King as more than just a great leader. They have argued he should be judged as the martyred victim of a government-inspired murder – killed because he became a dangerous revolutionary who struck fear into the hearts of the Washington power structure. King, they allege, had become a black radical, inspiring a revolution designed to bring about a new economic order and endangering US interests in South-East Asia and around the world. Those writers who reject these claims embrace an image of King that is less dramatic. Although a great African American leader, they maintain King was losing his grip on the movement he had helped to build. His position was gradually being usurped by younger and more radical elements within the black community. Taking this view, it becomes clear that the government had more of a vested interest in seeing him alive rather than dead.

In many ways the King legacy is central to the events surrounding his assassination – was it a powerful government conspiracy to kill a revolutionary on the rise, an idea in keeping with the greatness of King? Was it organized by J. Edgar Hoover, who hated King? Or perhaps the act of a hate group like the Minutemen, Ku Klux Klan, the National States Rights Party or other groups which had racial hatred at the top of their agenda. Was it the act of a hate group which the FBI knew had issued a 'bounty' on King's head? Or was it the act of a single racist killer?

Most reputable historians such as Gerald McKnight and David Garrow, as well as acclaimed writers Hampton Sides, William Bradford Huie, George McMillan and Gerald Posner, did not unearth any evidence that would implicate the Bureau in King's murder. But their works did not stem the tide of accusations that the agency conspired in King's murder.

Hoover had no reason to want the Civil Rights leader dead. After the assassination he told his aide Paul Letersky, 'I hope the son-of-a-bitch doesn't die. If he does, they'll make a martyr out of him.'[31] And, as Letersky wrote, 'The Director may not have cared very much that King had been killed but he cared a lot about finding his killer. Failure to do so would damage the Bureau's reputation and seriously embarrass the Director – perhaps to the point of costing him his job.'[32]

Ramsay Clark was the US Attorney General at the time of King's murder and was despised by Hoover because he was a liberal politician. Yet, Clark believed the Director had nothing to do with King's murder and in fact wanted to capture the assassin as swiftly as possible. 'Because of the way

Mr Hoover had presented himself [with regards to] Martin Luther King,' Clark said, he had to break the case quickly. There was nothing more important to him than the reputation of the FBI. Its reputation was at stake. He was afraid people were going to say he did it ... Agents were very anxious to solve this case.'[33]

The great irony was that the FBI, which tried to ruin Martin Luther King's life, was the very agency that was assigned the task of finding his killer.

Chapter 2

Murder in Memphis

When I stood in that rooming house bathtub, in Ray's footprints and looked down at where Dr King had stood, I said, 'My God, how easy it was!' ... I hadn't fired a rifle in 23 years. But with a rifle and scope exactly like Ray's and duplicating the distance and angle of the shot, I put ten straight shots in a circle the size of a silver dollar. Any twelve-year-old boy reasonably familiar with a .22 rifle could have killed Dr King from that bathroom window with the rifle Ray used.

Author William Bradford Huie

James Earl Ray came from a dysfunctional family. His father was a thief and his mother was an alcoholic. There were no family values in the Ray household; school was unimportant; morals were non-existent. In fact, the family came to be represented by a skewered idea that the brothers James, John and Jerry should support one another in crime.

Both John and Jerry had been close to their older brother James, especially Jerry. 'James would do anything for us and we for him,' John said.[1] The brothers had nick names for each other. James was usually called Jimmy but sometimes his brothers would call him T-Bone. John was known as Tongue due to his speech impediment but usually went by Jack. Jerry was called Egg. James' relationship with them would become the only close ties he ever experienced in his life. All three brothers spent most of their lives committing crimes.

James was born on 10 March 1928 in Alton, Illinois. Alton is situated in the southern part of Missouri where he and his brothers grew up. It was very much like the hill country in the South – white, poor, working class and very anti-black. It was known as 'Little Dixie'. The KKK attracted a great deal of support in the small towns and hamlets in the area surrounding Alton. In the 1930s and 1940s especially people like the Rays had pride in their race because it was the only thing they could have pride in.

On 10 October 1959, after a lifetime of robbing and stealing James was arrested for robbing a store in St Louis. James and his partner in crime James Owens got away with $120. Bystanders saw the two men change cars and reported it to the police. Officers spotted the car and both men were eventually arrested.[2] Although insisting on representing himself in court, his appointed lawyer said:

> [Ray was] a jailhouse lawyer … he pretty well ran his own trial. He knew what he wanted to do, and I pretty well had to go along with it. … when Ray took the stand of course the prosecution was then entitled to bring out his past criminal record before the jury. This utterly stupid action by Ray resulted in his getting the maximum sentence of 20 years, while his accomplice (Owens) was sentenced to only seven years. James was sent to Missouri State Penitentiary in Jefferson City, Missouri.[3]

John Larry Ray, born 14 February 1933 in Alton, Illinois, was three years younger than James. He was a stockier, more muscular version of the assassin; the same long nose, the same receding hairline and the same one-sided smile. From January 1968 John Ray owned and operated the Grapevine Bar at 1982 Arsenal Street in St Louis, a known meeting place for criminals. However, the bar's licence was in his sister Carol's name because John had a long criminal record. Like his older brother James, he was a bitter racist and hardened criminal, in and out of penal institutions for most of his life.

Jerry Ray, born 16 July 1935, was a younger and darker version of James. He was 6ft tall, 190lb and had receding black hair combed straight back. He had the initials JR tattooed on top of his lower left arm and a blue tattoo on top of his right lower arm. He went to reform school at the age of 14 and graduated to robberies of bars, petrol stations and other small businesses. He had convictions for grand larceny in 1954 and armed robbery in 1956. When his parole on the robbery conviction was about to become final in August 1958, he held up a gas station and was sent back to prison. He served an additional nine years at Menard State Penitentiary in Chester, Illinois. Following his release in 1960, he worked at odd jobs in St Louis and Chicago. In September 1964, he was hired as a night maintenance man at the Sportsman's Country Club in Northbrook, Illinois, a job he held until summer 1968. Jerry also frequently expressed his animosity towards African Americans.

Many years later Jerry and John would confess to helping their brother James escape from Missouri State Penitentiary in April 1967. Jerry said he caught a train on 24 April 1967 to Chicago to meet both brothers at the 'Fairview Hotel'. Jerry said his brother James looked 'pretty rough'. It was the day after James had escaped from prison.[4]

When the three brothers met they celebrated James' escape. John and Jerry handed their brother the money he had acquired working as a prison 'merchant', loaning out magazines to his fellow prisoners and selling amphetamines which had been smuggled into the prison by a corrupt guard.[5]

James told his brothers of his intention to cross the border into Canada, acquire false identification then join the Merchant Marines and possibly make his way to a country he greatly admired for its segregationist government. During the meeting they also discussed plans to make a 'big score' which included ideas about kidnapping and robbing banks.[6]

John returned to St Louis and Jerry back to Northbrook. James rented a cheap room outside Chicago. Over the following weeks James would often meet up with Jerry to play pool and drink beer.[7]

According to Percy Foreman, who became James' lawyer after his capture (and who referred to John and Jerry as a 'couple of morons'[8]), James and Jerry drove to Birmingham on 29 March 1968 where James purchased a .243 calibre Remington rifle at the Aeromarine Supply Company.

According to John Ray, James phoned him on 29 March 1968 and they arranged to meet in West Memphis, Arkansas, across the river from where James had been staying at the New Rebel Motel, on the outskirts of Memphis, Tennessee. They met up on the evening of 3 April 1968 at a 'back-alley' bar. John drove down from St Louis in his cream-colored Thunderbird with a machine gun and other weapons in the trunk. When they met his brother appeared edgy, John said, and worried about his future as a fugitive. John said he drank beer with his brother for a 'couple of hours'. The last image of his brother was walking 'down a back alley alone'. John said it was like a scene from the movie *Casablanca*.[9]

James had planned the 'big score' for the following day, 4 April 1968. But he didn't want his brothers around when he carried it out. He was protecting them. He was a fugitive and was well aware of the chances he was taking. His brothers on the other hand were free men who had been trying to stay out of prison by holding down legitimate jobs. At all costs, he wanted his brothers to remain free.

On the morning of 4 April Jerry received a telephone call from James, 'Jerry, tomorrow it will be all over. I might not see you and Jack for a while. But don't worry about me. I'll be alright! Big Nigger has had it!'[10]

James drove to Memphis in his white Mustang car and registered at Bessie Brewer's Rooming House situated across the street from the Lorraine Motel where Martin Luther King and his aides were staying.

* * *

On 1 March 1968, a month before King was killed, a presidential commission, set up to uncover the roots of urban riots that spread across US cities in the mid-1960s, concluded that the United States was moving towards two separate and unequal societies, one white and one black.

It was in this climate of fear that King journeyed to Memphis to participate in a sanitation workers' demonstration. The issue was simple. The workers were demanding better treatment from their employers and a 50 cents an hour raise. In the four months before King came to town the workers' strike had led to African American boycotts of downtown businesses.

The strike escalated into a confrontation between the city's mayor, 45-year-old Henry Loeb, and more than 200,000 African Americans. Trouble had been brewing for years. The problems included low wages, no job security and no insurance for the workers. The sanitation men used poor equipment, were made to eat their lunch in the street and had no facilities for washing up. The hours of work were long and their 7–3 shift was non-stop. If they did not complete their round on time, they were forced to continue without extra pay.[11]

On 1 February 1968 the garbage workers' anger increased when two workers, who had sheltered from the rain in a garbage truck, were crushed to death. The city government had refused the workers' families compensation. A few days later twenty-two workers were told to go out to work on a rainy day or return home without pay. They refused and after finding their pay had been docked, they walked off the job.

The strike developed from a workers' dispute into a Civil Rights confrontation with Memphis authorities. Protesters demanded better treatment for the city's African American community. Enthusiasm for the protest was developing because the issue of the treatment of the sanitation workers was clear cut. They were on the bottom of the socio-economic ladder, did a job that no one else wanted to do and their treatment seemed inhumane.

Loeb was stubborn and proud. His attitude to African Americans, while never overtly racist, was nevertheless conservative and patronizing. There is little doubt that his personality exacerbated the problem between the sanitation workers and the city government. Loeb had refused to negotiate with the strikers until they returned to work.

A protest march had been planned for 28 March. King had been asked to come to Memphis to lead the demonstration and then head a mass march to City Hall. His visit to Memphis was booked as a one-day visit in support of the strikers.

Once King took the 4,500 marchers onto Beale Street a group of young black militants infiltrated the marchers and began to throw rocks and smash the windows of local businesses. Rioters smashed store windows with the heels of their hands. Sticks from picket signs were used as weapons and looters jumped through the store fronts throwing out shoes, suits, television sets, musical instruments and anything valuable they could lay their hands on. Police fired tear gas at random and the marchers' leaders used bull horns in an attempt to bring order to the march. King's aides encircled him as the level of violence escalated. He was rushed to a white Pontiac car and taken to the eighth floor of the Holiday Inn, overlooking the river.

While the marchers milled about confused, police swept the street clean in a wedge movement injuring both looters and innocent marchers alike. The 3-hour conflict had produced at least 60 injuries, 280 arrests and the death of a 16-year-old African American teenager, Larry Payne, who, police said, had confronted them with a knife. He was killed by a shotgun blast fired by a police officer while the youth emerged from a basement in the Fowler Homes housing development. No charges were returned by a Shelby County grand jury.

For the first time in nearly a decade King had lost control of a demonstration. The violence of the march and the death of the teenager played a significant role in King's determination to return to the city to ensure a peaceful march. The idea was crucial to King's plans. If the march did not succeed, there was little chance that his Poor People's Campaign in Washington, planned for the coming summer months, would be non-violent.

The Memphis disturbances had been an embarrassment for King and the thought of returning depressed him. But the idea of not going back was too risky. If he did not return to Memphis, he would have to concede that his non-violent approach to securing equal rights for African Americans had failed. Before his second attempt at leading a peaceful march King sent his aides to the city to try and reason with the young militants. He then journeyed to Memphis to give a series of talks in order to make them see sense. He would stay in Memphis long enough to see if the courts had thrown out the city's injunction banning the march and return to Ebenezer Baptist Church in Atlanta on Sunday, 7 April to give a planned sermon. The second protest march was due to be held on Monday, 8 April.

On 3 April King and his party landed at Memphis airport on the Eastern Airlines Flight 381 from Atlanta. They were met by Community on the Move for Equality (COME) member Mrs Thomas Matthews, who picked King and his party up and took them to the Lorraine Motel in the poor end of town.[12]

Inspector G.P. Tines of the Memphis Police had assigned two African American police officers, Detective Edward Estes Redditt and Patrolman Willie B. Richmond, to go to the airport and begin surveillance on King. They were to report all King's contacts while in Memphis. A security detail of four senior white policemen was also deployed, led by Inspector Don H. Smith. However, the detail was rebuffed by members of the King party who turned down the offer of protection.

The reasons for refusing protection were complex. As many in the King entourage suspected, the offer of a police guard was to enable the gathering of further intelligence on King rather than to provide him with protection. During the previous week trust between COME organizers and the police detail had broken down. The police detail that had met King and his party at the airport was made up of high-ranking officers which did nothing to bridge the gap. And when the King party spotted the surveillance officers Redditt and Richmond at the airport, they suspected the police were not offering protection at all.

Ironically, if the head of one of the police teams detailed for the King visit had alerted King's party to a murder threat given to the police on 1 April, the King party may very well have accepted the protection on offer. King had received threats against his life from the time he became famous in the 1950s and he had come to accept them as a natural part of his life. During his visits to Memphis there had been two bomb threats but the FBI treated these with virtual indifference. The FBI's Washington headquarters notified the Memphis police, the Secret Service, the Shelby County Sheriff and the 111th Military Intelligence Unit but not King or his family. This had been gross negligence and was covered up by the FBI during the subsequent investigation into King's death.[13] By not alerting King or his aides to the threats against his life the FBI and the Memphis police were guilty of culpable negligence.

Throughout the period of the Memphis sanitation strike the Memphis Police Department had positioned numerous spies within the ranks of the marchers.[14] Some, like Louis McKay, had been spotted monitoring the marchers and the meetings and had been physically attacked and verbally abused. Detective Redditt and Patrolman Richmond had both been threatened by demonstrators. In fact, there had been a complete breakdown of trust between the Memphis police and COME officials who had organized the King visit. A total of nearly forty men had been assigned to King's security detail, day and night, by the new Police Director Frank Holloman. Holloman had been an FBI agent for twenty-five years, the last eight of them in charge of J. Edgar Hoover's office in Washington DC. Holloman's Memphis Internal Security Division was, in effect, a miniature FBI. At the time of the shooting there were at least a dozen officers from Police Tact Unit 10 taking a rest break around Fire Station 2, across the street from the Lorraine. In total there were approximately forty-four police officers in the vicinity of the motel.

A rally in support of the marchers had been scheduled for the night of 3 April, a Wednesday, at the Mason Temple. Ralph Abernathy had gone ahead to speak at the rally and inform the 2,000-strong crowd that King had been suffering from a cold and would not attend. However, on seeing the enthusiastic crowd of supporters Abernathy decided to phone King and try and persuade him to come to the Temple. King agreed and said he would speak for a few minutes. As soon as the crowd saw King arrive, they leapt to their feet and gave him a rapturous welcome. Abernathy spoke first and gave his friend an enthusiastic introduction. King began by making reference to the historical nature of his mission and the forthcoming march the following Monday. He also spoke about his attempted assassination in New York in 1958 and of how the doctors had informed him that if he had sneezed the letter opener would have ripped into his aorta and death would have been instantaneous.

King continued with his speech, gradually reaching an inspirational crescendo:

> And some began to talk about the threats that were out there, of what would happen to me from some of our sick white brothers ... Well, I don't know what will happen now. We've got some difficult days ahead. But it really doesn't matter with me now. ... because I've been to the mountaintop ... And I don't mind. ... Like anybody I would like to live. ... a long life; longevity has its place. ... but I'm not concerned about that now. ... I just want to do God's will. And He's allowed me to go up to the mountain. And I've looked over and I've seen the promised land. I may not get there with you, but I want you to know tonight that we as a people will get to the promised land. So, I'm happy tonight, I'm not worried about anything, I'm not fearing any man. Mine eyes have seen the coming of the glory of the Lord.

At the end of the speech the hall erupted in a frenzy of praise and admiration for the hero of the Civil Rights movement. King had become emotionally drained and collapsed as he left the podium. Abernathy caught him and led him to his seat. But some of his aides felt uneasy. King had never before spoken of his death in such emotional terms. Marion Logan was also disturbed when King told her of his readiness to die.

King spent most of the next day conferring with his aides in Room 306 of the Lorraine Motel. The motel, from a security standpoint, was a bad choice. It was located in a seedy part of town and there were some fears for King's safety.

Meeting with his aides, King sensed some doubts about the movement's non-violent policy, so he reiterated his belief that the only hope for the nation was through the power of passive non-resistance. He also told them he had conquered the fear of death. King's fears, however, soon gave way to a feeling of optimism. He had been in a good mood since the rally the previous evening and spoke of how the audience responded to his speech and the righteousness of the sanitation workers' cause.

King and his aides were preparing to go to Revd Billy Kyles' house for dinner. King had been looking forward to eating soul food. Kyles expected everyone around 6pm but invited his guests for 5pm because King always ran late. True to Kyles' expectations, King's aides began assembling in the Lorraine parking lot shortly before 6pm. King exited his second-floor room onto the balcony with Revd Kyles and made casual conversation with his associates. Stuffing in his shirt tails, King walked out onto the balcony of the motel and stood at the railing.

A white Cadillac would take King and his friends to Kyles' house. It had been loaned to the King party by a local African American businessman, a funeral director. The driver was Solomon Jones, a local man who had been appointed as King's chauffer and he was to drive King around during his stay in Memphis. Jones had been standing at the left front wheel looking up to King on the second floor of the motel. Also present in the courtyard area or on the steps leading to the second-storey balcony were King's men Andrew Young, lawyer Chauncey Eskridge, James Bevel, Ralph Abernathy, Hosea Williams and Jesse Jackson.

Standing on the balcony, King called down to Chauncey Eskridge and told him to tell Jackson he was to accompany him to dinner. It was a conciliatory act as King and Jackson had clashed over protest tactics. Abernathy returned to Room 306 for a moment to apply some aftershave and King said he would wait for him on the balcony. He spotted Jackson and gave the invitation in person.

Jesse Jackson introduced Ben Branch, a musician who was to play at that evening's rally. King asked him to play 'Precious Lord' and to play it 'real pretty'. Solomon Jones called up to King to take a top coat with him as the night air had been getting cooler. As King was about to turn to re-enter his room a loud muffled sound like a car backfire rang out. Kyles turned and saw King lying across the balcony in front of the door to his room.

Ralph Abernathy rushed to his friend, cradled him in his arms and patted his head. Blood was streaming from a hole in King's right jaw. One of the first to reach King after the shooting was police spy Marrell McCullough. Someone shouted, 'They shot Dr King.' Soon King was surrounded by his aides, some of whom pointed in the direction from which the shot had come, across from the Lorraine, a shabby row of buildings. It was the rear of South Main Street.

Earl Caldwell, an African American reporter for the *New York Times*, was covering King for the newspaper and had taken Room 215 at the motel. Shortly after 6pm he heard a sharp report that sounded like a firecracker. He also heard people yelling and initially thought someone had bombed the motel. Caldwell ran outside in his shorts and saw King's legs partly hanging over the ledge of the second-floor balcony. He ran back into his room, put on his trousers and a raincoat then grabbed a pencil and notebook.

Caldwell returned and witnessed a hysterical scene as a scattered crowd of people began shouting and screaming. Uniformed police officers began racing towards him and he started to believe it was the police who had shot King. Policemen DuFour and Baker were the first officers to reach King. Meanwhile Officer Ghormley saw Officer Landers scale a wall and enter the backyard of the rooming house.

A Memphis police officer described the chaos that followed the shooting. According to an FBI report, Officer Dollahite and other officers were inside the fire station when Dollahite heard someone yell that King had been shot. He immediately ran out of the door on the north side of the fire station, then ran east towards the Lorraine Motel, jumping over a fence, and then dropping down a 10ft concrete retaining wall which runs along the west side of Mulberry Street. Dollahite then ran to the driveway on Mulberry Street, which leads into the Lorraine Motel, to a point beneath the balcony where Dr King's body was lying. He stated that he heard an unknown 'Negro male' at the scene say, 'The dirty mother****** police shot him.' As Dollahite ran into the driveway, he dropped his firearm and had to stop momentarily to pick it up, then after checking it briefly continued to search the scene of the shooting. After seeing King's body sprawled on the balcony and observing other officers converging on the area, he immediately ran out of the driveway, moving north along Mulberry Street to Huling and west on Huling Street to Main Street, then South on Main Street.[15]

One police officer grabbed Caldwell and asked where the shot came from. The reporter was so shocked he could not speak. He then ran up the steps to where King lay and was horrified at what he observed. He knew instantly that King was dead. Caldwell ran downstairs, found a telephone and called his newspaper. He dictated the story over the sounds of hysteria.

Later Caldwell would startle assassination researchers with claims that he had observed a shooter in the bushes across the street from the motel. This was contradicted by Revd Kyles who had a complete view of the scene across the street from the motel. Kyles said he could not see any people or movements in the rear of the Main Street buildings, only bushes and a garbage-strewn plot of land.[16]

King did not speak. Abernathy comforted him, telling his friend everything was going to be alright. Abernathy said:

I heard what sounded like a firecracker. And I jumped. And when I jumped, I saw only his feet laying on the balcony. And I immediately rushed to his side and I started patting his cheek, saying, 'Martin, Martin, don't be afraid. Don't be afraid. This is Ralph. This is Ralph.' And I got his attention. And he calmed down. His eyes were moving and he became very, very calm. And finally, Andrew Young came up the steps and said 'Oh God, Oh God, Ralph. It is over.'[17]

Abernathy told Kyles to get an ambulance. Kyles tried but found all the phone lines were busy. King was totally unconscious, flat on his back, with his head turned slightly to the left side. Galyon observed a large gaping wound in the root of the neck on the right side. The wound had stopped bleeding. Galyon saw that King's clothes were covered in blood and his head was partially covered with a towel which had been used by King's aides to stem the flow of blood.

Later it was determined the bullet had entered King's lower right jaw, an inch to the right and a half inch below the mouth. The bullet hit the jawbone, exited and then re-entered just above the collar bone downward, toward the left striking vital blood vessels. The impact of the bullet then damaged three spine bones in the vertebrae. The major part of the bullet was recovered from King's upper left back as it rested just beneath the skin. Of the 150 grains, 64.5 were recovered, the remaining bullet fragments having scattered throughout the area of the two wounds. The autopsy report stated:

Death was the result of a gunshot wound to the chin and neck with a total transection of the lower cervical and upper thoracic spinal cord and other structure in the neck. The direction of the wounding was from front to back, above downward and from right to left. The severing of the spinal cord at this level and to this extent was a wound that was fatal very shortly after its occurrence.[18]

* * *

About 3 hours before the shooting, at approximately 3.15pm, a white man had appeared at a dingy rooming house, the rear of which was across Mulberry Street from the Lorraine Motel. The front of the rooming house was situated on South Main Street. It consisted of the top floors of 418 and 422, adjacent run-down brick buildings above stores that were situated at ground level. The two parts of the rooming house were connected by a covered passageway, each wing having stairs leading to ground level. Landlady Bessie Brewer's office was situated right off the landing at the head of the stairs of 422. The rooming house had ten apartments in the 422 section and six in 418.

The white male, who gave his name as John Willard, had entered from the front door, walked up the stairs and asked Bessie Brewer for a room. He was, said Brewer, dark, quiet, well-dressed wearing a suit and tie, about 6ft tall and aged about 30 to 35. Brewer observed he had an 'odd smile' or 'sneer'. It was so pronounced she said she would never forget it.[19]

Brewer showed Willard Room 8 which had a kitchenette but he turned it down saying he only wanted a 'sleeping room'; the room's window looked out onto the blank wall of the adjacent building. From this room the Lorraine Motel could not be observed. Willard asked for a 'back room', one of the rooms overlooking the Lorraine. Mrs Brewer showed him 5b, a small room with a torn mattress lying crosswise on bare bedsprings. The dingy bathroom, a short walk down the hall, had a perfect view of the Lorraine. Willard said the room would do fine and paid the $8.50 rent for the week. Brewer pointed out the shared bathroom facilities to Willard and told him that everyone in the area of his room was quiet but that the person next door usually drank a little. Willard replied, 'I take a beer once in a while myself.'[20]

At about 4pm a man answering the description of Willard entered the York Arms Company, a sporting goods store about half a mile from the rooming house. He looked at a number of binoculars before purchasing a pair for $41.50 from sales clerk Ralph Carpenter.

Following the shooting, which occurred at 6pm, police reconstructed the scene. King had been shot from the bathroom window. Memphis Police Officer Glynn King saw a footprint in the bathtub. He deduced the assassin's aim had been enhanced by placing one foot in the tub which allowed him a better firing position. Directly underneath, on the ground below the bathroom window, lay the window screen which had been pushed outwards. Placing the rifle on the windowsill of the bathroom, the police deduced, the assassin fired one shot which hit King. The range was 205ft 6in, a relatively easy shot using a rifle with a telescopic sight.

Charles Q. Stephens, who was renting rooms at 422 South Main Street, saw a man he later identified as Ray talking to Bessie Brewer on the afternoon of 4 April. Later that day, Stephens heard footsteps coming from Room 5b and furniture being moved around. He also heard footsteps going from 5b to the common bathroom. As he was sitting in his kitchenette, which was situated next to the bathroom, Stephens heard the report, opened his door and saw a man walking quickly down the hall away from the bathroom holding a long package. Following the shot, 'It immediately occurred to [him] that this was the same man he had seen earlier in the afternoon ... standing at the door to Room 5b'.[21] Stephens' common-law wife Grace Walden had been confined to her bed. According to an FBI memo, 'Mrs Stephens said she did not see anyone leave the apartment bathroom ...'.[22]

Another lodger, Willie Anschutz, had been in his room 4b, which was next door to Willard's room. He had been watching television with a friend, a deaf mute named Mrs Ledbetter, when the shot rang out. Anschutz knew that the shot had been fired nearby, but he could not tell if it came from the 'bathroom' or 'Room 5b'.[23] As he opened his door, he observed a man, who he later thought had been the roomer from 5b, pass him carrying a bundle. Anschutz then spoke to the man saying, 'Hey, that sounded like a shot.' The man held one arm across his face and answered, 'Yeah, it was a shot.'[24] After Anschutz had observed the man running down the hall he went to the bathroom and looked out of the window. A police officer in the backyard yelled for him to get back inside. Anschutz heard 'a girl' say that the shot came from the window he was looking out of.[25]

Police Lieutenant Papia was the first officer to run up the stairs of 422 after the shot had been fired. On entering the long hall of 418 he met a couple who were standing in front of the door to their room. Mrs Ledbetter gesticulated, pointing to the door of 5b. Anschutz told him, 'I heard what sounded like a shot come from the bathroom. A white man moved in today and I saw him run out just after I heard the shot. He ran out there [Room 5b].'[26]

Mrs Brewer and her husband Frank had been watching a television western, *Rawhide*, when the shot rang out. They walked to the rear entrance of the building. Mrs Brewer attempted to go outside but was told by a police officer to remain inside and return to her apartment. They could hear 'hollering' and 'screaming' at the back of the building.

When other police officers arrived, they searched the rooming house. Mrs Brewer told them a dresser had been moved away from the window in Room 5b and a chair placed there. It gave a clear view of the Lorraine Motel.

Shortly after the shot, the owner of an amusement store, Canipe's, which was situated next to the rooming house, said he had seen 'a white man, a little under six feet, pretty well dressed, dark headed, no hat, wearing a dark suit ... [come] by the door, dropped the stuff, I heard the thud, that's what made me look up just in time to see his back, walking away, going south'. He said that moments after he had spotted the man, a white Mustang pulled away sharply with only one person in the car, and he told police, 'he sure burned leather'.[27]

Two customers at Canipe's Amusement Store, Bernell Finlay and Julius Graham, who had finished work at 5.20pm, drove there because they wanted to look at old phonograph records. They were the only two customers. Both men heard the bundle dropping in the doorway, looked up and saw a man walk past from the direction of the rooming house entrance. They heard the screech of tyres as the Mustang pulled away.

Seconds later a police officer, Lieutenant J.E. Ghormley, from the TAC squad who had been observing the King party from the nearby fire station, rushed to the front of the rooming house but had just missed confronting the fugitive. He found a bundle in the front entrance to the store. A dirty green and brown herringbone-patterned bedspread covered a blue suitcase and a long cardboard box with the barrel of a rifle sticking out of it. Later, police examined the contents of the bundle which included a Remington Gamemaster rifle, model 760, 30.06 calibre, serial number 461476, with a spent cartridge in its chamber. The rifle had a mounted Redfield telescopic sight, one pair of Bushnell 'Banner' 7-power binoculars, metal-jacketed 'soft-point' Remington Peters bullet and a Peters cartridge box containing nine 30.06 cartridges. Police also found a 'blue suitcase'.

During the hours that followed, the Memphis police took control of the crime scene. Officers were deployed to interview everyone in the vicinity of the crime, including the rooming house residents, King's party and the staff of the Lorraine. Within a short time, however, President Johnson, in consultation with Attorney General Ramsay Clark, ordered the FBI to take over the case. The official reason came from a possible violation of Title 18, Section 241 of the US Code. The statute prohibited 'conspiracies to injure, oppress, threaten or intimidate any citizen in the free exercise or enjoyment of any rights or privilege secured to him or her by the Constitution or laws of the United States'.

* * *

During their investigation the FBI discovered a total of twenty-six finger-prints on the material left at the scene of the crime. It was an item in the list, a pair of pliers, that started the manhunt for King's killer. Every known customer of the Los Angeles Romage hardware store where the pliers were purchased was contacted and interviewed.

Soon the FBI had another name apart from John Willard. From the rifle abandoned in the bundle they were able to trace it to a Memphis gun shop who said it had been sold to a Harvey Lowmeyer, who paid cash for it on 30 March 1968.

On 11 April the FBI found the best lead yet. The hunt for the laundry mark found on clothes in the blue suitcase had been traced to the Home Service Laundry at 5880 Hollywood Boulevard 6, two blocks from the Romage hardware store. The records showed that the 02B-6 laundry mark had been issued to an Eric S. Galt who had used the laundry service. Therefore, the man who had dropped the bundle in the doorway of Canipe's Amusement Store had used the laundry service between 4 and 18 March 1968.

Meanwhile, the Mustang with Alabama licence plate number I-38993 was found in Atlanta. Inside the car the police discovered some clothes, a pillow and pillowcase, sheets and a container that once held a Polaroid camera. The car had also been registered to Eric S. Galt of 2608 South Highland Avenue, Birmingham, Alabama.

The FBI had been checking motels in the Memphis area asking if anyone recalled a white man with a white Mustang. Roomers at the New Rebel Motel, not far from Memphis, confirmed that a man fitting this description had checked in at 7.15pm the night before King's murder and checked out before 1pm the following day. He gave his name as Eric S. Galt.

The FBI now tied Galt to the Mustang, a motel in the Memphis area and the laundry marks found on items at the scene of the crime. The search continued, specifically in the Atlanta and Memphis areas. The search also centred around the Los Angeles area. A vehicle security sticker on the car had shown the name E. Galt, 1535 North Serrano Street, Los Angeles.

The FBI did fibre analysis of the evidence recovered from the Mustang, the bundle and Room 5b. The FBI discovered that the green bedspread that wrapped the bundle had the same fibres that were found on the bed and pillow in Room 5b. The same green fibres were present on a sweater, sheets, a jacket, pillowcase, walking shorts and rugs found in the Mustang abandoned in Atlanta. Hair taken from the hairbrush in the bundle dumped in the doorway of Canipe's Amusement Store was found to be similar to hair retrieved from the Mustang.

On 19 April the FBI tied Eric S. Galt to fugitive James Earl Ray. It came about through FBI investigations in the Los Angeles area arising from the laundry marks. Agents interviewed Marie Martin and her cousin Charlie Stein, who has become acquainted with Ray during the few months Ray had stayed there and recognized the name Eric S. Galt. Galt's remark to Stein that he took dancing lessons led agents to the National Dance Studio, not far from the St Francis Hotel, in Long Beach, California. Ray had taken lessons there from 5 December 1967 to 12 February 1968. The studio produced the first photo of Galt. It bore only a slight resemblance to Ray as he had closed his eyes when the photo was taken; a ruse that criminals often used. An FBI artist later drew the eyes in.

Concurrently, agents had examined all money orders cashed in the Los Angeles area and found one bought by Eric Starvo Galt, made out to the Locksmithing Institute of Bloomfield, New Jersey. Their records produced an address – 113 Fourteenth Street, Atlanta. Agents staked out the address then made a surreptitious entry. A map of Atlanta was discovered in the room and it contained fingerprints. Together with the twenty-six prints they had found from the evidence material in the bundle, the FBI began searching through 53,000 sets of prints which matched the criteria which had been established. FBI Assistant Director Cartha DeLoach knew there were millions of fingerprints in the FBI files and it would take months to look at them, so he worked on a hunch. From what agents had already discovered the assassin was acting like a 'fugitive' always on the move. So DeLoach asked the fingerprint team to concentrate on examining the prints of escaped convicts who were white, male, under 50 etc. The 700th set of prints matched – the name was James Earl Ray.

Later the FBI connected the Eric S. Galt signature with Ray when they obtained an undated coupon from the Modern Photo Bookstore in New York. It was mailed by Ray in September 1967 when he was living in Birmingham, Alabama. The FBI found a latent fingerprint on the coupon identical with the left thumbprint of Ray.

Until this time the hundreds of agents assigned to the case had been pursuing an elusive prey from coast to coast. The 'John Willard' who had registered at the Memphis rooming house became the 'Eric Starvo Galt' who had bought the white Mustang ultimately identified as the getaway car, who had been the 'Harvey Lowmeyer' when he purchased the Remington Gamemaster rifle in Birmingham, Alabama, identified as the murder weapon. Now they were able to build a fuller profile of the fugitive and place him on the FBI's Top Ten list.

Chapter 3

Manhunt

... if you want my impression of Earl Ray ... and from what he told me ... Gentlemen, for what it is worth, I haven't any doubt in my mind that he did it on his own. For whatever reason he did it ... on his own. If it had been anything, or anybody behind him on that particular job that during the various and many conversations I had with him it would have come out.

Alexander Eist, James Earl Ray's police escort in London

That's where I made my mistake. I should have pulled a hold-up [in Canada]. But I didn't. And I let myself get on that plane to London without enough money to get where I intended to go.

James Earl Ray

The pursuit of James Earl Ray read like a tale from an international mystery bestseller and it ended at Heathrow Airport, London, on June 8th 1968, when the man wanted for the murder of Martin Luther King was arrested trying to board a flight to Brussels. From the time of the assassination, he had been hunted from country to country, a man in flight holing up in cheap hotels and finally trying to secure passage to Rhodesia where he hoped to become a white mercenary. He had led law-enforcement officers on a 25,000-mile chase through the US, Canada and Europe before he was finally caught.

* * *

On 23 April 1967 career criminal James Earl Ray had stowed away in a bread truck and escaped from Missouri State Penitentiary where he was serving a twenty-year sentence for robbery. He was assisted in the escape by his brother John and his old friend 'Catman' Gawron who arranged to meet James once he was outside the walls of the prison. 'I'll jump off at the stop sign in Jefferson City,' James said, 'but if I can't make it out of the box right away, I'll be under the bridge that crosses the Missouri River a few miles upriver.' However, John was confused about which bridge James had been talking about and the rendezvous with his brother was aborted.[1] The following day, John said, James phoned him and the younger brother picked James up near New Franklin. Both brothers headed to St Louis. John gave him his Social Security ID. According to John, the brothers then took a Greyhound bus to Chicago to meet up with their brother Jerry.[2] Some days later James found work as a dishwasher under the alias John L. Rayns. Although Ray feared that authorities had launched a manhunt, they made few efforts to locate him beyond issuing standard wanted posters offering a $50 reward.

Ray left his job after a month and briefly joined his brothers in the St Louis area, where, FBI investigators believe, they robbed an Alton bank of nearly $30,000. He purchased a used car and drove to Montreal, Canada, arriving on 17 July 1967 and leasing a room under the name Eric S. Galt. He hoped to obtain a Canadian passport but, finding this difficult, left on 21 August and travelled to Birmingham, Alabama, where he remained for six weeks. Ray purchased another car, a white 1966 Mustang, in a private-newspaper ad sale and succeeded under Alabama's lax regulations in registering it and obtaining a driving licence as Eric Starvo Galt.

Fearful of discovery, Ray left in early October and journeyed to Nuevo Laredo, Mexico. He spent a few days smuggling goods across the border, then rented a room in Puerto Vallarta, Mexico. He claimed to be a writer and spent most days drinking and visiting brothels. He resumed drifting after five weeks, this time settling, on 19 November 1967, in Los Angeles. Ray attended 'self-hypnosis' sessions, took dance lessons and enrolled in lock-smithing classes and a bartending course. He sought work briefly but, lacking social security identification, he feared appearing suspicious. In February 1968 he underwent cosmetic surgery to reshape his nose before he travelled to the Deep South in March 1968.

* * *

Following the assassination Ray had driven to Atlanta where he abandoned his Mustang. He then caught a bus to Cincinnati, changed buses and arrived in Detroit on 6 April before crossing the Canadian–US border by taxi and arriving in Windsor, Ontario, and then catching a train to Toronto.

On his arrival in Toronto Ray rented a room and then searched a graveyard for names of men who had birth dates near his. However, he found what he was looking for at the offices of a Toronto newspaper. He was under the mistaken belief that he needed a guarantor so devised a plan to use two identities, one for the alias and the other for the guarantor. He began by scouring newspapers in the Toronto library for identities. Then he posed as a passport official over the phone to check whether or not passports had already been issued to Ramon George Sneyd and Paul Edward Bridgman. This reduced the risk of the passport office becoming alarmed at the issue of a second passport. Ray quickly adopted these aliases from a list he had gathered for his journey to London.

There is evidence that Ray kept watch on the homes of Paul Edward Bridgman and Ramon George Sneyd to ascertain whether or not they looked like him. The general appearance of both seemed to be similar – medium build, late 30s, dark hair, not short, not fat or of a different ethnic origin.

On Wednesday, 10 April 1968, Ray applied for duplicate birth certificates for Bridgman and Sneyd and the following day had passport photos taken. Ray decided to adopt Sneyd's identity for his passport. His initial plan was to appear at the passport office with his false birth certificate, leave the office, disguise himself as Bridgman and swear he had known 'Sneyd' for at least two years. However, the Kennedy Travel Bureau saved him the trouble by telling Ray they would apply for the passport for him. To circumvent the rules about having someone vouch for him the travel agency told him he could make a 'declaration' instead. It was notarized by Kennedy Travel Bureau manager Henry Moos.

At Missouri State Penitentiary it was common knowledge that a passport could be easily obtained in Canada. It simply entailed a visit to a Canadian City Central Lending Library to view copies of newspapers bearing a date near your own date of birth, copying the names of perhaps a dozen men (or women) born around that time then making a record of their dates of birth and parents' names, particularly the maiden name of the mother. A check could then be made against each name in the telephone directory.

This procedure would have enabled a forger to choose a person who was still alive. To make sure, it would simply be necessary to pose as a salesman and phone the chosen person. The forger would then apply for a birth certificate. On its receipt an application for a passport could then be made. To enable a criminal on the run to act independently it would be necessary to falsely state that a guarantor could not be found. The passport office rules during the 1960s stipulated that if no guarantor was available, a simple sworn statement would suffice – 'A Statutory Declaration in Lieu of Guarantor'.

It was also common knowledge within the criminal fraternity that prosti-tutes were always willing to act as 'guarantors' for a small stipend. Ray was knowledgeable about some, but not all, these procedures. What is clear is that he knew that passports had previously been easily obtained by criminals he had associated with.

Ray admitted that he studied how to obtain a false passport during the time he spent in Missouri State Penitentiary. 'In prison I studied about how a broker named Burrell or Birrell got a Canadian passport and escaped to South America,' he said.[3] It was likely Ray had read an issue of *Look* maga-zine from 27 February 1962. *Look* carried a story about a New York securities worker, Lowell Birrell, who had committed fraud then fled to Brazil with a forged Canadian passport.[4]

Two years before Ray's 1967 escape, another inmate of Missouri State Penitentiary, George Edmondson, had escaped and fled to Montreal. He assumed a new identity after illegally obtaining a passport and birth certifi-cate in the name of Alex Borman. Edmondson was recaptured and returned to Missouri State Penitentiary. He told FBI agents that Ray had associated with all the St Louis inmates at the prison and Ray was familiar with the procedures to obtain an illegal Canadian passport.[5] According to the HSCA, criminals on the run regularly purchased a 'complete set of false identifica-tion in [any] neighbourhood for as little as five dollars'.[6] This was, said HSCA Chief Counsel Robert Blakey, evidence that Ray did not have assistance in obtaining false passports or identities.[7]

Ray's initial plan was to go directly to South Africa but was told that the plane ticket would cost $820. As Ray did not have sufficient funds, the next best thing, he thought, would be to ask for a round-trip ticket to London. (This in itself was proof that if Ray had committed the assassination for money, he had not collected a bounty issued by racists groups by the time he arrived in Toronto.) He requested this type of ticket as he thought it would arouse less suspicion than a single ticket. It cost $275. He chose 6 May for his departure date. In the meantime, Ray travelled to Montreal as a back-up plan in which he might secure passage on a ship that would take him overseas without asking for a passport. He was unsuccessful and returned to Toronto on 26 April.

During his time in Toronto, he was visited by a man conspiracy advo-cates referred to as the 'fat man' co-conspirator. The man arrived at Ray's Toronto rooming house and handed him an envelope which, conspiracy advocates alleged, could have contained instructions or money related to the assassination. However, he was an innocent bystander named Robert McDoulton, a paint-company salesman who worked near Ray's rooming house in the Dundas Street area. He had found an envelope in a public telephone booth in the vicinity of Ray's rooming house at 962 Dundas Avenue, bearing the name Ramon George Sneyd. He thought it contained some sort of job application form. When Ray telephoned the travel agency, he had written the flight time to London on the back of the envelope. He then left the telephone booth without retrieving the document. The letter had contained the birth certificate he had applied for in order to obtain a passport. Ray's rooming house landlady identified McDoulton as the man who had called at the house. According to the Toronto police they were satisfied that McDoulton was a 'respectable citizen' and had nothing to do with the assassination.[8]

Ray believed he could travel from London to a country in Africa which did not have extradition agreements with the United States. He thought Rhodesia, an international pariah because of its racist government, would be the perfect hide-out. Rhodesia had attracted a great deal of publicity in the mid-1960s. In 1965 Rhodesian Prime Minister Ian Smith made a Unilateral Declaration of Independence and the country had been the subject of news stories and editorials in the National States Rights Party's organ 'The Thunderbolt' which was read by Ray. Following the assassination Ray's brother Jerry was later hired by the organization's leader J.B. Stoner.[9]

Ray had first considered the possibility of escaping to a country in Africa during his time in Missouri State Penitentiary. In December 1967, eight months after he escaped from prison, he wrote to the US-based American South African Council asking about emigrating to Rhodesia. Ray wrote:

> Dear Sir,
> I recently read an article in the Los Angeles Times on your council. The John Birch Society provided me with your address. My reason for writing is that I am considering immigrating to Rhodesia, however, there are a couple legal questions involved: One: The US government will not issue a passport for travel to Rhodesia. Two: Would their [*sic*] be any way to enter Rhodesia legally (from the Rhodesian point of view?) I would appreciate any information you could give me on the above subject or any other information on Rhodesia.

Ray knew that if Rhodesia could defy the world it would likely refuse any extradition deal with the United States, a country that supported the British government's efforts to bring black majority rule to the British colony. Ray also considered the possibility of securing work as a mercenary, possibly ending up in Angola where a war was being fought using mercenary soldiers.

But first Ray had to solve a problem that had arisen with the new passport the travel agency had arranged for him. His name was spelt RAMON GEORGE SNEYA instead of Ramon George Sneyd. However, he felt he could have the mistake corrected when he arrived in London. On 6 May he caught his flight and arrived at Heathrow airport at 6.40am on 7 May. The mistake in his name went unnoticed. After hanging around the airport all day he then exchanged the return portion of his ticket for a flight to Lisbon which he caught at 10.55pm that night. On his arrival in Lisbon an airport official wanted him to correct the mistake on the passport and Ray agreed to have the matter dealt with.

Ray spent ten days in the Portuguese capital. He knew the city was an international recruiting centre for white mercenaries. According to Ray:

> After a couple of days I located a small passenger ship whose rates I could afford and that was leaving soon for the Portuguese colony of Angola. But when I tried to book passage, the ticket agent said I'd have to have a visa from the security police. Reluctantly, I went through that motion. The police said the process would take seven days – the ship was sailing in three.[10]

Ray tried the South African embassy, the Rhodesian mission and the unofficial legation for Biafra but they could not help him. He decided to return to London on 17 May. But before returning he visited the Canadian embassy and was issued a new passport. However, he was informed he had to present *both* passports when going through customs.

If Ray had had sufficient money, it is likely he would have waited in Lisbon for his visa, due to be issued by 15 May, and then sailed to Angola. Ray feared that robbing a bank in Portugal, a country where he did not speak the language and was unfamiliar with the currency, was too risky. Instead, he decided to return to London in the likelihood that it would be easier to rob a bank there.

* * *

On 19 April the FBI identified Ray as the same person as Eric Starvo Galt, wanted for the murder of Martin Luther King. However, the 'Sneyd' passport was not issued in Ottawa until 25 April and the RCMP had to search through 50,000 passport applications to identify Ray. On 20 May the RCMP and the FBI discovered that he had left Toronto for London on 6 May. On 23 May the FBI learned from the Canadian embassy in Lisbon that on 16 May Ray (Sneyd) had been issued a new passport and they also discovered that Ray had flown from Lisbon to London on 17 May.

The FBI informed Scotland Yard that Ray was in London. The assistance of British police was requested by John Minnich, an FBI agent attached to the American embassy in London. An all-ports warning was issued on 6 June requesting that if a man named Sneya or Sneyd presented himself at Immigration Control, he be detained and Scotland Yard detectives informed.

* * *

Meanwhile, Ray had been busy keeping his head down in London and trying to think of ways to get to Africa. He told author William Bradford Huie, 'In London I tried to find out all I could about getting in the mercenaries.'[11]

Ray contacted a *Daily Telegraph* reporter, Ian Colvin, who he learned had connections to mercenary groups working out of Brussels. He said his brother was a mercenary and asked Colvin if he could have the telephone number of mercenary leader Major Wicks so he could try and contact his brother. It is likely Ray read about Wicks in London papers of 19 May. This would have been two days after Ray returned from his abortive mission to Lisbon where he tried to secure employment as a mercenary. What probably caught Ray's eye was the background information in the newspaper reports that Wicks was an ex-mercenary more recently engaged in supplying Biafra with soldiers.

At about 5pm on 4 June, Colvin said, a man named Ramon Sneyd phoned him and said he was a Canadian who had a brother who had been to Angola and he wanted to get in touch with Wicks. Colvin was wary of informants who had troubled Wicks, seeking information about volunteers for Biafra and then denouncing Wick's organization. He therefore told Ray he would contact Wicks who could then get in touch with him. The message was passed to the mercenary leader but he did not recognize the name given to him.

Ray's London rooming house manager Jane Nassau told detectives she had listened in on the calls to ensure the correct connection:

He had read in the Telegraph about a man ... who had been deported from 'Pogo Land' [*Author's Note*: a racist description of African nations] and he [Ray] wanted to know the man's address. He was most persistent in the enquiry to trace this man. Because he was so incoherent nobody seemed able to help him. I now remember that the man who was deported was a captain or major. In the end I think he got this man's address. I do not know who he spoke to at the Daily Telegraph.[12]

Ray persisted and phoned Colvin again on 6 June. According to Colvin:

Mr Sneyd ... said that his brother was not really missing, though he had not heard from him for four months. The fact was that he would like to join him and become himself a mercenary. Mr Sneyd did not revert to enquiring for Major Wicks and seemed content to discuss his problem with me instead. As I had just published a book about Mr Tshombe in which the mercenary force in the Congo is frequently mentioned, this did not strike me as extraordinary, and as the man seemed to be in some sort of troubled state of mind, I was patient and listened. Now and then the conversation was interrupted, as he was telephoning from a phone box. I said to him that the mercenary forces had largely left Africa. He might find the remnants of them in Belgium and Jean Schramme was certainly there. There were ex-servicemen's associations and welfare organisations for the former settlers in Africa who might put him in touch with his brother. I had no idea of their addresses but mentioned to him the name of a research editor on Congo affairs, M. Jean Gerard-Liebor of CRISP, the Centre de Recherches et Informations Sociales et Politiques who could tell him where to inquire next.

Colvin said Ray's purpose and manner, 'gave an odd, almost unbalanced impression'.[13]

On Wednesday, 5 June, aware that the British authorities might be looking for him, Ray moved to a new rooming house at The Pax, a backstreet hotel situated at 126 Warwick Way in Pimlico. He was later identified by the hotel owner Anna Thomas, who said he had registered under the name Ramon George Sneyd, 'speaking with a schooled Canadian accent'. She described Ray as having made:

... a bad impression ... was nervous, furtive, locked his bedroom door at night and stayed in bed most of the day. I always thought he slept in bed with his clothes on she said. When I brought his breakfast tray, he told me to leave it outside, like he was still in bed. Then, a minute later,

before I had gone a step, he was at the door fully dressed, picking it up
… he was so neurotic.[14]

On Saturday morning, 8 June, Ray left the hotel and went to Heathrow
airport to catch a fight to Brussels. He had booked a seat on British European
Airways Flight 466 which was due to leave at 11.50am. Ray was carrying a
loaded pistol and £51 sterling. After checking in with BEA and handing
over his luggage, Ray approached Immigration Control at Terminal 2 and
handed over his passport. As he closed the wallet Immigration Officer
Kenneth Human noticed another Canadian passport inside it. Human
questioned Ray about the two passports. Ray explained that it had been a
mistake made by Canadian authorities. A minute or two after Ray had presented himself a Police Special Branch officer approached the desk. While
Human and Ray engaged in conversation, Detective Sergeant Phillip Birch
had searched his suspect index and became aware that Sneyd was a fugitive
from US justice.[15]

Birch asked Ray to accompany him to the Special Branch office at
the airport. On searching Ray, he found in his right-hand back trouser
pocket a Japanese .38 Liberty Chief Special revolver loaded with five
rounds of ammunition and asked him why he had been carrying the gun.
'Well, I'm going to Africa and I felt I might need it,' Ray replied. 'You
know how things are out there.' Ray was detained until the arrival of
Detective Chief Superintendent Thomas Butler, the police officer who
led the hunt for the perpetrators of the Great Train Robbery in 1963, and
Detective Chief Inspector Thompson of Scotland Yard. Butler began by
informing the suspect, 'We are police officers. I understand you have in
your possession two passports in the names of Sneya and Sneyd. What
is your name?' Ray said, 'I can't understand why I am here. My name is
Sneyd.' When Ray said he did not hold a valid firearm licence he was
arrested and told he would be taken to Cannon Row Police Station, a
stone's throw from Big Ben and the Houses of Parliament. The police
station was situated in the area of Old Scotland Yard in close proximity
to 10 Downing Street.[16]

Ray had been placed in a cell and told he had to wait until further enquiries were made. Meanwhile, Detective Sergeant Peter Elliot and Detective
Constable John Whitham had been sent to retrieve Ray's luggage from the

BEA returning Brussels flight and discovered a brown jacket with a label bearing the name of 'Mr Eric Galt', dated 21 July 1967 and order no. 11526.[17]

After being charged with the possession of an illegal firearm, a British lawyer, Michael Eugene, was appointed to defend him. Ray asked him to contact F. Lee Bailey, a US lawyer who had represented Sam Shepard in a famous murder trial of the previous decade. Bailey refused to defend Ray citing his friendship with Martin Luther King. Ray also asked Eugene to contact Melvin Belli who had achieved notoriety by representing Lee Harvey Oswald's killer Jack Ruby. Belli did not respond to any overtures.[18] During his discussions with Eugene, he surprised the solicitor by requesting he contact his brother Jerry Ray – only moments before he had denied he was James Earl Ray.[19]

Another lawyer Ray asked Eugene to contact was Birmingham, Alabama, lawyer Arthur Hanes. It prompted a positive response. The lawyer and his son, Arthur Hanes Jr, travelled to London and Hanes Sr eventually met Ray on 5 July 1968 in Wandsworth Prison. The two men met in a small interview room and could see and talk to each other through a glass partition. During the entire period of the Hanes' visit to London they were kept under surveillance by Scotland Yard detectives. A report of their activities was prepared by Scotland Yard for the FBI.[20]

Hanes explained to Ray that fighting extradition to the United States would be seen by many as a sign of guilt. He advised Ray to go along with the US government's extradition efforts to get him back to Memphis to stand trial. Hanes also counseled Ray not to get involved with lawyer J.B. Stoner, an avowed racist who had expressed an interest in defending Ray. Getting involved with Stoner, Hanes advised, would prove to many that his crime had a racist motive. He also told Ray he would only take his case if Hanes and his son were his only defence team and if Ray would agree to the publication of his story after the expected trial. Hanes explained this would guarantee funds to pay for Ray's defence.[21]

As the appeal period terminated on 17 July, Ray decided to abandon any further efforts to remain in Britain. Ray wrote to his brother Jerry from his cell and signed the letter, 'Lord R.G. Sneyd', a joking reference to his incarceration in a British prison. He told Jerry, 'I could appeal my extradition hearing but I am getting tired of listening to these liars so I might close it up on Tuesday.'[22]

* * *

In 1978 the circumstances of Ray's stay in London were examined by the HSCA and investigators sought the testimony of a British police officer who had guarded Ray. In 1968 Sergeant Alexander Eist had been appointed to the Flying Squad and was assigned to escort James Earl Ray between prison and the magistrates' court. He had not been asked to give an account of his conversations with Ray in the period between the assassination and the HSCA hearings.

Eist retired as a Detective Chief Inspector after serving twenty-eight years on the police force. In 1978 he decided to come forward after he related his story to a US major stationed in England who advised him he should contact the FBI. Eist was asked to give testimony to the HSCA and was interviewed at the Greenman's pub, Six-Mile Bottom, in Cambridge, by committee investigators Edward Edwards and Robin Lindley.

On 4 August 1978, Eist told the investigators:

> Recently, about two months ago I think it was, there was a bit of publicity over here about certain things happening to do with Earl Ray and the shooting of Martin Luther King. There were inquiries and things going on. And I have a lot of Americans coming here, and I was talking to an American couple who said this was probably important to the country's sake and I should do something about it and get in touch with the author-ities, which I did, I phoned the FBI.[23]

Eist testified to the committee that he had many conversations with Ray. In particular, Eist said, Ray told him, 'there was no way that they would actually be able to pin the murder on him except that he had thrown the gun away; that was the mistake he had made'. Eist recalled Ray as saying he had seen 'a policeman or police vehicle and panicked and thrown the gun away, and his fingerprints would obviously be found on this weapon'. Eist also said that Ray had never expressed any regret about King's death. Eist told the committee he believed that, 'from what he told me ... for what it is worth, I haven't any doubt in my mind that he did that [assassination] on his own ... If it had been anything, or anybody behind him on that particular job that during the various and many conversations I had with him it would have come out.'[24]

Eist's testimony to the HSCA was disturbing to both Ray and his lawyer Mark Lane. Typical of conspiracy advocates, Lane decided to attack the integrity of the witness by alleging Eist had been a corrupt police officer.

And in his autobiography Ray wrote, 'Evan Williams, an investigator in Clwyd, North Wales, found that Eist had been indicted for several jewel robberies and for falsely claiming to have obtained confessions. British authorities refused to release documents from Eist's trials confirming this.'[25]

However, Lane had used an unreliable source to make his claims about Eist and, in the process, had destroyed the reputation of an innocent police officer. Eist had not been dismissed from the police force but had instead retired on the grounds of ill health. Furthermore, the only suspicious circumstances connecting Eist to corrupt police practices involved a case in which Eist had been fully absolved of any wrongdoing.[26]

* * *

In July US marshalls escorted James Earl Ray on a flight to Memphis. Ray left England at 12.38am on Friday, 19 July. During the flight Harold Light said Ray was no problem, docile and he declined food and drink. At one point during the trip Ray complained of a headache and was given two aspirins.[27] On arrival at a US military base the detectives boarded the aircraft with Ray, removed his handcuffs and transferred the prisoner to the care of the escorting FBI agents.

Ray was then turned over to Sheriff William Morris and taken to the Shelby County Jail, where a special block had been prepared on the third floor. Ray's cell was in a block which contained five separate cells. Steel plate was installed outside the windows and those of the adjacent County Office building were also secured. The cell block had two television monitors and an audio monitoring system. A group of fourteen specially selected deputies were assigned to Ray's custody. Two guards were in the cell block at all times keeping Ray under constant surveillance and maintaining a written log. Food was selected on a random basis from food served to other prisoners.

Meanwhile, the nation began to wonder if authorities had the real killer of Martin Luther King in custody. Americans, fed on a diet of Kennedy conspiracy theories, began to doubt that a common criminal like James Earl Ray had the know-how to implement a sophisticated political assassination. They would have to wait a full ten months before the case came to trial. Only then, Americans believed, would the whole truth about the murder of Martin Luther King be revealed.

* * *

In March 1969, 41-year-old James Earl Ray was led into the tight security of a Memphis, Tennessee, courtroom to stand trial for one of the most infamous crimes in US history.

Shelby County District Attorney Phil Canale laid out the case prosecution of Ray:

> Gentlemen, this was not a man being fed money by conspirators. Wherever he could, he economised. He lived like a beachcomber. When they found his white Mustang, it was full of crackers and canned food. He ate his meals in his car when he was on the road; when he stayed in motels, they were the cheapest, and he prepared and ate his meals in his rooms, buying the cheapest foods. He travelled with everything he needed, from soup and coffee, heaters to condiments. He probably never ordered a full meal in a restaurant: he lived on hamburgers, candy, pizza, potato chips, and beer. When he was captured in London, in his pocket was an advertisement he had clipped from a newspaper advertising cheap airline rates to Africa.[28]

Canale went on the describe how Ray took a flight from Toronto to London 'on the cheapest possible excursion ticket' and lived frugally and when he was arrested in London, he 'had less than 125 dollars on his person. ... Every step of the way from his escape to his capture, he himself did everything required in the preparation and carrying out of the murder'.[29]

Canale then addressed the issue of whether or not Ray could have been part of a conspiracy and argued that if Ray had been involved in a conspiracy he would not have been 'so exposed'. Canale went on to explain how Ray bought the rifle used to kill King and the Mustang used for his escape from the scene of the crime. 'He rented the rooms himself wherever he went,' Canale said, '[and he] bought his own clothes, made his own telephone calls; nothing was done for him'. Canale said there was no evidence that anyone helped him, 'and [he] went about picking up travel folders and information, buying the airline tickets, applying for the passport, picking up photographs, tickets, and passport'.[30]

Canale said that if it had been a conspiracy:

> ... his fellow conspirators would have kept him hidden as long as possible, so that the man who fired the fatal shot would have remained out of sight until then, a stranger, someone not easily identifiable – someone not

likely to be captured and so put in jeopardy the others in the conspiracy. What conspirators would have allowed such a man to leave such a trail?[31]

Canale and his fellow prosecutors in the case produced a map of Atlanta found in Ray's rented room in Atlanta. The map had several locations circled indicating areas that were in the vicinity of Martin Luther King's home, church and offices. Ray's travel itinerary indicated he had been stalking King.

Evidence was also introduced that proved Ray had spent the night of 22 March 1968 in a motel in Selma, Alabama, as King conducted his business nearby. Newspaper reports said King would be in Selma on 22 March recruiting for his Poor People's Campaign. As it turned out King's route was changed and he appeared in a town near Selma. However, Ray drove to Selma on 22 March and registered at the Flamingo Motel. William Bradford Huie wrote about these events for *Look* magazine in late 1968 and the article was approved by James Earl Ray before publication. Later, Ray insisted he was in Selma only because he got lost on the road from New Orleans to Birmingham.

The circumstantial and eyewitness evidence appeared to be overwhelming. The FBI had determined by fingerprint matching, handwriting analysis and chemical analysis that the LOWMEYER who bought the murder rifle (fingerprints, signatures) was the GALT who drove the white Mustang (hair samples, signature on the driver's licence) was the WILLARD who stayed in Room 5b (fibres of Willard's bedspread matched fibres found on the Mustang's upholstery and fibres embedded in Room 5b's rug) was the JAMES EARL RAY who escaped from Missouri State Penitentiary (GALT'S fingerprints were RAY'S) was the BRIDGMAN who obtained the birth certificate (necessary for a passport) in Toronto (BRIDGMAN'S handwriting was Ray's) was the SNEYD who was arrested in London (SNEYD'S fingerprints were RAY'S).

The prosecution said that handwriting and fingerprint experts linked James Earl Ray to the purchase of the rifle. Ray's fingerprints were on the gun and the telescopic sight. Ray had purchased the weapon five days before the murder under the alias Harvey Lowmeyer. The real Harvey Lohmeyer had worked in a prison kitchen with Ray's brother John in Illinois during the late 1950s. Lohmeyer told the FBI that he had heard about James Earl Ray but had never met him.

Ray had bought the gun from the Aeromarine Supply Company in Birmingham. Ray actually bought two guns. The first, a .243-calibre Winchester, Ray may have thought would not accommodate the bullets he had previously purchased. An examination of that weapon showed some hardened Cosmoline in the breach, making it difficult to operate. Ray had returned this first gun and exchanged it for the Remington. The prosecution alleged that the markings on the bullet removed from King matched the general rifling characteristics of the Remington. General rifling characteristics are the consistent features inside the barrel of all rifles of the same model.

Prosecutors had used Robert A. Frazier's ballistics evidence in their presentation. Frazier, chief of the firearms identification unit of the FBI, had examined the cartridges, the hull from the chamber of the rifle and the slug removed from Dr King's body. He said that the death slug was identical in all physical characteristics to the five loaded 30.06 Springfield cartridges found in the bag in front of Canipe's Amusement Store. He stated that the death slug contained 'land and groove' impressions consistent with those present in the barrel of the rifle. He could not positively certify that Ray's rifle fired the death slug.

The details of the binoculars and a suitcase full of clothes which had been dropped in front of the Canipe's Amusement Store minutes after the shot was fired were presented to the court. The FBI had taken possession of the physical evidence and an FBI agent took them to the FBI laboratory in Washington DC. The agent also took the murder slug with him. Two days later the Memphis police sent the T-shirt and undershorts which had been found in the suitcase. These items were important as they had laundry marks on them.[32] On Monday morning, 1 April Ray had taken his clothing to the Piedmont Laundry at 1168 Peachtree Street in Atlanta. The laundry had been managed by Mrs Estelle Peters. She remembered Ray clearly as his clean-cut image made him stand out from her regular clients who lived in the hippie district.[33]

The prosecutors stipulated that James Earl Ray, under the alias Eric S. Galt, had spent the night of 3 April 1968 at the New Rebel Motel, Memphis. Investigations at motels in the vicinity of Memphis to identify persons who might be driving a white Mustang disclosed that an Eric S. Galt of 260 Highland Avenue, Birmingham, Alabama, had spent the night of 3 April at the New Rebel Motel.

The following day, 4 April 1968, Ray checked into the rooming house in Memphis at 422 South Main Street at about 3pm. Ray signed in under the name John Willard. Prosecutors believed he rejected a room in a part of the house which did not afford a view of the Lorraine Motel and accepted Room 5b where the motel could be observed. Ray could watch all the activity on King's balcony. From that window, however, it would have been an awkward shot. Ray would have had to lean far out the window and contort his body to target King. A better view, although partly obscured by trees and bushes, could be obtained from the bathroom window down the hall from 5b. After the shooting Bessie Brewer identified James Earl Ray as the John Willard who had rented Room 5b. She observed that the furniture had been moved – a dresser had been dragged away from the window and a chair had been drawn up to the window. (This evidence indicated the assassin had kept watch on the Lorraine Motel.) Through the serving of a legal paper the exact location of King's room had been publicized; Ray had bought a copy of the *Memphis Commercial Appeal* giving that information. His fingerprints were on the newspaper.

Evidence was presented to prove that Ray bought binoculars from the York Arms Company in the late afternoon of 4 April. The binoculars were later found in a bag which had been dropped in front of Canipe's Amusement Store shortly following the shooting. The binoculars had Ray's fingerprints on them. Binocular straps were later found in Room 5b and were subsequently matched with the pair Ray had bought from the York Arms Company.

The pale-yellow Mustang, visually identified as 'white', was observed at the scene of the crime. It did not have a licence plate in front but held red and white 1968 Alabama plates in the rear of the vehicle. Two Mexican tourist stickers stamped October 1967 were on the windscreen. Threads and dirt samples from Ray's Mustang and the sofa in Room 5b contained fibres from the dingy green bedspread used to wrap up his belongings.

The prosecution created an assassination scenario using testimonies of the rooming house witnesses. Willie Anschlutz, who had the room next to Ray's, 6b, said that he had tried to use the bathroom twice shortly before the shooting but had found it occupied. Anschlutz complained to neighbour, Charles Q. Stephens, in Room 4b, who told him that the 'new boarder' was using the bathroom. Anschutz could not positively identify Ray because the man exiting the bathroom after the shot was fired had raised his hand and arm to his head to conceal his face.

The prosecution stated that Ray had made several trips to the bathroom, locking the door and standing in the bathtub to monitor the activities in Room 306 of the Lorraine Motel, 205ft away at a downward angle. The prosecution stated that Ray had observed King standing on the balcony and talking to some friends in the courtyard. He then hurried to his room, got his rifle and one bullet, returned to the bathroom, locked the door, stepped into the bathtub, rested his rifle on the windowsill and, at exactly 6.01pm, fired the shot that killed King. Ray's rifle had recoiled so sharply that it left scratches on the windowsill. The FBI later took the windowsill for examination and inconclusively stated that a groove on the sill matched the barrel of the rifle.

Ray unlocked the bathroom door and walked towards his room. Charles Q. Stephens, who was working on a radio in his kitchenette next to the bathroom wall, heard a shot, walked to his doorway and observed a man he later identified as Ray walk to Room 5b. Ray jammed the gun into the cardboard box, threw all his belongings, except the binocular straps, into a dingy green bedspread and hurried down the stairs. Emerging onto the pavement, he turned left and trotted toward his car 60ft away. Ray then drove off at top speed. Amusement store owner Guy Canipe testified that within minutes of the shooting he heard the thud of a bundle dropping in his doorway and saw a neatly dressed man drive off in the Mustang. Skid marks were found on the street.

Many years after the assassination Alexander Eist told the HSCA why Ray dropped his bundle including the rifle before he got into his car. Eist said Ray told him:

> … there was no way that they would actually be able to pin the murder on him except that he had thrown the gun away; that was the mistake he had made. I recall he said to me he had seen a policeman or a police vehicle and panicked and thrown the gun away and his fingerprints would obviously be found on this weapon.[34]

* * *

That he did not go to trial was, in some part, Ray's own fault. On 10 November 1968, two days before he was originally scheduled to go on trial, Ray fired his first defence lawyer Arthur Haynes, of Birmingham, Alabama, and replaced him with Houston lawyer Percy Foreman, a nationally recognized figure. Hanes had been dismissed without warning by Ray after he had already pleaded Ray not guilty to the charge of murdering King.

Ray's new lawyer told Ray, 'There's a 100% chance you'll be convicted and a 99% chance you'll get the death penalty. I would consider it one of the most significant accomplishments of my career if I could save your life, I think pleading guilty would save your life.' Foreman also told Ray that Memphis juries had been hard on first-degree murder defendants and he would probably receive a long sentence – ninety-nine years – if he pleaded guilty, but this would not be a real problem for Ray. If Ray had received the minimum sentence for murder, twenty years for the State of Tennessee, this would effectively mean that Ray would have to serve the rest of his life in prison, for no sooner had he completed the Tennessee sentence he would immediately be arrested and extradited to Missouri to complete his original twenty-year sentence.[35]

After the prosecutors met with Foreman and told him they would not ask for the death penalty if his client pleaded guilty, Ray was faced with a choice – either plead not guilty and face the overwhelming evidence against him or plead guilty and avoid execution. Ray chose the latter.

Chapter 4

Jailhouse Lawyer

[The pathological liar] spins tales that appear plausible on the surface but do not hang together over time. Fact and fiction are woven together in an interesting matrix until the two are virtually indistinguishable. Unlike a delusional psychotic person, they will abandon the story or change it if confronted with contradictory evidence ...

Charles M. Ford, MD

Ray always greets us with a silly, sheepish grin which is higher on the left side of his face than on the right. He seems to be enjoying a joke which only he knows. When I walk into his cell, I always feel that he has just pulled a fast one on me and I arrived a minute too late to catch him at it. When Ray is talking, if he is lying, his eyes blink and keep shifting downward. If his lie is challenged, he will shake his head briefly, then drop his head and admit his lie.

Ray's first lawyer, Arthur Hanes

Central to an understanding of James Earl Ray's motives and his pleas of innocence is an appreciation of how he used lies and deception through-out his life to manipulate friends, colleagues and law-enforcement officials. As his biographer William Bradford Huie told the *St Louis Post Despatch*, 'Ray has practiced deception since the day he was born. It's highly unnatural for him to tell the truth. . . . he is a born fabricator.'[1]

Throughout his time as an armed robber and burglar prison officials and law-enforcement officials testified to Ray's emotional scars. According to East Alton Police Chief Harold H. Riggins, who had arrested Ray on a number of occasions:

We suspected [Ray] was in need of mental help because he was in a mixed-up state of mind. He was a liar, there's no doubt about that. We feel sure he had been slapped around in his life. I would say he had no respect for the law as he was bitter, unremorseful, sarcastic and overbearing. He's the type of fellow who would do anything for a fee. He could be swayed to do anything.[2]

Understanding Ray's value system had its roots in his teenage years and developed as he began to spend more of his young manhood incarcerated in prisons. Ray was a victim of anomie – a lack of social or moral standards in his upbringing. He was also a 'born loser', beginning at the bottom of the totem pole of life and staying there.

Ray was the eldest of nine children of George (who sometimes used the name James Gerald) and Lucille Ray. One of Ray's brothers died in a car crash, two others wound up in jail, one of his sisters died in a fire and another was in and out of mental institutions.

The parents were married on 26 April 1926 in Florida. George Ray changed his name so many times during his life, his children became confused. George used the surnames Raynes, Ryan or Raines when it suited him, usually to fool the authorities who wanted to question him about various crimes or debts.

The Ray children all suffered from the terrible burden of having inadequate parents. Lucille was a woman who suffered from low self-esteem and depression and became an alcoholic. The father had committed numerous criminal offences as a young man. He displayed little respect for authority or officialdom. When he was 21, he was sentenced to a term in prison for breaking and entering.

At first, George and Lucille lived with Lucille's parents and then moved around the area, living in Quincy, Illinois, Ewing, Missouri, and back again to Quincy. The family never escaped from grinding poverty, trouble and misfortune and lived hand to mouth in run-down, shabby neighbourhoods. Even working class whites looked down on them. But they were not peculiar. There were millions of families like the Rays during the 1930s Depression.

James' mother tried her best to keep the family together and did what she could with a meagre income and a rundown farmhouse. However, the debilitating poverty left her unable to cope. In 1952 George left her for another woman and she drifted into chronic alcoholism. Numerous arrests followed for drunkenness and disorderly conduct. She died in 1961.

By 1953 five of the Ray children had become wards of court and tragedy seemed to follow them around. Marjorie Ray was born in 1930 and died as a child when she set herself on fire with a box of matches. John and Jerry followed the criminal career path of their father and older brother. Franklin was born in 1944 and died prematurely in 1964 when the car he was driving hit the guard rail of the Quincy Memorial Bridge and plunged into the Mississippi River killing him and the girl who was riding with him. Younger sister Melba suffered from a mental illness and was frequently in and out of psychiatric wards. Carol Ray was the youngest and lived with and cared for her father in later years, then married a petty criminal, Albert Pepper.

Ray's father, nicknamed 'Speedy' because he spoke with a slow drawl, had a reputation as a recluse but he nevertheless frequently visited saloons, drinking to excess. He was 69 years old at the time of the assassination and lived in Center, Missouri.

Speedy was a feckless individual whose habits and inability to 'bond' with his children led his sons, in later years, to claim he was dead, although they knew he was very much alive. In 1946, 17-year-old Ray wrote on his army enlistment application that his father was dead.[3] He told prison officials his father had died.[4] According to author George McMillan, '[James Earl Ray] was very much disillusioned about Speedy as a man and as a father by the time he left Ewing … From that time on, for the rest of his life, Jimmy was forever afterwards to insist, whenever he was asked, "Father?" … Jimmy would answer, "Dead".'[5]

Speedy's antisocial values were passed on to the children. McMillan, who got to know the father well while researching his book *The Making of an Assassin*, judged him to be a man 'who sees life so differently, his values are so opposite. He is proud of things that others would deplore.'[6] Speedy felt he had been relegated to the bottom of society and he was just a pawn to be exploited and brutalized.[7]

In 1935 the family moved to Ewing, Illinois, and bought a smallholding for $600 with money provided by Lucille's mother. It was the year that James started school. He was painfully shy and was seen by many as a 'Huck Finn' character. As a child he had suffered from bedwetting and troubled sleep, became introverted and found it difficult to communicate, a trait that never left him. At 8 he had an odd experience while he lay in bed. He lay jerking and twitching for nearly half an hour. It was later believed he had suffered an epileptic fit. One night when he was 10, he awoke and couldn't see. Doctors diagnosed an attack of hysteria. It was the first of many psychological problems that were to haunt Ray throughout his life and caused him, following his 1967 escape from prison, to seek the help of psychologists and hypnotists to address his ailments.

It is clear that Ray never bonded with his parents, never had any deep feelings for them. There are no recorded statements about the death of his mother or his relationship with his father. Missouri Director of Corrections Fred T. Wilkinson, who had known Ray for a number of years, said, 'Ray was indifferent to people around him …'.[8]

Ray also appeared to have inherited his parents' reclusiveness. Throughout his life he never felt a need to engage in long conversations with others and in later years his fellow inmates described him as a person who 'kept himself to himself', an introvert who rarely spoke of his family, friends or had any voiced ambitions in life.

Throughout his life Ray was unable to 'connect' with women. His relationships were always superficial and were predicated on a need for sex which was why he frequented prostitutes. He had no need or desire for any emotionally intimate relationship. Ray's friend 'Uncle' Jack Gawron described Ray as very shy when meeting a girl for the first time and that he would lisp or stutter. When Ray wanted a girl Gawron usually found one for him.[9]

Ray's real role model was his Uncle Earl, an ex-convict, racist and, from all accounts, a mean and dislikeable man. James worshipped him. He admired how Uncle Earl stole, gambled and conned people. Even when Earl threw acid in his wife's face James apparently approved of his uncle's act; at least he felt it was not 'wrong'. As a young man Ray took stolen goods to Earl to 'fence'.[10]

When he was growing up James was not without friends. He was often seen with three boys who lived nearby. They hunted, swam, played with slingshots and often complained of hunger. Sometimes they would hunt in the woods for rabbits or squirrels. At school James' progress was slow. Like most children who come from dysfunctional families, the stress of poverty and parental neglect left him without the physical or mental stamina that are required for schooling. James' IQ was tested and he achieved a score of 108, slightly above average. (Later, prison tests showed he had an IQ of 105 and 111.) However, he made no effort to apply himself and was never encouraged by his parents.

James' attitude towards school was entirely negative. He broke all the rules and was judged to be dishonest and impolite. He was suspicious of others and was disaffected with the world around him. His fifth-grade teacher Mrs Ina Kitson recalled James as being 'rather shiftless', but he never carried a grudge. He didn't care too much about things but I think that was caused by his environment. He was hard to understand but he always had a devilment about him that made you think he was up to something.'[11]

A classmate, Emmet Washburn, had no respect for the young James. Following a theft at school, Washburn said, the young Ray pointed the finger at him. 'Jimmy was a thief,' Washburn remembered. 'He got me in on it in the 5th grade. They discovered that the lunch money was missing and they caught Jimmy. He said he took it, all right, but the rat said I put him up to it. I didn't have a thing to do with it but that's the kind of individual he was.' Washburn's story was confirmed by Superintendent Leach of the Ewing School system, who said, 'I do remember that Washburn was one of our brighter students and we definitely proved that [Ray] had taken the money himself and was just trying to drag Washburn in.'[12]

In 1943, when Ray was 15 years old, he went to Alton to stay with his grandmother on his mother's side and obtained work in a shoe factory. It was at the factory that Ray had his first encounter with radical politics, an interest that would remain with him for the rest of his life. Ray made friends with Henry Stumm, a German immigrant who harboured overtly Nazi sympathies. Ray's 'Uncle Willie' believed that the older man greatly influenced Ray and that his nephew began to adopt the same fascist ideology.[13] Ray began speaking out against Jews and 'niggers', made statements in admiration of Hitler and described Germany in glowing terms. He later told prison officials he came from a 'German-English family'.[14]

When Ray joined the US Army in 1946 as a 17-year-old, he asked for a posting to Germany. He found himself in Nuremberg, home of the Hitler rallies and the war crimes trials. He became a driver of refrigerated trucks but found he was unable to manoeuvre them properly. He received a 'poor' rating from his superiors.

Ray was transferred to Bremerhaven but soon got into difficulties. Ray also contracted VD numerous times, went absent without leave on four occasions and was often drunk. He was tried and convicted by a Special Court-Martial for being drunk in quarters. Ray was sentenced to be confined to hard labour for three months and to forfeit $45 per month for four months.[15] It was the first of many drinking related offences for which he received army discipline. In 1948 he was discharged. He was described by his last commanding officer as 'inept and as a soldier with a general attitude of indifference'. Ray returned to the United States.[16]

For the following decade Ray's life centred around a dislike for regular employment and a desire to steal. Louis Chief William H. Peterson said, 'He was a dirty-necked thief who slept all day and stole all night. His record is as dirty as he is.'[17]

When Ray was discharged from the army, he tried his hand at a number of jobs and at one time considered becoming a private detective, abandoning the notion when he found the work was not as glamourous as the movies portrayed it. He moved to Los Angeles but was arrested on 7 October 1949 following an attempted robbery of the third-floor office of the Forum cafeteria. He was given three months in the county jail. During his trial he denied everything even though the evidence against him was overwhelming. Ray had fled from the scene of the crime but only after he inadvertently dropped his ID papers. He first told police officers his ID papers had been stolen. Days later he changed his story. He now said he had indeed been there, but he had only entered the building to eat at the restaurant.[18]

Years later, in the first edition of his autobiography *Tennessee Waltz* (1987), he again changed his story to claim he may have been drugged by a woman and left to sleep in the hallway of the building. All this in defence of a burglary where an assistant manager at the restaurant walked in and caught Ray red-handed. The incident was telling and proof that Ray had concocted stories that placed him at the scene of the crime but only as an unwilling supplicant – an innocent victim of circumstances.

On 6 May 1952 Ray robbed a taxi driver, was arrested by police and later in court denied he had used a gun. He said the police were mistaken and that actually he had employed a piece of lead pipe. In fact, each and every time Ray was arrested, he would vehemently deny everything.

On 23 March 1955 Ray was arrested with accomplices Walter Rife and Catherine Doris Buskirk near Hannibal, Missouri. Ray and Rife were charged with forging postal orders stolen in a burglary at a Kellerville, Illinois, post office. Ray had bought ID from Willard McBride for use in cashing the money orders. They had cashed eight at Hot Springs National Park, Arkansas, and one money order at Tallahassee, Florida. On 1 April 1955 Ray and Rife pleaded guilty. Ray received three years and nine months and Rife received three years. Ray spent his sentence at Leavenworth Prison and was released on 20 May 1958.[19]

From a poor start, Ray had begun to master the rudiments of the thief's skills under his Uncle Earl's tutelage. Although he was later characterized as a bungling burglar, he was by no means lacking in skills after his first long period of incarceration. Close associate in crime Walter Rife believed Ray 'grew up' in Leavenworth Prison. 'He learned how to behave around big-time criminals,' said Rife, '[and] he was permanently committed to a life of crime.' James Louma Owens, who befriended Ray in 1959 and committed armed robberies with him, said Ray was 'very smart', a 'thinker [who] plans every angle before he makes a move'.[20]

In summer 1959 Ray met Joseph Elmer Austin, a 60-year-old criminal and cellmate of Walter Rife, who had recently been paroled. On 11 July 1959 Ray and Austin robbed the Kroger Supermarket at 131 North Euclid Street, St Louis, of $1,200. They were later identified in photographs taken by a store security camera. On 21 August 1959 both men robbed another Kroger Supermarket in Alton and got away with $2,200. After a police chase Austin was captured while Ray escaped but was indicted for the crime on 27 October.

On 10 October 1959 Ray robbed another Kroger Supermarket in St Louis, accompanied by James Owens. They got away with $120. This time a bystander saw the two men change cars and reported it to the police. Officers spotted the car and waited for the men to return to it. They arrested Owens, who allegedly told police where Ray was staying. Two detectives arrested him.[21]

Foolishly defending himself during his court case, Ray couldn't provide the jury with any real evidence to exculpate him and instead acted as a jailhouse lawyer pleading his constitutional rights had been infringed and stating his confession had been 'beat out of me'.

Ray denied culpability and tried to will the crime away. He recanted his confession despite the appearance of four customers who positively identified him as the robber. Detective Harry Connors, who questioned Ray and put it to him that the evidence against him was overwhelming, said, 'He sat there with a silly grin on his face and said, "I can't deny it but I'll never admit it."'[22] One of his lawyers said, 'Ray thinks he can rearrange reality to suit himself. If he doesn't want a chair to be in a room, he wills it away. It's not there for him.' Owens frequently saw Ray in Missouri State Penitentiary. However, their relationship had soured as Ray blamed Owens for his arrest. Later his brother John said that if James ever saw Owens again that '[James] would kill [Owens] on site'.[23] Ray would remain in prison until his successful escape in 1967.

Ray defenders argue that as Ray had always been captured following his offences, he could never have committed a sophisticated crime like King's murder. What they often overlook, however, is the fact that those close to Ray have described him as anything but an incompetent criminal. Close family friend 'Uncle Jack' Gawron spoke of numerous robberies and burglaries that Ray had committed but avoided detection. 'Uncle Jack' had become acquainted with Ray's mother Lucille when he was paroled from prison in 1954. When he escaped from prison in 1956, he was harboured by Ray's mother and grandmother. By his own estimate Gawron had spent forty-five years in prison. During a period of several months in 1959 he became close friends with Ray and taught James to be a more efficient burglar. Together they carried out approximately twelve successful burglaries in northern Missouri and Illinois.[24]

Ray's lawyer Percy Foreman told *Newsweek* reporters, 'Ray is very smart like a rat. He has a strongly developed fundamental instinct to be somebody. He would rather be a name than a number. . . . He's cunning. Had he had the education he could have become a very useful citizen.'[25] William Bradford Huie said Ray 'has a sharp mind. He has done some self-educating in prison and is far from being a stupid man.'[26]

* * *

Ray's Uncle Earl, who had spent much of his life in penitentiaries, advised his nephew to 'always keep your head down' in prison. Although conspiracy advocates have always characterized Ray as a model inmate, the real truth about him is somewhat different and a wealth of evidence exists on record to show that Ray harboured violent traits in prison.

Ray's brothers Jerry and John said that James always had a bad temper.[27] Ray's uncle believed James had the capacity to 'kill' and said, 'I knew the boy was badly in need of psychiatric attention upon his release from military service. . . . I should have helped more …'.[28] Friend Walter Rife, who committed numerous robberies with Ray in the 1950s, said that Ray had a sharp temper and once stabbed a patron of a bar they visited.[29] Speedy Ray told FBI agents, following the murder of King, that his son was 'probably extremely ill mentally and … urgently in need of medical help'.[30] He told author George

McMillan that James had a violent temper and, 'You'd go along with Jimmy and everything would seem OK and then – Wham!'[31]

On one occasion, the FBI discovered, when an African American inmate called Ray 'Grey', Ray started a fight.[32] An FBI report also stated that:

> It was also believed that Ray had stabbed one inmate while still in the Missouri State Penitentiary down on the dock by the garbage cans, but his identity was never discovered by prison officials. It was believed that [redacted] held this inmate while Ray stabbed him with a knife. It was not believed that this was a mortal wound, but simply an assault with a knife.[33]

The FBI was able to assemble a full and revealing picture of Ray during the time he spent in Missouri State Penitentiary between 1959 and 1967, the year he escaped. Agents interviewed over a hundred inmates and their reports are part of the FBI's MURKIN (Murder of King) file. However, conspiracy advocates have dismissed information contained in the reports as tainted, believing inmates would have given any negative story about Ray as a method of securing an early release. Some Ray defenders believe some inmates used the interviews to get even as they were Ray's adversaries in prison. And it is evident from the interviews that some inmates did indeed seek some form of reciprocity for the information they supplied to FBI agents.

But, contrary to claims made by Ray defenders, 'deals' with convicts were never considered. According to an FBI memo that discussed the interviews with inmates:

> It is incumbent upon you to insure that [redacted] fully understands that the FBI cannot be a bargaining agent between him and any tribunal nor can the FBI act as an intermediary between [redacted] and any other individual in such a matter as this. The Bureau should not be put in a position for any individual to be able to state at a later date that such a proposal was taken under consideration by the Bureau ... and to leave no doubt in [redacted] mind that we cannot intercede in the sentence that he is serving.[34]

There were a number of inmates interviewed by the FBI who embraced the unwritten code of professional criminals – 'never rat'. In spite of these problems, most prisoners gave common descriptions of Ray. From defenders and adversaries alike Ray emerges from the reports as a habitual 'loner' with few friends; a prisoner who was always devising some scheme to break out of prison; a schemer who was involved in various money making ventures, including buying and selling amphetamines, loaning out a large collection of books and magazines and lending money to other prisoners.

From the interviews, it is clear that some inmates did not agree that Ray had a potential for violence, sold drugs or held racist views. As the names in the MURKIN files are, for the most part, blacked out it was difficult for researchers to determine how long each inmate had known Ray, whether or not they were indeed a cellmate of Ray and whether the inmate was simply repeating an accusation made by someone else. However, in 1997 author Gerald Posner was able to determine the identities of the inmates who gave interviews to FBI agents and he established which prisoners had known Ray well, worked with him in prison or celled with him.[35] According to Posner, 'Once the identities were known it was evident that many of those who claimed Ray was merely a passive prisoner with no racial hatred were themselves often accused of having been Ray's drug suppliers or prison protectors.'[36]

For some inmates, admissions about Ray's real activities in prison would have caused grave difficulties and even resulted in further charges made against them. Typical of this type was one inmate who told the FBI, 'I remember Jimmy Ray but I don't know anything about him now and if I did know anything about him, I wouldn't tell any representative of law enforcement.'[37]

However, many of the inmates who spoke of Ray's drug dealing, racist remarks and sometimes violent behaviour had been released from custody by the time they were interviewed by the FBI and did not have to say anything at all. Especially revealing to the FBI were the inmates who expressed no interest in any reward, hoped Ray would never be captured and that they would render no assistance to the FBI that would aid in Ray's capture. The FBI interviewed one inmate, who was close to and sympathetic with Ray, who described him as 'very deadly', not the 'rabble rousing type' and that if anyone wronged him Ray would 'immediately contrive means to get him'.[38]

Ray devoted only a small part of his autobiography to his time spent in prisons. It is revealing in that he omits to mention his medical reports and the incontrovertible evidence that he dealt in drugs. Ray arrived at the Missouri State Penitentiary with Ray Pruitt with whom he became friendly. Soon he developed a reputation as a 'lone wolf' and this phrase arises time and time again when inmates spoke about Ray to FBI agents in the weeks and months following the assassination. Most of the interviews were held before Ray was captured. He read frequently, preferring sex books and James Bond novels and had eclectic tastes in his reading. Ray did not trust anyone; he believed all convicts were 'stool pigeon material' and because he had been 'done in a couple of times'.[39]

Ray was also well schooled in the law and was seen as a 'jailhouse lawyer'. Many inmates viewed Ray as 'one of the nuts' or 'cowboys' who were small-time hoodlums who would be involved in 'petty thievery' or 'gangsterism' going on in the prison.[40] Ray liked country and western music and when a number of musical groups visited the prison Ray would never miss the performances. He often talked about going to the Lake of the Ozarks when he was released.[41] Some inmates told of how Ray believed he had a talent for locksmithing.

Wes Snider, a 31-year-old inmate, had cell 187 at the Missouri State Penitentiary from 1962 to 1965, 10ft away from Ray who had cell 191. Snider was interviewed only weeks after the assassination. His veracity lies in the information he gave to agents; information that had not been disseminated by the media at the time he gave the interviews. Snider's description of Ray included the identifiable trait of nervously pulling at the left earlobe. Snider said that, 'Ray never trusted anyone, that he was suspicious of everyone and had a feeling that everyone was out to get him … that on occasion he and Ray had talked about the philosophy of Friedrich Nietsche the philosopher, and he stated it was Ray's feeling that "man can do anything as long as it seems right for him".[42] Another inmate described Ray as a 'loner with no close friends, having a bad nervous condition and definitely having a mental problem'.[43]

Together with four other inmates, Ray and his group 'had a little thing going for them' selling amphetamine pills and other stimulants to inmates. It was estimated the group made $1,000 a month and had access to the amphetamines through a crooked guard who smuggled the pills into the prison.[44] Ray also personally used drugs. Typical of drug users, during his time in Missouri State Penitentiary his weight fluctuated considerably over the years and he experienced periods of paranoia. According to an ex-inmate:

> [Ray] was addicted mentally to stimulants, amphetamines, not the pills but powder. He got it the way you get anything you're not supposed to

get in prison and he injected it. Because of this he didn't eat – no appetite – and he was thin, about 150 pounds. I know he was paranoid. Never mind what the prison psychiatrist said ... he was smart and cool and he didn't trust anybody.[45]

Snider told agents that he worked with Ray in the kitchen baking bread. He described Ray as a 'loner' but considered him 'a "friend" on amphetamine powders'. According to an FBI memo:

The inmate said that Ray always had an 'outfit' in his cell stating that an outfit was 'a nose dropper with needle' to shoot a solution made up of amphetamine powder. Ray would purchase a spoonful for from $50 and then would break it up and sell it in smaller packages. Ray was a main line shooter for a number of years and because of this was highly nervous.[46]

Ray had gotten the kitchen job through another inmate, Neal Aeby, who, according to ex-guard James R. Dickson, was a 'big supplier of drugs'. Ray was named as a drug taker or pusher by inmates Richard L. Menard, Leo Harold Parker, Orlan Eugene Rose, Harry Sero, Carl Benton Drake, Lewis Raymond Dowda and Kenneth Lee Wade. Snider told agents that if amphetamine powder was not available Ray would break up 'Bennies'. According to inmate Frank Joseph Guinan, Ray was addicted to them and obtained his supply from a guard named 'Stout'. Snider also said that Ray, perhaps once or twice a month, would get money from the outside to buy amphetamine. Ray would get a letter smuggled out to his contact who would send a cheque directly to the inmate Ray was purchasing the drug from. As soon as the cheque cleared Ray would get the amphetamine.[47] Ray made some purchases from 'Jim Bradley ... top con ...'. The FBI agent's informant did not ask for any special treatment for the information he provided and also asked that his name not be revealed as he feared retaliation.[48] Other inmates named Missouri State Penitentiary guard Harold Schaeffer as '[Ray's] source for dope [and is] said to have been negligent in Ray's escape'.[49]

Ray's drug dealing was confirmed by his brother John, who told FBI agents that when his brother escaped from prison he had plenty of money as a result of dealing in amphetamines.[50]

The compelling evidence that Ray dealt in and took drugs is independently corroborated by Ray family friend 'Uncle Jack' Gawron, who told agents he believed Ray trafficked in drugs or barbiturates in prison. Gawron said he purchased inhalers for Ray, the request being made through Ray's sister Carol. Gawron said that on three separate occasions he was contacted by a prison guard who would pick up the inhalers and take them to Ray in prison and that the guard was paid $100 for each trip.[51] Further confirmation of Ray's dealing in drugs was made by Scotland Yard detectives when they discovered he had left a syringe needle in a waste bin at one of his London rooming houses.[52]

However, some stories told to FBI agents by serving or former inmates must be suspect. Ray Curtis' statements about drugs are compelling and are corroborated by others, but his stories about Ray threatening Martin Luther King have been called into question as he changed his story over the years and was involved in financial arrangements with tabloid newspapers.

From the FBI files it is clear that Curtis also invented part of his story of how Ray had been in league with a group of racially motivated conspirators and was supposed to be spirited away on a houseboat on the Mississippi River following King's murder. The FBI discovered that the owners of the houseboat Charles Willie and his wife (not Willet as Curtis alleged) had no connection with Curtis. The couple were cleared by the FBI. Moreover, Curtis admitted to the FBI that he had made up the story for a fee of $5,000 from *Ebony* magazine.[53] Curtis' allegations have not been used for my background research into Ray's activities in prison.

Ray was also involved in money lending schemes during his incarceration at Missouri State Penitentiary. James Owens, who had participated with Ray in the Kroger Supermarket robbery for which Ray received his twenty year sentence, said Ray had operated a 'three for two loan business', loaning two dollars and expecting three in return.[54]

Ray's prison files show he repeatedly lied to prison authorities. Typical of pathological liars, many of these lies were irrational. He told authorities that both his parents were dead; that he had an aunt in Quincy, Illinois, when it was actually his mother who lived there; that his education went as far as the eighth grade; and that he had graduated from a Chicago night school with the equivalent of a two-year high-school education.[55]

Despite his lucrative money making schemes in prison, Ray was determined to escape and he made a number of attempts. In March 1966, following a failed attempt to escape, he claimed to hear voices and said he did not remember trying to escape. Ray was sent to the state mental hospital but a day later changed his mind. He now insisted that he suffered from confusion, neuritis and anxiety. Ray's change of mind may have had something to do with his discovery that the mental hospital treated amnesia with electro-shock therapy.[56]

Prison staff were convinced that Ray had wanted to go to the mental hospital as it provided a better opportunity for escape. However, before he could put his escape plans into operation, the doctors decided there was nothing wrong with him and he was returned to the prison. The incident is telling in that it reveals a side to Ray that has been denied by conspiracy advocates. Ray was not bumbling and inept but cunning and deceitful. Some of his earlier criminal acts were ill-thought-out but Ray had the ability to learn from his mistakes. Prison officials believed some of his escape attempts were ingenious, especially his successful effort in 1967.

On 23 April 1967, just prior to the 5pm inmate count, Ray was discovered missing and could not be found within the prison grounds. It was not until ten days later that the authorities discovered that Ray had escaped by hiding in a large bread box. The box was taken by an open truck from the main prison to Renz Farm, a prison establishment that was outside the main prison walls, 5 miles north of the prison. Before the truck reached its destination, Ray made his escape.[57]

* * *

Throughout the following year Ray lied and stole his way across the United States. During his period on the run he also visited Mexico. His ideas of building a porn business there came to nothing after his attempt to secure Mexican citizenship failed when he discovered that marrying one of his prostitute friends did not guarantee citizenship.

In Los Angeles Ray had plastic surgery on his nose before he returned to the Deep South in March 1968 and attempted to seek help from a psychologist and a hypnotist for a cure for his depression, feelings of low self-esteem and severe headaches. According to Dr Mark O. Freeman, a clinical psychologist, Ray said that he wanted to 'overcome his shyness, gain social confidence and learn self-hypnosis in order that he could relax, sleep and learn to remember things better'. Freeman thought Ray was 'young and immature'.[58]

During his visits to Los Angeles and Mexico Ray became involved in violent skirmishes. Following an argument in a Los Angeles bar he dragged the offending woman to the door and loudly berated her for supporting African Americans.[59] In Mexico he had been ready to use his pistol in a skirmish with African American sailors.[60] During his stay in Los Angeles Ray met a number of people who later told FBI agents what they could about this Southerner who rode around in a car with Alabama licence plates and spoke in a 'countryfied way'. A dance instructor, Sharon Rhoades, described him as a strange character who was 'very ill at ease in crowds ... who always fidgeted [and] pulled at his ears, played with his hands and looked in every direction but at the person with whom he was conversing'.[61]

Dyrell Dennis, who resided at the St Francis Hotel and knew Ray from the fugitive's time at the bar there, told FBI agents she had spent 3 hours with Ray. She had been in the Sultan Room on the first floor of the hotel when she was approached by a man named 'Eric'. He appeared 'nervous, had pointed facial features and spoke with a nasal twang'. Dennis persuaded Ray to give her $20 after which they went to another nightspot. On returning to the hotel, Dennis said, Ray told her, on more than one occasion, that he 'could become violent'. Dennis thought he sounded unstable and was 'probably a psychopath', so she left. Later when she saw him in the Sultan Room Ray became belligerent and asked for his $20 back.[62]

* * *

Nearly ten years after King's death James Earl Ray agreed to an interview with *Playboy* magazine and also participated in a lie-detector test. The test was conducted by Douglas Wicklander, an expert in his field. The polygraph revealed that Ray had been lying and that he had indeed killed Martin Luther King. The polygraph also indicated that Ray had acted alone in the commission of the crime.

Ray's lawyer at the time, Mark Lane, tried to counteract the bad publicity generated by the *Playboy* article by getting Ray to agree to another polygraph, this time administered by another top expert in the field, Chris Gugas. Because of Gugas' expertise and experience in administering these kinds of tests he discovered that Ray had been trying to beat the polygraph. During important questions Ray would apply pressure to the machine's blood pressure cuff in the hope it would give a favourable reading. Gugas revealed that the test indicated that Ray had shot King and there was no conspiracy.[63]

The HSCA appointed experts to examine all the polygraph tests that Ray had undertaken. They concluded that Ray had killed King but felt that the tests could not positively dismiss the possibility of conspiracy.[64]

The evidence that Ray had murdered Martin Luther King was established over a thirty year period. Investigations also demonstrated that Ray had lied repeatedly to distance himself from the murder. However, there remained questions about whether or not Ray had some assistance and why he had killed King.

Chapter 5
Distorting the Truth

I think [the conspirators were] the United States of America. There is a movement in this country to preserve racism financed by a substantial amount of money ... People like James Earl Ray are preyed upon. They are merely pawns.

Ralph David Abernathy, quoted in *Newsweek*, 24 March 1969

Many doubts about the case, which were to multiply as the years went by, began when Ray stood up in court and pleaded guilty. The doubts arose, in part, because the US media did not fully cover the trial. In fact, the case against James Earl Ray was fully disclosed in court on the day of the hearing and was available in the official transcript. The public was given only the dramatic highlights of the case and out of that inadequate accounting, doubts and incredulity began to emerge. To the average American the federal and state governments seemed to be hiding the truth. However, it was also obvious that the defence did not have the opportunity to challenge the evidence in an adversarial setting therefore the truth was never established to the satisfaction of the public. From these proceedings, suspicions arose that the State of Tennessee and the federal government had no desire in seeing the evidence closely scrutinized.

For the past fifty years or so conspiracists have entered the fray, painting a picture of Ray as a dupe who realized he may have been framed for the murder of King. They have also posited the theory that, before his capture at Heathrow Airport, he may have received assistance from government co-conspirators during his April 1967 escape to Canada and his post-assassination stay in London. Speculation also centred around the possibility that Ray had received financial assistance during his time on the run.

From the time of his capture many people questioned how a small-time criminal like Ray had the sophisticated knowledge to obtain a false passport and numerous aliases with documentary support. Some conspiracy advocates claimed Ray was a pawn in the hands of foreign or domestic intelligence agencies.

It also appeared too implausible for many Americans that a white man could kill the most famous African American in the United States and flee the scene of the crime. Despite a wealth of evidence proving Ray had been the shooter and presented at Ray's trial, the country was still unconvinced he killed King or that he had acted unaided.

Notions of a government-led conspiracy centred around a number of issues that were chronicled in conspiracy books in the years following the assassination:

- There was an alleged last-minute change in Dr King's hotels from the Rivermont to the Lorraine. There was also an alleged change of room at the Lorraine which was interpreted by some to suggest King had been set up.
- A number of witnesses, specifically King's chauffer Soloman Jones and *New York Times* reporter Earl Caldwell, reported seeing someone in the bushes across from the Lorraine Motel immediately after the shot that killed King was fired.
- There were allegations that another white Mustang car was parked in front of Jim's Grill within 100ft of the Mustang parked in front of Canipe's Amusement Store.
- There were concerns that the FBI laboratory was unable to conclusively match the bullet taken from King's body to the rifle found at the scene of the crime.
- Critics pointed to the absence of Ray's fingerprints in Room 5b of Bessie Brewer's Rooming House.
- Many critics believed Ray's claim that a mysterious man named Raoul had hired him as an unwitting co-conspirator, guided his movements and given him money to buy the Mustang and the rifle. They alleged conspirators had used both items to frame Ray. Even though he pleaded guilty at his trial, Ray insisted that he was a 'patsy' and that 'Raoul' was the real killer and the person who financed his time on the run following the assassination.
- There were reports cigarette butts had been found in the Mustang's ashtray. Critics said that as Ray was a non-smoker and that the butts may have been left there by a co-conspirator.
- There was a widespread belief that Ray had been given large amounts of money for his time as a fugitive.
- Critics pointed to the fact that two African American firemen had been removed from Fire Station 2 across from the Lorraine Motel shortly before the assassination. They alleged the men were removed

to prevent them from exposing a plot to kill King involving the Memphis Police Department (MPD).

* * *

Hiring and firing various lawyers, Ray fought in vain for a new trial, claiming that his lawyer Percy Foreman had pressured him into confessing because he wanted to benefit from a book deal with author William Bradford Huie; the deal was contingent upon Ray pleading guilty. And the fact there was no trial combined with Ray's subsequent claim he was not the killer contributed to a general suspicion Ray may have been used as a patsy to take the blame for the King killing. Additionally, even though King's widow Coretta Scott King had approved Ray's guilty plea, she blamed the FBI for the assassination.

As the years passed allegations about a conspiracy multiplied and the original FBI investigation was criticized ad nauseum. Innocent events – the so-called 'second Mustang' – the damaged scope on the rifle found at the scene of the crime – policemen jumping down from the wall opposite the Lorraine Motel – the allegations King's security had been dropped – Jesse Jackson's movements during the shooting – all came under suspicion.

King's Security

Conspiracy advocates cite the presence of Marrell McCullough at the Lorraine Motel at the time of the assassination. McCullough was a Memphis undercover police officer who had infiltrated the 'Invaders', the black militant group that had allied itself with King's Memphis protest. According to William Pepper, McCullough's real mission was to report to the 111th Military Intelligence Group headquartered at Camp McPherson, Georgia, on King's movements and plans.[1]

McCullough later went to work for the CIA which inspired conspiracy theorists to claim he was a co-conspirator. However, the HSCA extensively investigated McCullough's role and found nothing connecting him to the federal government at that time nor any involvement in the assassination.

In the late 1990s McCullough's role in the assassination of King became clearer. He told investigators he wanted to resolve the issue and speculation which had raged for years and said he was willing to take a lie-detector test conducted by the United States Secret Service. According to a Justice Department report:

[McCullough] was aggressively questioned and consistently denied that he had any knowledge about a plot to assassinate Dr King. . . . The results of the polygraph examination show that [McCullough] was truthful when asked whether he was involved in an assassination plot. ... Apart from interviewing and polygraphing [McCullough], our investigation reviewed records (including CIA files) pertaining to his activities and interviewed people who have had contact with him both at the time of and after the assassination. Our inquiries revealed nothing to contradict his contention that he had no part in the assassination and was never in Jim's Grill. Moreover, he affirmed in a sworn affidavit that Jowers' allegations about him are false, that he was never in Jim's Grill or met Jowers, and that he was not involved in a plot to kill Dr King.[2]

There were a number of reasons why the Memphis Police Department had been unfairly criticized for failing to protect King. During their time in Memphis King and his party refused to accept police protection. Secondly, the removal of overt police protection outside the Lorraine Motel at 5.05pm on 3 April was a result of a complaint made by the King party who did not welcome the presence of police officers as they suspected them of 'spying'. Police Chief James C. MacDonald and Police Director Frank Holloman had responded to the wishes of the King party to remove the officers but quietly assigned three or four TACT police units to patrol the area near the motel. They served two purposes – to protect King without being conspicuous and to provide on-the-spot reserves in case a replay of the rioting of 28 March occurred.[3]

The Bushes
Many proponents of a government-led conspiracy believe the shot that killed King did not come from the rooming house bathroom window but from the bushes behind Jim's Grill and across the street from the Lorraine Motel. The allegations began shortly after the assassination when a witness, Harold 'Cornbread' Carter, was interviewed by the MPD and FBI. Carter was a 66-year-old man who had a long history of heavy drinking and had suffered a stroke some years before. He lived in Room 9 of the rooming house. Carter said he had been in his room when King was shot.

Some days after the murder Carter changed his story and now said he had been sitting in front of a bank of bushes across the road from the Lorraine drinking wine. He heard a shot from ground level and said someone had fired a gun nearby then kicked gravel in his face as he ran by.

However, prior to Ray's trial Carter changed his story once more and said he was not at all sure what he had seen. He recanted his story and refused to act as a defence witness.[4]

A number of other statements added to the growing suspicion about the possibility of a rifleman seen in the bushes. Both King's chauffeur for the Memphis visit Soloman Jones and *New York Times* reporter Earl Caldwell gave statements indicating a rifle shot came from the bushes. In the 1990s witnesses Olivia Catling and James Orange came forward to relate how King had been killed by a shooter in the bushes.

Jones said he believed he may have seen a policeman or fireman with a pale-blue crash helmet which looked like a white hood or sheet at that distance. During the period of the 1969 trial, Ray's lawyer Percy Foreman decided not to use Jones as a witness – Jones stated at this time he could have been mistaken in all the excitement and perhaps he didn't see a man with something white over his face immediately after the shot was fired. As the years progressed, Jones would resurrect the story about the bushes when he was interviewed by various conspiracy writers.[5]

During the HSCA investigation Jones testified under oath that he did not see what he reported until 'almost' the time police arrived at the scene of the shooting. He said he looked across the street only after he was pulled to the ground by Andrew Young. He also said that he was never certain that he had seen a man in the bushes. Jones said, 'I don't know whether it was a person or what it was, but it was something white'. He could not ascertain where in the bushes he had seen something 'either laterally or vertically'. The HSCA concluded Jones was mistaken and cited the fact that Memphis Police Department TACT officers in the fire station, who responded to the shot, would have been visible when they ran through the bushes above the retaining wall and dropped to the street. Photographs taken immediately after the shooting show police activity in this area.[6]

In 2000 the Justice Department made further enquiries about the truthfulness of Jones' allegations. The report stated, 'when the shot rang out, several persons in the parking lot instantly hit the ground and remained there, taking cover until they felt it safe to stand. Since Jones, according to his testimony, was one of the individuals who went to the ground, there was a delay before he made his observations'.[7] These facts are supported by the testimony of Chauncey Eskridge who had been in the courtyard of the Lorraine Motel when the shot rang out. He looked behind him but saw nothing except the back of a decrepit two-storey, red-brick building and a window on the second floor partly open, below was the backyard filled with bramble bushes and garbage. He ran from the courtyard, turned right to Huling Street, looked both ways and saw nothing except a car disappearing. At this moment several police officers jumped over the retaining wall, one of whom asked Eskridge where the shot came from.[8]

In 1989 Earl Caldwell changed the story about the bushes he had given to author Gerold Frank in 1969. When Caldwell spoke to Frank, he said nothing about seeing a shooter in the bushes. In fact, Caldwell was too late on the scene to see anything of value. He only emerged from his motel room, according to his own account, after police had arrived on the scene.

James Orange alleged he 'ducked down' after he heard the shot and saw King's leg dangling over the balcony:

> When I saw the leg … I looked back and saw the smoke. It couldn't have been more than 5 to 10 seconds. The smoke came up out of the brush area on the opposite side of the street from the Lorraine Motel. I saw it rise up from the bushes … I also noticed quite early the next morning around 8 or 9 o'clock that all the bushes were cut down and cleared up. It was as though the entire area of the bushes from behind the rooming house had been cleaned up. I will always remember the puff of white smoke and the cut brush and having never been given a satisfactory explanation. When I tried to tell the police at the scene [what] I saw they told me to be quiet and get out of the way.[9]

However, Orange's story was different to the one he told at the time of the assassination. No mention had been made of 'smoke'.[10]

Conspiracy theorists have often cited an unpublished Associated Press photograph, unearthed by *Memphis Press-Scimitar* reporter Wayne Chastain, which had been taken from the rooming house bathroom window shortly after the assassination. Allegedly, the bushes had obscured the view between the rooming house and the Lorraine Motel making it difficult if not impossible to fire the shot from the bathroom window. However, the story was bogus. At the time of the assassination there had been a clear view of the Lorraine Motel from the bathroom window and contemporary photographs of the scene of the crime show that even if the bushes had been in full bloom the trajectory would not have been obscured.[11]

There was no physical evidence to support the allegations that the shot that killed King had been fired from the area behind Jim's Grill. On the night of 3 April there had been heavy rainfall and at 6pm on the evening of 4 April the ground was still wet and muddy. Within moments of the shooting Officer Torrence Landers had climbed the retaining wall in front of the bushes and searched the area. He found only two isolated footprints in the entire area. If the assassin had fired from the bushes there would have been a trail of footprints. Furthermore, the second-floor balcony of the Lorraine Motel offered an excellent view of the area behind the rooming house. Three persons with that vantage point – maid Ceolar Shavers, South African news producer Joseph Louw and Revd Kyles – reported seeing nothing unusual or anyone in the backyard.[12]

In the year following the assassination independent researchers had discovered that the City of Memphis sanitation department had cut down the trees and bushes at the rear of the rooming house shortly after the assassination. Critics suspected the area was cleaned up to destroy any evidence that assassins had been positioned there.

The day after the assassination the area at the rear of Jim's Grill was cleaned up for the police to look for evidence. Director of Memphis Public Works Maynard Stiles had received a telephone call from a representative of the Police Department. The request was for assistance in cleaning up the rooming house lot. The workers, Stiles said, would have followed directions from the police. According to Stiles the police wanted the area cleaned up so they could look for additional evidence. Journalist Kay Pitman Black spoke with city officials on the morning of 5 April. She went to the South Main Street rooming house and saw the trees that lined the embankment. The area had been cleaned, she said, 'to make it look better for all the people coming into town'.[13]

The bushes were not cut down until *four months* after the assassination. Additionally, the bushes had no real import. They did not obscure the line of sight from the bathroom to the second floor of the Lorraine Motel.[14]

Conspiracy advocates never addressed the issue of why the bathroom screen would be missing if the shot that killed King had been fired from the bushes. At the time of the assassination Memphis police officer Lieutenant Papia had been the first officer on the scene to check the bathroom. He noticed the window had been pushed up and had stuck. There had been a screen outside lying on the ground.[15]

It is clear that some witnesses, confused by the chaos that engulfed the assassination scene, mistook police officers for 'shooters' in the bushes. As Justice Department investigators concluded, 'Photographs taken within moments of the assassination confirm that law enforcement officials were visible in the immediate area of the brush across Mulberry Street very soon after the shooting ... Two pictures [by Joseph Louw] ... taken through his window even before he exited his room show law enforcement officials in mid-air dropping from the retaining wall and crossing Mulberry Street.'[16]

The State's Star Witness

Conspiracy advocates invariably point to the alleged unreliability of the main prosecution witness, 46-year-old Charles Q. Stephens. Stephens was the only rooming house resident who had been able to positively recognize Ray as the man who left the bathroom immediately following the shot that killed Dr King.

Charles Stephens said that on 4 April 1968 he saw and heard a man standing with Bessie Brewer, the manager of the rooming house, near the entrance to Room 5b. He assumed that the man was looking for a room. Following the sighting of Ray with Brewer, he had heard someone in Room 5b. Stephens and his common-law-wife Grace Walden occupied the room next door, Room 6b. The wall separating Stephens' kitchen from the bathroom was made of plywood and he could clearly hear any sounds or movements in the bathroom. Stephens said, 'I heard footsteps and heard them leaving and coming past my room and into the common bathroom at the end of the hall ... On the first couple of times he did not stay long. On the third time the person stayed there what seemed like a long time towards the end of the afternoon between 5 and 6pm.'[17]

Stephens had served in Italy during the Second World War and was familiar with gunshots. He had been wounded and still bore the scars of his gunshot injuries. When he heard the shot emanating from the bathroom he had been repairing a radio in his kitchen. During the period 5–6pm, the roomer in Room 4b Willie Anschutz had angrily complained to Stephens about the 5b roomer who had been making frequent trips to the bathroom and preventing residents from gaining access. Stephens told him it was the resident of Room 5b.

Stephens believed the shot that came from the bathroom sounded like a 'German .88':

It was very loud. I could tell that it came from the bathroom because it was very loud. I heard through a broken pane in my window a lot of voices and hollering from the building across the road. I saw a lot of people milling around near the motel. About a minute after hearing the shot I went to my door and opened it. The bathroom door was open. When I went to the bannister I saw a man running near the end of the hallway. He was carrying a bundle in his right hand. It was at least three or four feet long and six to eight inches thick. It was wrapped in what looked like newspaper. Although I did not get a good look at him, I think it was the same man I saw earlier with Mrs Brewer.

Stephens also stated that when he opened his room door, he observed William Anschutz say something to the man who was walking away.[18]

Conspiracy theorists claimed Stephens would have been unable to make sense of any of the events that occurred in the rooming house during the time King was shot because, they alleged, he was drunk. According to taxi driver James McCraw, a friend of the downstairs grill owner Loyd Jowers, he had been called to the rooming house shortly before 6pm on 4 April and found Stephens lying on his bed intoxicated. He said Stephens was too drunk to stand. Many years later, Memphis police officer Tommy Smith claimed that Stephens had been drunk when he questioned him shortly after 7.15pm on the night of the murder. Smith said Stephens had to lean on his doorframe as he was too drunk to stand unaided.

The HSCA investigated McCraw's story and his 1968 taxi firm records were subpoenaed. They showed that McCraw had been lying. The taxi driver had no pickup from the rooming house from the time he started his shift at 3.15pm to the time of the assassination.[19]

William Anschutz, Police Captain Ray and other police officers who spoke to Stephens after the assassination all stated that although he had been 'slightly intoxicated', he was in full control of himself.[20]

Memphis police Lieutenant Papia also confirmed that Stephens' speech was not impaired and it was his opinion that Stephens was not intoxicated. Additionally, Glynn King was one of the first police officers to go to the rooming house following the shooting. He first spoke to the landlady Bessie Brewer and then Charles Stephens, who, he said, did not appear to be intoxicated.[21]

Conspiracy theorist Mark Lane dismissed the idea that Stephens had been a credible witness and claimed Stephens' common-law-wife Grace Walden had been the only witness who could have identified the stranger in Room 5b. She said that immediately following the shot she had seen a man run past her door and it was not Ray. Lane accused the authorities of putting her in a mental institution to cover up the crime. Following the assassination Walden had given a statement to the Memphis police and said she had not heard or seen anything in the moments following the King shooting.

In fact, FBI agents noted, she was 'confined to bed'. Additionally, Stephens had stated that at the time of the shooting his wife had been lying in bed and was not in a position to see anything that happened with regard to the bathroom and landing.[22]

In the months following the assassination Walden was traced to a mental institution by Lane. This was positive proof for him that the state had deliberately tried to hide a witness who could validate claims that James Earl Ray did not kill Martin Luther King. However, the true circumstances of Walden's incarceration were investigated by the HSCA in the 1970s and the Justice Department in 2000. Both investigations concluded there were no sinister implications in her incarceration.[23]

The Fire Station

On the afternoon of 4 April 1968 Ed Redditt, an African American police detective, was removed from his surveillance post at the newly constructed Fire Station 2 situated across the street from the Lorraine Motel. Redditt had been watching King and his party since 10am that morning. He carried a newspaper and a pair of binoculars. The previous day he had torn off an inside page and cut out two slits in the centre, taping the paper over the glass panel in the door for the purposes of watching the Lorraine Motel across the street without being seen. He had a perfect view.

Redditt recorded in a notebook everything he saw. He was accompanied by his partner Patrolman W.B. Richmond. They were to keep a close eye on King and were to report any comings and goings of people who were visiting King at the motel. Frank Holloman, who was in charge of Memphis' Internal Security Division, was fearful further trouble on the forthcoming (and previously aborted) peaceful march in Memphis could be connected with some of King's visitors. Memphis was still in a state of emergency following the disorder that erupted during the sanitation strike.

The previous evening Redditt and Richmond had attended the Mason Temple as part of their surveillance of King, but had left before King arrived. They had been approached by an African American preacher, Revd Blackburn, who had been in the audience. Blackburn had been angry because he knew the two officers had been spying on King.[24] There was a tense atmosphere around the policemen. Revd Lawson had been speaking to the audience before King's arrival and he had been talking about a young African American youth who had been killed earlier in the day. Richmond and Redditt feared Lawson might point them out to the audience.

Shortly after noon a fireman came into the locker room and informed Redditt he had a telephone call. A woman's voice threatened him. Redditt passed the information to his superior Police Director Holloman. Concurrently, Holloman had also received information that someone was coming to Memphis to kill Redditt. Intelligence Inspector Graydon Tines sent Lieutenant Eli Arkin to bring Redditt to police headquarters, where the officer was told to move himself and his family to a safe motel. Richmond remained at his post and continued his surveillance. Redditt had also received threats from the King party the previous day, at the airport.[25]

On the same day Philip R. Manuel, a staff member of Senator John McClellan's Congressional Investigating Committee, was in Memphis discussing with the MPD the upcoming strikers' march which had been re-scheduled for 8 April. Manuel had received a telephone call from his Washington office informing him they had received information from an informant within the Mississippi Freedom Democratic Party that a black police lieutenant's life was in danger. Unfortunately, Manuel believed the caller was talking about a Memphis police lieutenant. In fact, the call was about a police officer in Knoxville, Tennessee.[26]

The day before King's murder the only two African American firefighters at No. 2 station, Floyd E. Newsum and Norvell Wallace, were removed from the fire station and reassigned elsewhere. Conspiracy advocates, notably Mark Lane, tried to link the removal of Redditt and the reassignment of Newsum and Wallace to the idea that African American workers had been removed from the scene of the assassination to better facilitate King's murder. Floyd Newsum had attended King's 'Mountain Top' speech the previous evening and was deeply moved by King. He was aware that Redditt and Richmond had been surveilling King from the fire station. He actually confronted Redditt about the 'spying' and Redditt, searching for an excuse to alleviate tensions, replied he was only in the fire station for the purposes of King's protection and not spying. Of course, his real role was spying on King.

The conclusions reached by conspiracy advocates ignore a simple but crucial part of the story. If authorities had been concerned that local government workers sympathetic to King had been removed, why would they leave African American police officer W.B. Richmond at his post? If Redditt had been removed because of his race, then Richmond would also have been removed from the scene. As historian Gerald McKnight wrote:

> Lane's stock as a citizen investigator in the King case would rise or fall depending upon Redditt's veracity. Unfortunately for Lane, Detective Redditt turned out to be an accomplished self-promoter who completely misrepresented virtually everything Lane attributed to him. It is puzzling that Lane did not suspect that there was something shady about Redditt's story during the 3 days he was sounding out witnesses, some of whom were movement activists and very knowledgeable about the racial crisis in Memphis that reached fever heat during the sanitation strike. All of them knew that Redditt was an MPD intelligence officer who spied on Dr King, the sanitation workers, and their allies and that he was distrusted and even hated by many in the black community.[27]

Redditt wrote a report to Inspector Tines, prior to the assassination, that the two firemen could impede his surveillance because of the firemen's support for King and the strikers. Inspector Tines said he remembered that Redditt and Detective Arkin had complained about an African American fireman who could 'blow' (Redditt's and Richmond's) 'cover'. The firemen, then, were removed not to facilitate the assassination, but to lessen tensions between them and Redditt.[28]

Redditt was called to testify before the HSCA in the late 1970s. Since the time of the assassination, he had been colluding with conspiracy authors and embellished his story that he had been removed from the scene of the assassination because he was an African American. He told conspiracy advocates that he was assigned to 'protect' King. However, during questioning Redditt dissembled. He admitted that he was assigned only to surveil King and not to provide protection. Furthermore, he confessed that the 'perimeter plan' (sealing off the area around the Lorraine in the event of an attempt on King's life) was a hoax. He also confessed that the removal of Newsum and Wallace from the fire station was the result of a memo he and Richmond wrote to Inspector Tines requesting to the latter facilitate the firemen's transfer. Redditt inferred it was conspiracy theorist Mark Lane who had misinterpreted his story.[29]

The Mustang

The Mustang car was purchased by James Earl Ray from William Paisley in Birmingham, Alabama, in August 1967. When it was found on 10 April the contents of the vehicle were collected by FBI agents and sent to Washington DC for examination. There were some news reports of cigarette butts having been found in the car's ashtray. Since that period conspiracy advocates have pointed to these facts in support of the idea that Ray had an accomplice as Ray did not smoke. From the start Ray's lawyer Arthur J. Hanes promoted this story and it caught on.

Conspiracy advocate Michael Newton wrote:

> Surely had the facts been given to that [1969] jury, one of them would have wondered why the ashtray of Ray's famous Mustang 'getaway' car was overflowing with ashes and cigarette butts when it was found by the FBI. Ray supposedly was acting alone when he gunned down King in Memphis, got into the car and drove it to Birmingham where he deserted it. [*Author's Note*: Ray actually abandoned the car in Atlanta] The members of the jury never got to hear that Ray was a virtual fanatic for cleanliness and had been a life-long non-smoker.[30]

The issue was never successfully addressed by anti-conspiracy authors or the government investigations of the crime. The FBI files are somewhat contradictory on the subject. One memo stated 'material from ashtray received from FBI, New Orleans'.[31] Another memo stated there were 'no cig butts or ashes'.[32]

In 2000, Justice Department investigators reported that:

> No witness whom we interviewed or whose statement we reviewed recalled seeing the ashtray overflowing with cigarettes. . . . a 13-year-old boy recalled only a cigar butt in the ashtray and he and his mother remembered cigarette or cigar ashes on the floor of the automobile. In addition, former [FBI] agent Claiborne 'was fairly certain' he saw a couple of cigarette butts in the ashtray when he searched the car, but the inventory of evidence records nothing about the ashtray.[33]

When FBI agents searched Ray's Atlanta rooming house they found, 'Three cigarette butts from top of wardrobe, Room 6. One cigarette butt from under wardrobe, Room 6.'[34] There was no evidence, in the days before DNA analysis, that the cigarettes had been smoked by Ray. According to FBI interviews of fellow inmates of the Missouri State Penitentiary, Ray had smoked cigarettes up to the time he gave up due to stomach problems.

However, there is evidence that he did not give up the habit altogether. FBI agents Robert Barrett and William Saucier interviewed a former inmate, name redacted from the files, who told them, 'Ray ... smoked Winston cigarettes ... and had a Zippo lighter with the initials J.R. scratched on it'.[35]

Cathryn Norton, a dance instructor at the National Dance Studio in Los Angeles, frequently gave dancing lessons to Ray from December 1967 to February 1968. She said he was not friendly with any of the other students or instructors. According to Norton, Ray attended a party, arranged through the dance studio, at the home of Paul Carson. About twenty people attended including herself. Norton said Ray was evasive in conversation and that he smoked filter cigarettes. She also noted he had a nervous habit of pulling on his earlobes with his fingers, a trait that had been noticed by numerous people who knew Ray.[36]

Donald J. Jacobs, a student at the Los Angeles bartenders' school Ray attended, was interviewed by FBI agent Hubbard. Jacobs said he had engaged in some conversation with Ray at the Dance Studio. Ray told Jacobs that he had been a cook in the Merchant Marine and had worked on barges on the Mississippi River. Jacobs described Ray as, 'white male, 5'11", 185–190 pounds, dark brown hair with some grey; hair tended to be unruly and stand up; late 30's early 40's, large build, low voice, neat, *smoked cigarettes*, white shirt'.[37]

There is also further compelling evidence that Ray occasionally smoked. When Ray had been extradited from England to the United States, he was taken to Lakenheath Air Force base and transported by plane. Before the plane took off Ray was examined by a British doctor at '19.35 EDT 18 July 1968'. According to the medical report, the doctor had examined Ray's 'extremities', the medical term for fingers. The report stated, 'Extremities – Tobacco stain P, index finger, otherwise normal.'[38]

Conspiracists insisted that two identical white Mustangs had been parked outside the rooming house on 422 South Main Street in the period leading up to the assassination. For conspiracy advocates this meant only one

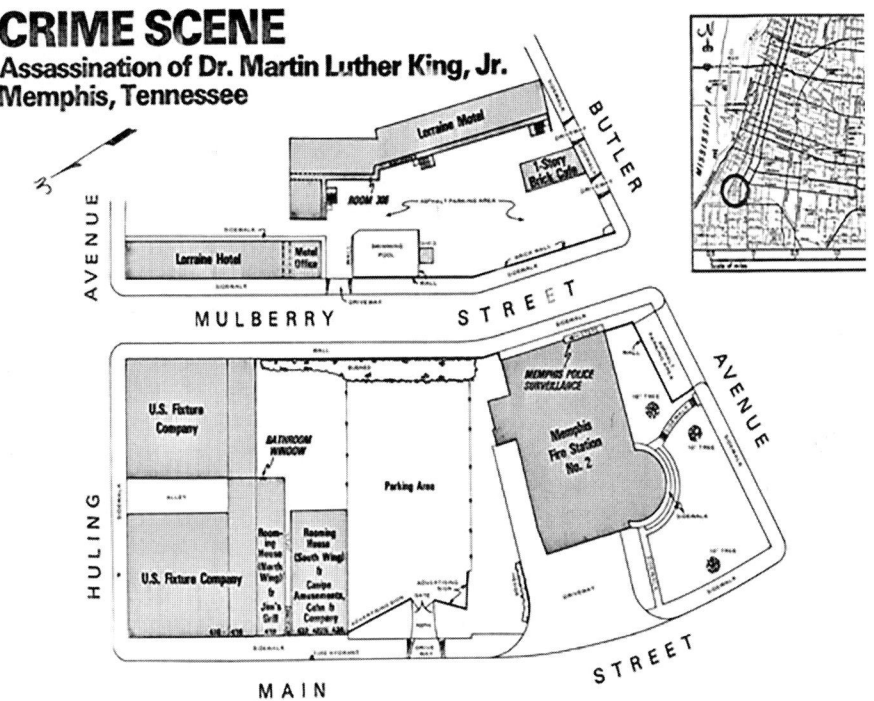

Map of the crime scene for the murder of Martin Luther King Jr. (*National Archives*)

The exterior of Room 306 of the Lorraine Motel. The wreath marks the spot where King was shot on 4 April 1968. The balcony looks towards the rear of Bessie Brewer's Rooming House.

The rear of Bessie Brewer's Rooming House, 422 1/2 South Main Street at the time of the assassination, across the street from the Lorraine Motel. The bathroom window from where Ray fired the shot that killed King is circled. (*National Archives*)

Ray's view of the Lorraine Motel from the bathroom which was situated near his room, 5B. Standing in the bathtub, Ray rested the rifle on the windowsill and fired one shot at King, 203ft away. The area behind the rooming house was strewn with garbage which may have prompted city officials to have the area cleaned up before the world's press descended on Memphis and in turn contributed to accusations of a police cover-up. (*National Archives*)

Entrance to Bessie Brewer's Rooming House, South Main Street, Memphis. In the centre of the photograph is the canopied door to the stairs leading up to Ray's room, down which he fled after shooting King. (*National Archives*)

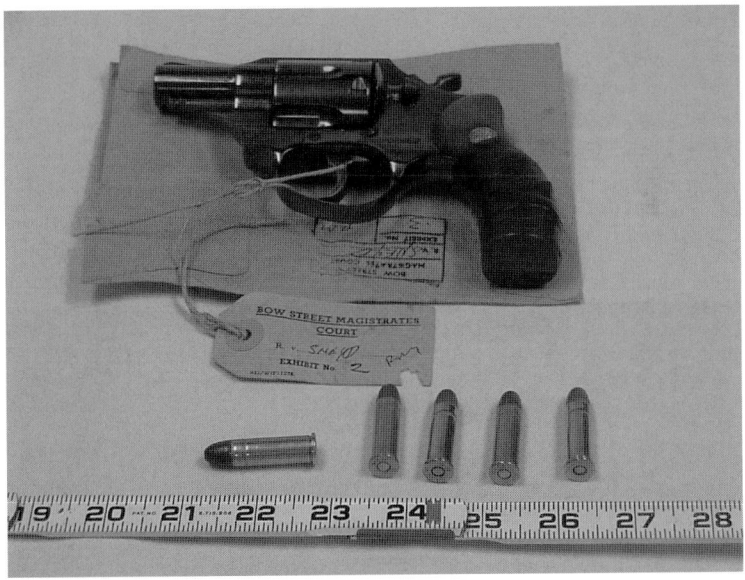

Ray's pistol. This Japanese .38 Liberty Chief Special was used by him to rob a London jewellery store on 27 May 1968 and a Trustee Savings Bank in Fulham, London, on 4 June 1968.

North–south view of South Main Street near Canipe's Amusement Store. On the afternoon of 4 April 1968, there were police cars parked all along this road. This was the likely reason Ray dropped his bundle, including the rifle, in the doorway of Canipe's Amusement Store after becoming alarmed at the police presence. (*National Archive*)

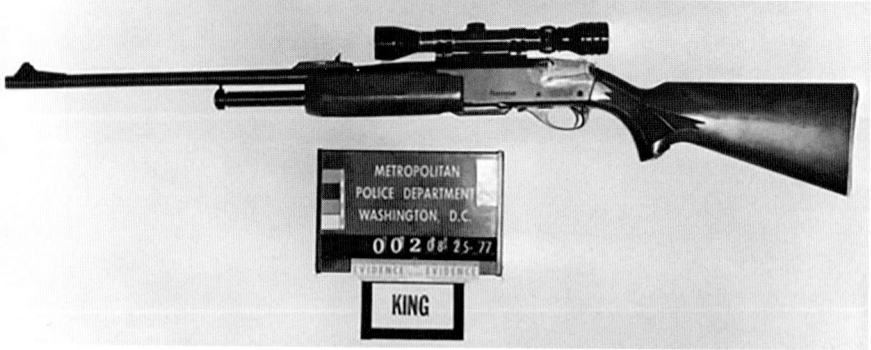

James Earl Ray travelled to Birmingham, Alabama, and together with his brother Jerry Ray purchased a Model 760 Gamemaster .30-06-calibre rifle, a telescopic sight and a box of twenty rounds from the Aeromarine Supply Company. (*National Archives*)

Above: The entrance to Canipe's Amusement Store showing Ray's bundle and the rifle. To the left of Canipe's is the stairway down which Ray fled after the shooting. *Below*: The contents of the bundle which includes the binoculars he used to spy on King and various personal items from which the FBI collected fingerprints and laundry tags. (*National Archives*)

Ray's Ford Mustang car found abandoned in Atlanta after the shooting. The pale-yellow Mustang was sometimes identified as 'white'. (*National Archives*)

James Earl Ray graduated from a Los Angeles bartenders' school in March 1968, and a photograph at his graduation shows him posing with the owner. He closed his eyes, as if to avoid being recognized by anyone who saw his picture. (*National Archives*)

James Earl Ray's Canadian passport which incorrectly spelled his fake name 'Sneya'. (*National Archives*)

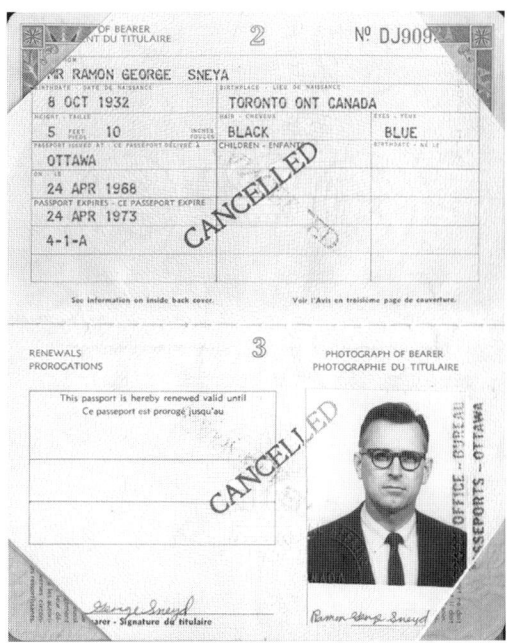

James Earl Ray is taken into custody by Memphis police after his extradition from England in July 1968. (*Shelby County Register of Deeds*)

Ray's brother Jerry (left). The House Select Committee on Assassinations said Jerry was the likely candidate for Ray's bogus 'co-conspirator Raoul'. Jerry is seen here with National States Rights Party lawyer J.B. Stoner who had prior knowledge of Ray's escape attempts and may have inspired and/or encouraged the Ray brothers to kill King. (*National Archives*)

John Ray who assisted his brother James in escaping from the Missouri State Penitentiary in April 1967 and met up with his brother in West Memphis, Arkansas, across the Mississippi River from Memphis, Tennessee, the night before James killed King. (*National Archives*)

thing – conspirators had used a decoy car in order to lead the Memphis police away from the real shooter.

However, the witnesses were confused by Ray's coming and goings at the rooming house on the afternoon of the murder. The first trip was to buy a pair of binoculars from the York Arms Company a few blocks away. He arrived there at approximately 4pm and returned at about 4.30pm. During that time, he had lost his parking space outside Jim's Grill. He now had to park about 60ft away near Canipe's Amusement Store. This issue is critical as Ray needed to get into the rooming house with the rifle, a long package that was sure to attract attention. At 4.30pm workers at a business across the street had just finished their shift and were waiting for their husbands to pick them up. Ray waited in the car outside Canipe's until there was a quiet period and he could return to his room. He sat in his car for approximately 15 minutes up to 5pm. He was noticed by workers Peggy Hurley and Elizabeth Copeland. The Mustang was certainly empty by the time two men entered Jim's Grill at a few minutes past 5pm.[39]

The Mustang was also central to Ray's story of how he first heard about the shooting of King. Ray said that on returning to the rooming house after his tyre had been fixed at a local garage, he observed a police car blocking off roads. Ray wrote:

> What in the hell could have brought on a roadblock, I wondered. Had the law latched on to Raoul? I switched on the radio and continued driving, intending to stop at the south end of town and phone Raoul's man in New Orleans to see if he could tell me anything. As I neared the state line, however, I heard a bulletin that Rev. Martin Luther King had been shot. Soon after the announcer said the police were looking for a suspect: a white man in a white Mustang. My car and I were too close to that description for comfort. I couldn't do anything about my skin colour, but I could lose the car.[40]

However, the car radio did not work. According to a 12 April 1968 FBI memo signed by agents Jack B. Simpson, Richard H. Davis and Jack T. Beverstein, 'On April 12th 1968, 1966 Mustang, Vehicle Identification Number 6TO7C190467, was examined at the FBI garage in Atlanta, Georgia … The radio in the vehicle was noted to be a Ford radio (FOMOCO), and not in working order. No holes were noted as having been drilled in the dash of the vehicle …'.[41] The memo is important because it was written *before* Ray's capture and his subsequent story of having heard news broadcasts about the assassination on his car radio.

Finances

Ray had become a successful prison entrepreneur during a seven-year stay in the Missouri State Penitentiary in Jefferson City. He first ran a library of 300 books in his cell, renting them out for cash and cigarettes. He made beer in his mattress cover and peddled eggs for a dollar a dozen, $30 a crate.

In 1963, Ray became friendly with a guard on his cellblock who smuggled in drugs, mostly speed, known as 'splash', which Ray sold to fellow prisoners. After skimming his share, the guard mailed the remainder in $100 bills to Ray's sister Carol and his brother Jerry. When Jerry got his money, he would write 'OK' on a piece of paper and mail it back.[42]

The FBI's MURKIN files show how numerous Missouri State Penitentiary inmates talked of Ray's money making schemes, including selling food from the kitchen to supplying amphetamines. However, during the investigation into Ray's background, following the assassination, the Missouri prison authorities tried to protect their reputation by denying Ray had been a 'merchant' in the Missouri State Penitentiary prior to his escape in 1967.

However, there is a telling comment by Warden Harold Swenson, the Missouri Corrections Commissioner, which suggests at least the possibility the prison authority's claims may not be accurate. Swenson confirmed that Ray's prison record showed he had committed a violation of prison rules by dealing in contraband such as coffee and cigarettes. So, at the very least Ray had been a 'merchant'.

Ray escaped from the prison in a bread truck on 23 April 1967. Shortly after, the Ray brothers met at the Atlantic Hotel in Chicago – the first time in twenty years that all three had been out of prison at the same time. Both John and Jerry handed him money and his sister later gave him money he had earned as a 'prison merchant'. She withdrew the money from the bank a few days after James' escape. In 2011 Jerry Ray admitted he robbed a 'gambling joint' with James in Chicago in July 1967 which, he said, netted them $1,800 plus jewellery and handguns.[43]

After Ray was arrested in London and brought to Memphis, county prosecutor Philip Canale estimated he had $7,000 available to him from the time of his jail break until he was arrested. By following Ray's path for those fourteen months, author George McMillan figured his expenses – in Los Angeles, New Orleans, Birmingham, Atlanta, Toronto, Lisbon and London – at $6,800. Running out of cash, Ray robbed the Fulham branch of the Trustees Savings Bank in London on 4 June, taking away about £100, or $240. At the time of his capture on 8 June, he was carrying $123.54 in cash.[44]

FBI Assistant Director Cartha DeLoach believed there was sufficient evidence to say that Ray had committed robberies to finance his travels. DeLoach wrote:

> We believe that one robbery and two major heists provided him with more than enough funds to carry out his scheme. We had sufficient evidence to suggest that Ray had planned and executed these robberies, but we didn't have quite enough proof to bring him to trial and convict him. Had it been necessary to prove the robbery charges to get a murder conviction, I'm convinced we could have produced sufficient evidence.[45]

In the mid-1970s the HSCA investigated Ray's movements and finances from the time he escaped from the Missouri State Penitentiary on 23 April 1967 to the time of his capture at Heathrow Airport on 8 June 1968. The Committee established that he broke out of prison with approximately $300. When he fled to Winnetka, Illinois, he earned $664 as a dishwasher.

The HSCA believed that on 13 July 1967 Ray and his brothers John and Jerry held up a bank in Alton, Illinois, getting away with $27,234 – with Ray's take being sufficient to finance his travels to Mexico, Los Angeles, New Orleans, Birmingham, Atlanta, Memphis, Canada, Portugal and England. The HSCA said there was 'substantial, albeit circumstantial evidence that the Ray brothers, including James, pulled off the bank job'.[46] Furthermore, Jerry Ray had spoken of how he had fooled a polygraph examination when he denied robbing the bank.[47] Authors Frank and McMillan supported the HSCA's conclusions about the Alton robbery.

The HSCA said Ray therefore had sufficient funds to pay for an apartment in Canada, buy $250 worth of new clothes and purchase a holiday in a Canadian ski resort. After his 1967 trip to Canada, Ray paid for plastic surgery to his nose and spent $125 to attend a bartenders' school in Los Angeles. He also bought expensive camera equipment as he was considering setting up a pornography business.

The issue of James Earl Ray's alleged drug dealing is important. The FBI was unable to conclusively prove the Ray brothers robbed the Alton bank and the HSCA's conclusions had to rely on evidence that could never be established.

Many contradictory statements by former inmates about Ray's drug dealing were made to investigating FBI agents. However, the allegations were not dependent on criminals who may have had an axe to grind in pointing the finger at Ray. They were corroborated by family members, friends and acquaintances. Furthermore, George McMillan spoke to three different Missouri State Penitentiary wardens and a number of custodial officers who confirmed drugs were indeed sold within the prison and that it had been possible to smuggle money out through corrupt guards.[48]

A former Missouri State Penitentiary inmate who knew Ray told FBI agents that in 1966 Ray got 'Kenny Hurtt' to send out $15 for him to a 'Mr and Mrs [name unrecalled] … Stationery Company in St Louis, but no stationery arrived'. Ray later confessed to Hurtt that he was using him to smuggle money out of prison.[49] The FBI confirmed the information supplied by the inmate by checking Missouri State Penitentiary records which established that a 'Kenny Hurtt' had been an inmate at Missouri State Penitentiary and, on 20 January 1967, had sent a money order for the amount of $15.25 to the Albert J. Pepper Stationery Company, 712A Shenandoah Street, St Louis, Missouri. Albert Pepper was married to Ray's sister Carol.[50] Jerry Ray told McMillan that he handed $4,900 to his brother James when they met in Chicago following James' escape in 1967. Jerry said the money was handled in prison by a corrupt prison guard who took his share and mailed the rest of the money to Jerry.[51]

It was estimated that the total amount of money James Earl Ray smuggled out of prison from 1963 came to $6,400 – the approximate amount of money Ray was to spend between the time of his escape and his capture at Heathrow Airport. Memphis prosecutor Phil Canale's investigation confirmed that Ray sent 'about 7,000 dollars' out of prison and it was banked by Ray's sister Carol in Maplewood, Missouri.

Chapter 6

The Hoax Conspiracy Trial

The deceit of history, whether it occurs in the context of Holocaust denial or in an effort to rewrite the story of Dr King's death, is a dangerous impulse for which those committed to reasoned debate and truth cannot sit still. The more quickly and completely this [Jowers trial] jury's discredited verdict is forgotten the better.

Washington Post, 12 December 1999

Two figures loom over the way in which the Kings have succeeded in making themselves into national laughingstocks. The first is Pepper, Ray's lawyer, whose outlandish claims of government involvement in King's slaying have been disproven and destroyed by both ABC News' Turning Point and CBS News' 48 Hours. The Memphis district attorney's report highlights 'the pervasive mention of monetary reward that key witnesses relied upon by Dr Pepper refer to in their statements'. In the current Time magazine, long-time civil rights journalist Jack E. White accurately characterizes Pepper as 'either a credulous buffoon or a con artist'. Most people who've seen Pepper's work up close would vote for the second.

Pulitzer Prize-winning author Professor David J. Garrow

Ever since his conviction for the murder of Martin Luther King, James Earl Ray was aware that criticisms of the FBI were increasing in popularity with the US public. He also realized those criticisms could assist in his efforts to secure a new trial. Ray promoted and encouraged the idea of FBI involvement at every opportunity. 'I don't know who actually did it.' Ray said in 1993, 'but in my opinion, Cartha DeLoach, who was J. Edgar Hoover's number three at the FBI, orchestrated it. He was more of a political agent than an FBI man who was into everything. He was running dirty tricks for the FBI.'[1]

Throughout the two decades following King's death conspiracists repeatedly called for a new independent inquiry into the Civil Rights leader's assassination. However, it was during the 1990s that the case attracted increased attention. Ray's defenders were now united in accusing the government of organizing the assassination. From 1991 to the beginning of the new millennium the King assassination was rarely out of the public eye as startling new revelations and developments brought the controversial issue of conspiracy to the forefront.

William Pepper, who became Ray's defence lawyer in the 1980s, conducted his own enquiries into the murder of King and alleged there was a 'local conspiracy' in Memphis involving the Memphis Police Department and the Mafia and a 'broader conspiracy' beyond Memphis that 'reached into the higher levels of the government of the United States and some of its agents and officials …'.

Pepper said the Mafia, the CIA, President Johnson, the US military and government agencies conspired to kill Dr King. James Earl Ray had been the 'patsy'. King was shot by a professional assassin, he said, who had been positioned in the bushes across from the Lorraine Motel. The contract was allegedly taken out by the local representative of the Marcello family, Frank Liberto, but at the bequest of the local FBI. For the next decade Pepper threw his accusations around without thought or reason.

As incredible as Pepper's allegations appeared, his theories persuaded the King family that the government was involved in the assassination. In a television programme broadcast in the United States, Coretta Scott King and several of the King children announced their support for Pepper, their belief in Ray's innocence and the existence of a government plot.[2]

* * *

Pepper's ideas about a government plot to kill King gained traction in December 1993 when an assassination 'witness', Loyd Jowers, the owner and operator of Jim's Grill, situated below Bessie Brewer's Rooming House, confessed to being part of a conspiracy to murder Martin Luther King. Appearing on ABC's *Primetime Live*, Jowers said he took the rifle that killed King from a sniper who had been positioned in the yard behind his restaurant, wrapped it in a cloth and hid it underneath the bar counter without being seen.

Jowers' alleged role in the assassination dates to the time of the murder. As owner of Jim's Grill which was situated below Ray's rooming house, Jowers had been interviewed by Memphis police shortly after the killing. On 4 April 1968 he told police that he knew nothing about the shooting. Jowers said he was behind the counter when he heard a loud noise and went to the kitchen to investigate. When he saw nothing unusual, he returned to serve his customers.[3]

Jowers' original non-conspiracy story was corroborated by the cafe's customers who told investigating police and FBI agents that nothing out of the ordinary occurred at the time of the shooting. Waitress Rosie Lee Dabney and Harold E. Parker were typical in how they described the activity within the restaurant at the time of the assassination. Dabney told agents that, 'she came on duty at about 3pm. She stated that everything seemed normal up until 6pm when she heard that a shooting had occurred. She added she saw nothing out of the ordinary, and could provide no further information.'[4]

According to FBI agents:

> Harold E. Parker was in Jim's Grill having his evening meal of chilli and beer. He said he was sitting in the last booth in the Grill with … George Harding. . . . Mr Parker added there were a number of people in the Grill during the entire time that he was there and that there were several young men playing the shuffleboard ping-pong machine and the jukebox. He said he was not aware of any activity outside Jim's Grill until a Deputy Sheriff entered Jim's Grill sometime after 6pm and told everyone in the Grill to remain there until they were advised they could leave.

Parker's account was supported by George Rowland Harding, Richard Sanders, Franklin Wilson Ray and Robert D. Wheeler.[5]

With the assistance of a few friends who bolstered his story, including taxi drivers James McCraw, Willie Akin and others, Jowers began to promote his conspiracy tales with financial gain always at the forefront of any discussion. According to friends and relatives he hoped to make money from the new and embellished account of his alleged role in the assassination.

Jowers first hinted he was willing to talk more about the assassination when he was interviewed by Jack Saltman, the producer of a mock HBO James Earl Ray television trial, in December 1992. He told Saltman he wanted more than the standard $40 witness fee the producers had arranged. However, with no large amounts of money forthcoming he essentially stuck to his original story given at the time of the assassination, that he was in Jim's Grill and nothing untoward occurred. And, as Justice Department investigators observed, 'Jowers has only confessed in circumstances where candour has not been required by law or where he has not been required to reconcile his prior inconsistencies.'[6]

In late 1993 the Memphis District Attorney received a letter from Memphis lawyer Lewis Garrison requesting immunity for certain individuals who he claimed had knowledge of a plot to kill King. One of his clients was Jowers. The District Attorney rejected the offer.

Then, in December 1993, Jowers confessed on *Primetime Live* that he had been paid by Mafia-connected 'produce dealer' Frank Liberto to kill Dr King. He appeared with a 'co-conspirator', Willie Aiken, who stated he was involved after the fact. Jowers stated he had been told there would be a decoy in the plot to kill King and the police 'wouldn't be there that night'. Jowers said that Frank Liberto, now deceased, had a courier deliver $100,000 for Jowers to hold at his restaurant.

Jowers stated that the money was used to hire Frank Holt, an African American, to do the shooting. Allegedly, Holt was handed the rifle by Jowers, and shot King from the bushes behind the restaurant. Holt then came into Jim's Grill and gave the gun to Jowers, who hid it behind the bar. Holt ran to the front of the restaurant and went out the front door where he ran into a police officer who pushed him back inside. Jowers claimed that he still had the rifle in the cafe on 5 April and showed it to taxi driver James McCraw and his girlfriend Betty Spates, who saw him hide it behind the counter. Jowers said he was visited the day before the murder by a man named Raoul, who brought a rifle into his restaurant.

Following Jowers' appearance on *Primetime Live*, reporters from *The Tennessean* newspaper had found Frank Holt in Florida and he denied he had been paid by Jowers to shoot King. A lie-detector test was arranged by the newspaper and Holt passed with flying colours.[7]

In response, Jowers then began to reinvent his story. For the next five years he named several different new 'assassins', and with the assistance of a small circle of friends, he began to develop a new story to implicate various Memphis police officers.[8] He also made numerous contradictory statements about his role in the assassination to friends, relatives and Ray's lawyers but none were made under oath.[9]

In 1998 Jowers changed his story once more when he met former King aide Andrew Young and King's son Dexter. In a 2-hour taped confession Jowers now said the planners of the plot included undercover Memphis policeman Marrell McCullough, Memphis Police Department Lieutenant Earl Clark (who died in 1987), a third police officer unnamed and two men Jowers did not know but thought were federal agents. Jowers told Young and King that immediately after the shot was fired, he received a smoking rifle at the rear door of Jim's Grill from Clark. Jowers broke the rifle down into two pieces and wrapped it in a tablecloth which 'Raoul' collected the next day. Jowers said he did not see who fired the shot that killed King but he believed it was Clark, the Memphis Police Department's 'best marksman' as he described him. Incredibly, Jowers denied he knew the purpose of the plot was to kill King. Subsequently, he refused to say more unless he was granted immunity.

William Pepper believed Jowers and decided to bring him to court through a 'civil trial'. Before the trial began he made an agreement with Jowers' lawyer that the only damages that would be claimed would be a token $100. Lewis Garrison told the jury that his client did indeed play a part in a conspiracy but his role 'was insignificant'. Garrison rarely objected to any of the evidence presented by Pepper.

The demands of a criminal trial are not present in a civil trial. The burden of proof in civil cases is not 'beyond a reasonable doubt', the standard in criminal cases. In civil cases, the plaintiffs must prove their case with a 'preponderance' of the evidence – whether something is 'probably true' and 'more likely true than not true'. As the defence in the Jowers trial was in agreement with most of the issues raised by the 'prosecution' it was unlikely during the trial that any real truth would emerge. Rather than scrutinizing the totality of the evidence in the case lawyers for both sides argued in favour of evidence that appeared to suggest Ray was innocent.

During the period between Jowers' confession and the trial Pepper had managed to discover new 'witnesses' and they were called to give evidence. He also built his case around 'witnesses' who contradicted their original statements to the Memphis police and the FBI. Some of those witnesses, including Jowers' friends, also spoke of the possibility of making money from their revelations.

Pepper's witnesses continually changed their stories to accommodate new realities. Pepper tried to whitewash these facts by claiming that the witnesses had been, 'often fearful of becoming overly involved, at a time close to an event will frequently hold back pieces of information only to let them out at a later time when somewhat of a relationship has been developed with an investigator'.[10] Among the new witnesses were people who had observed a man fleeing the area of the bushes, a fire chief who testified that army agents had climbed on to the roof of the fire station to observe King (see Chapter 5 above) and friends of Jowers who supported his conspiracy story.[11]

And conveniently, evidence that Pepper planned to present to a jury claiming it would support his conspiracy allegations had gone missing, including the rifle he alleges was used to shoot King (at the bottom of the Mississippi River), the Memphis Police Department shooter (dead before his accusers went public), the Mafia organizer of the conspiracy (dead before his accusers found evidence of his role in the crime), photographs showing James Earl Ray did not shoot King (they have never surfaced) and members of an army sniper team (never 'named' and 'living in another country').

One of the 'long-lost' witnesses discovered by Pepper was Olivia Catling who had apparently managed to keep her conspiracy story secret for over twenty-five years. Catling, who lived a short distance from the Lorraine Motel, said she had planned to walk down the street on 4 April in the hope of seeing King. She testified at the trial that when she heard the shot a little after 6pm she ran with her two children and a neighbour's child to the corner of Mulberry and Huling streets and allegedly saw a man running out of the alley beside a building across the street from the Lorraine. The man jumped into a green 1965 Chevrolet just as a police car drove up behind him. He gunned the Chevrolet around the corner and up Mulberry past Catling's house. She said the police ignored the man and blocked off the street leaving his car free to go the opposite way. She said the man she saw was not James Earl Ray. She also said that she heard a fireman on Mulberry Street call to a police officer that the shot came from the bushes across the street from the Lorraine.

However, during a later interview, she contradicted her original story. She insisted she had seen a man on Huling Street before the police arrived at the intersection, not after they set up their roadblock. She also told the investigators that she was accompanied by her 11-year-old daughter and a neighbour's 12-year-old girl. The investigators interviewed the police officers who had set up the roadblock. They denied anything happened as related by Catling. More importantly, Catling's daughter contradicted her mother's version of the events.[12]

Betty Spates, Jowers' girlfriend and waitress at Jim's Grill at the time of the assassination, did not testify at the trial but her statement (one of many that changed over the years) about seeing Jowers enter the back of Jim's Grill with a rifle was presented. But the jury was unaware of her history of lying. One month before Ray pleaded guilty in March 1969, the District Attorney's office learned of a witness who alleged that Jowers was involved in the King assassination. Spates had claimed Jowers found a gun behind the cafe and may have shot King. Two days later Spates told prosecutors she was offered $5,000 to make up the story. Spates said the bogus story originated with King supporters.[13]

In 1994 Spates had backtracked on her allegations that she had seen Jowers enter the back of Jim's Grill with a rifle. In an affidavit for the Office of the District Attorney General she retracted her conspiracy story. She told investigators that she was certain she did not see Jowers with a gun in Jim's Grill at 6pm on 4 April 1968. She also told them she had agreed to say she had seen Jowers with a rifle to share in the royalty money which Jowers hoped to receive after selling his story.[14]

The jury was also unaware that within minutes of the shooting a deputy sheriff entered Jim's Grill and instructed Jowers to lock the door. Thereafter, police officers compiled a list of every witness inside. Spates' name did not appear on the list nor did any witness place Spates in the restaurant at the time of the assassination.[15] Additionally, Spates' claims that Jowers had a rifle at the time of the assassination were contradicted by a number of people who were in Jim's Grill during that period, including Billy Ray Hoard, Franklin Wilson Ray, Steven Cupples and Barry Tubbs.[16]

Spates' sisters Alta Mae Washington and Bobbie Balfour also said her story about seeing Jowers with a rifle was bogus. Washington said she did not start work at the restaurant until October 1968 and the money she saw being placed in a stove in Jim's Grill in April 1969 was put there so Jowers could hide a small amount, perhaps $1,000, from his estranged wife.[17] Both sisters said Betty Spates 'was not a truthful person'.[18]

During the years following his 'confession' Jowers changed his story each time in the telling. One tale he told described a group of police officers he met in Jim's Grill who were planning the assassination and that one of them was the assassin. He named the shooter as Lieutenant Earl Clark of the Memphis police, and the other plotters were an 'undercover officer', a 'TACT Inspector', a 'Homicide Inspector' and a 'former partner' of Jowers when the grill owner was briefly a police officer in the 1940s. Jowers' claims were also supported by his friend taxi driver James McCraw. Although McCraw had died in 1996, his statements were used by Pepper during the trial to bolster the claims of a meeting of conspirators in Jim's Grill.

In 1969 McCraw added to his story by saying he had seen another white Mustang at the rooming house, failing to mention anything about his friend

Jowers. Twenty years later he expanded on his original stories by claiming he had seen Jowers with the assassination rifle inside Jim's Grill. Although the jury clearly believed McCraw's story, Justice Department investigators concluded that because McCraw had changed and exaggerated his stories over the years they were 'untrustworthy'.[19]

Earl Clark's first wife Rebecca A. Clark was called to testify for the 'defence' at the 'trial'. She had divorced the now-deceased former Memphis police lieutenant in 1975. She testified that she had worked until 4pm on the day of the assassination and that her husband came home fairly soon after she had arrived, perhaps 10 or 15 minutes later. Her husband had been taking a quick nap and then was planning to have a shower and change his clothes, when she heard a broadcast on his police radio that King had been shot. 'He could not have been anywhere else, I was listening to the radio and heard it with my own ears,' she said. When asked if she was lying to protect her children she said, 'Sir, I am just telling the truth. It never entered my mind to protect my children, not that I wouldn't protect them. I love them dearly but I would not lie.'[20]

No independent or credible witness or any other corroborative evidence has confirmed Jowers' story about police officers meeting in his restaurant to plot King's assassination.[21] And, as William Hamblin, a former taxi driver and also a former employee of Jowers', said, '[Jowers and McCraw] have named every policeman in the graveyard. Every time they get scared, they'll name another policeman as being the murder man.'[22]

Two years after the trial the Justice Department concluded there was no credible evidence that Earl Clark had participated in the assassination of King nor was there any credible evidence that would implicate the other Memphis police officers in the crime. After interviewing numerous witnesses, colleagues in the police department and reviewing the court transcripts they found no reason to believe that Clark either knew Jowers or had met with him in Jim's Grill. They established that Jowers had never been a 'hunting partner' of Clark's, as Jowers alleged, or that a conspiracy meeting had taken place in Jim's Grill.[23]

The more outrageous claims made at the trial by William Pepper centred around possible involvement of the Mafia, the FBI and the US Army in King's murder.

The 'Mafia connection' cited by Jowers had not originated with him. It was investigated on a tip-off by the FBI on 7 April 1968 and the Bureau found the story not credible. Memphis resident John McFerren believed he had stumbled on the conspirators in the hours before the murder. At about 5pm on 4 April 1968 he was walking through the last warehouse on his rounds when he overheard a man's voice say, 'Hell, no, you're not going to get your pay until you do the job. You do the job, then you get your pay.' Two men had been sitting in an office, alleged McFerren, then one of them said, 'You can shoot the son of a bitch on the balcony.'[24]

The man McFerren recognized was Frank Liberto. Liberto was a businessman who had owned the warehouse. The FBI interviewed McFerren but decided his claims were based on wrong assumptions and snatches of conversation which could have been misinterpreted. According to a memo from the 1968 FBI files:

> Investigation disclosed that the individuals referred to in connection with the telephone call received at the LL and L produce Company are Frank Camilla Liberto and James William Latch, President and vice-president respectively of this company. They have denied ever discussing the possibility of shooting King or having knowledge of the person responsible. They stated they may have made derogatory remarks about King because of the loss of revenue caused by his activities.[25]

The FBI also found evidence that McFerren had not always been trustworthy when it came to making complaints about Civil Rights violations. During their investigation agents found that, 'McFerren has participated in civil rights activities in and around Somerville, Tennessee for a number of years. He has previously reported incidents to our Memphis office, many of which were found to be without any substance in fact.'[26]

It was clear to many observers of the trial who knew about McFerren's decades-old story that Jowers had hi-jacked the story told initially by John McFerren, then interwoven his own story with that of McFerren's to create a plausible but unproven and unsubstantiated allegation of Mafia involvement in the assassination.

In the late 1970s the HSCA thoroughly investigated McFerren's claims and found them not credible and that much of what McFerren claimed was based on conjecture.

One of the many fanciful claims McFerren made was that James Earl Ray had worked for Frank Liberto in Memphis, in 1967. HSCA investigators, who had tracked Ray's movements since his escape from prison in April 1967, discovered it had been impossible for Ray to have worked there at the time McFerren alleged.

McFerren claimed he had identified Ray in photographs supplied by FBI agents. In fact, he selected another man who looked nothing like Ray. McFerren had described Ray as having a dark complexion and thought he was Cuban, Mexican or Indian, 25 years old with coarse black hair, jaundiced skin and scars and pockmarks on his cheeks. The descriptions did not fit Ray's profile.

When McFerren testified to the HSCA the committee discovered he had embellished his original story as told to FBI agents. He now claimed that the two conspirators he had overheard had mentioned Ray by name and that George Wallace had been behind the assassination. However, a weak point in his story was that shortly after the assassination when he was interviewed by FBI agents, he did not name Ray – the FBI had not, at that point been able to discover Eric Starvo Galt's real identity. His claims were eventually discredited, especially following his allegations that the same man who had killed King had also murdered JFK. By the time McFerren was called as a defence witness at the Jowers trial his preposterous tales had been long forgotten.[27]

The Liberto 'Mafia connection' was re-investigated in 1998–2000 by the Justice Department. They found that McFerren had told his story to David Caywood, a lawyer, who reported that McFerren had recounted the story about Liberto calling him a 'son of a bitch' but nothing about a shooting on a balcony. Caywood said he would have remembered the 'balcony' part of the conversation as they both appeared on that same balcony with King the day before the assassination.[28]

The Justice Department also looked into the allegations made by some of Jowers' friends who purported to have had knowledge that Frank Liberto had threatened to kill King. Investigators interviewed taxi driver Nathan Whitlock and his mother Lavada Addison who said that sometime in the 1970s Liberto had confessed to them he 'had King killed'. The allegation was not made until 1993. During the Jowers trial Whitlock expanded on his story to say that government agents had threatened him. The Justice Department investigators characterized Whitlock as 'paranoid' and with having financial motives in testifying at the trial. They also believed Lavada Addison's interpretation of Liberto's comments as 'macho boasting'.[29]

The Justice Department investigators also found no evidence to support the allegations that Liberto had any ties to the Mafia. They:

... initiated a review of Department of Justice and FBI organised crime investigative records [and] found no information in these records showing that either Frank or Salvatore Liberto [Liberto's brother] had any affiliation with the Mafia. Our review of the remaining historical record also revealed nothing to support the claims concerning Liberto's Mafia involvement ... we found no credible evidence to suggest that organised crime was involved in the assassination.[30]

Investigators also looked into Jowers' finances and concluded there was no evidence to suggest he had come into any large sums of money. According to the report:

In 1968 [the assassination payment] was a very large sum of money. Consequently, if Jowers profited from the assassination ... his financial position should have dramatically improved. The financial records we reviewed did not reveal any significant improvement in Jowers' lifestyle at any time after the assassination. Nor did any witness we interviewed, including family members, detect that Jowers received a substantial windfall.[31]

The truth of the Justice Department's comments about Mafia involvement in the assassination came as no surprise to police and government investigators who had been involved in organized crime investigations during the 1960s. The Mafia has always been a loosely linked organization of criminals, spread throughout the United States, who came together to settle 'territorial disputes' and conflicts between Mafia gangs. Their sole purpose has been to increase their ill-gotten enterprises without attracting publicity. Mafia crime families had built their enterprises by avoiding conflict, wherever possible, with federal, state or local police forces. Particular 'targets' were 'off-limits' including police officers, judges, politicians or federal law-enforcement officials. Whenever these unofficial rules had been broken the government's response had been swift and severe. It is inconceivable that the Mafia would burden themselves with an unnecessary plot that would have no benefit whatsoever. The Civil Rights movement in the United States existed as an irrelevance to mob bosses and their aims did not clash. As ex-FBI agent Bill Roemer observed, '[The Mafia do not] go after judges, they don't go after reporters, they don't go after FBI agents or cops – they will only go after these people when they have stolen money from them or double crossed them.

It's counterproductive ... it's not the way these "businessmen" would have acted'.[32]

William Pepper had urged the jury to believe there was a motive for the killing – J. Edgar Hoover detested King and Lyndon Johnson wanted rid of a charismatic African American leader who was proving problematic on the issue of the Vietnam War. Although there was no credible evidence whatsoever to argue this point, Pepper instinctively understood that the demonization of Hoover and Johnson that had spread through the media since the 1970s would provide enough motive. In linking the preposterous claims of Loyd Jowers to the FBI's abuse of power he was able to create enough doubt in the jury's mind.

Pepper had no interest in seeing Loyd Jowers go to jail. The whole thrust of his efforts was in trying to prove that Jowers was merely a tool in a larger conspiracy involving the FBI, the Military, the CIA and the Mafia. Pepper's thesis centred around the reasons why the government wanted to eliminate the Civil Rights leader. During the trial Pepper said:

> The State regarded him [King] as an enemy because he opposed it [the war in Vietnam]. But what does it really mean, his opposition? I put it to you that his opposition to that war had little to do with ideology, with capitalism, with democracy. It had to do with money. It had to do with huge amounts of money that that war was generating to large multinational corporations that were based in the United States.[33]

And Loyd Jowers had no fear of arrest following the jury's verdict. There was simply no credible evidence to charge him with anything. The trial was a mockery of justice and leading commentators believed that the King family had misplaced their trust in William Pepper. As historian David J. Garrow said:

> [Jowers was] an ostensible defendant ... who for six years now has been going out of his way to plead guilty. During the trial Jowers' inconsistent stories were never introduced; crucial witnesses were never called and the defence was virtually non-existent. No one told the jury that Jowers had bragged about getting rich off his television appearances and had practically begged people to implicate him.[34]

* * *

In December 1999 the civil trial jury concluded that Martin Luther King was assassinated by a conspiracy involving Loyd Jowers and 'others, including government agencies'.[35] William Pepper now had official support for his government-centred theories about the assassination and he said it was 'vindication'. However, the one-sided presentation of the case allowed for no other result. David Garrow said the jury's verdict 'was meaningless'.[36]

The 'trial' made headlines around the world and convinced many that the truth about the case had now been uncovered. Pepper had persuaded the King family that Jowers' confessions had been truthful and that the circumstances of the murder indicated FBI, CIA, Military Intelligence and Mafia involvement. As King's son Dexter left the courthouse, he told reporters, 'I think this is history being created. Anyone who would question whether the truth would come out, this is the last form of democracy that's still alive where you have independent jurors rendering a verdict. So, we're very happy.'[37]

However, the idea that the trial's outcome was confirmation of a conspiracy was not universally accepted. Former Tennessee state prosecutor, John Campbell, said the trial was a one-sided affair and featured witnesses passing on second- and third-hand hearsay with little cross examination:

> What does a jury do under those circumstances when everybody agrees, and all they want the jury to do is just basically approve it ... They've been provided a very narrow view of Dr Pepper's conspiracy theory. They have not seen all the warts. They have not seen a lot of the conjecture that came up in '93 and '94 with witnesses who apparently were not called at this trial.[38]

Before the Jowers trial began Shelby County District Attorney William Gibbons had conducted a four-year investigation into Jowers' 1993 allegations which had later been central to the Jowers-trial proceedings. His findings were published a year before the Jowers trial. The report concluded there was no evidence that would suggest anyone other than Ray was involved in the murder of Martin Luther King.[39]

Gibbons and his team were also able to invalidate every allegation made by Jowers in his increasingly embellished stories. The twelve-page report did not rule out the possibility that Ray received some assistance from his brothers John and Jerry Ray, yet found there was no evidence that would warrant charges against anyone but James Earl Ray for the murder of King. Gibbons said, 'The District Attorney's Office remains absolutely convinced of James Earl Ray's guilt in the murder of Dr King ... The evidence against him is overwhelming ... There is simply no credible evidence to support a new trial for Mr Ray'.[40]

The District Attorney's report also concluded that Jowers' claims to have been involved in a plot to kill King were motivated by a desire to make money. Investigators interviewed six people who were in Jim's Grill on the day of the assassination and spoke with members of Jowers' family. They found that Jowers had been taking a very active role in getting people to make statements that implicated him. One witness, Prentis B. Purdy, who was in the cafe the day of the assassination said Jowers contacted him and told him 'there was money to be made if he cooperated'. Among the numerous discoveries the investigators made was one in which an alleged 'assassin' confessed to the crime. Investigators discovered that the self-confessed assassin, James C. Green of Springville, Tennessee, was in prison at the time of the murder.[41]

Historian Gerald McKnight was also not persuaded by the trial's result and rejected the claims made by Pepper that J. Edgar Hoover had conspired to murder Martin Luther King. McKnight wrote:

> Had Hoover and the FBI elites actually planned to neutralise King by assassination it is reasonable to assume they would have called off their COINTELPRO campaign against him and destroyed these records once the decision was finalised. Any truly independent federal investigation into the King assassination uncovering this kind of incriminating evidence would place the FBI at the top of its list of prime suspects. It is equally untenable and baseless to imagine that the Hoover FBI, a virtually independent security state within a state that had succeeded as spectacularly over almost 50 years under the operational premise that control was the name of the game, would conspire with parties outside the Bureau to kill King.[42]

It should have been clear to members of the jury that a conspiracy involving the government would, out of necessity, require a cast of hundreds if not thousands. In an era when even the lowliest government worker has been able to spill the beans on the abuse of power, Pepper's claims become preposterous.

In June 2000 the Justice Department released the results of their eighteen-month investigation which had been called for by the King family after the trial. The inquiry involved investigators with the postal service, Alcohol, Tobacco and Firearms and the Marshals service. No FBI agents took part because of long-standing suspicions that the Bureau had somehow been involved in King's death.[43]

It was the fifth official investigation of the assassination. The report concluded that the Justice Department was satisfied that there was no reliable evidence supporting any involvement of a long list of alleged conspirators – including people who were allegedly involved in the Kennedy assassination, the Mafia, African American ministers who were close to King, the Military, the CIA or the FBI. Nor was President Johnson culpable.

According to the 2000 report the allegations made at the Jowers trial were promoted through supposition and hearsay and the evidence to prove claims made by purported 'witnesses' were non-existent. Investigators found that a number of Jowers-trial witnesses had related 'double hearsay' and accusations concerning government involvement which had absolutely no foundation in truth. The report stated:

> A limited amount of ... trial evidence was offered in an attempt to suggest that the FBI ... were involved in the assassination. Several witnesses made vague accusations that the FBI failed to investigate thoroughly or suppressed evidence related to the murder and that its leadership wanted Dr King killed. No specific trial evidence, however, supported these accusations and we found nothing to confirm the speculation.[44]

The report confirmed the findings of the HSCA which discovered that while the FBI had acted disgracefully with regard to their spying on King and made efforts to discredit the Civil Rights leader, it did not conspire to assassinate him.

Contemporaneous with the publication of the Justice Department's report the HSCA's Chief Counsel G. Robert Blakey said the conclusions of the 1976–9 HSCA investigation were consistent with the new findings of the Justice Department investigators. Blakey said the HSCA's reasons for coming to their conclusion that the FBI had no part in King's death were sound. Blakey told *Salon* magazine:

> ... we took the FBI and we figured, all right, Hoover killed him. Well, who are Hoover's associates? The FBI agents who were spying on King? OK, which ones had any contact with James Earl Ray? We got no

connections. We had unlimited access to the FBI files, including their
informant files. We went into the whole COINTELPRO operation that
was designed to discredit Dr King. Let me tell you, I had every incentive
in the world to prove that the FBI did it, with Ray or without Ray. Well,
you can imagine the book I would have written? 'FBI Kills King, Blakey
Proves It.' And look, I worked for [African American Congressman] Lou
Stokes. You think he didn't have an incentive to prove it if he could've?
What about Walter Fauntroy, King was his friend. You think Walter
Fauntroy wasn't on me, watching me? ... If Ray had been paid by the
FBI to shoot King, why hasn't Ray given up the FBI? And, if you posit
this paranoid's vision of an all-powerful, no-holds-barred government,
able to kill people by hiring assassins, why would they leave a witness?
If Ray could give up the Bureau, do you really think he would have sur-
vived this long?[45]

The Justice Department Report also demolished the claims made at the
Jowers trial that the army had been involved in the King assassination.[46] The
report stated:

In addition to reviewing records, we located and interviewed five surviving members of the 111th MIG who were in Memphis on April 4, 1968.
They all claimed they were not aware that military personnel from any
other unit, including the 902d MIG, were in Memphis around the time
of the assassination. . . . Additionally, no one from the 111th MIG had
first-hand knowledge that any military personnel were in the vicinity of
the Lorraine on the day of the assassination or that military personnel
ever conducted surveillance of Dr King ... we found nothing to indicate
that surveillance at any time had any connection with the assassination.[47]

At the conclusion of the investigation Barry Kowalski, the man who headed
the Justice Department investigation, told reporters, 'We found no credible
evidence to support allegations of any conspiracy to kill Dr. King involving
Jowers, Raoul, the Mafia, Memphis police officers, figures involved in the
Kennedy assassination, federal agents, U.S. military personnel or African-
American ministers close to Dr. King. We are convinced of our conclusions
beyond a reasonable doubt.'[48]

The new investigation did not prevent William Pepper from continuing on his quixotic mission to persuade the US public of Ray's innocence.
Building on the evidence he had acquired for the Jowers trial, Pepper spent
the following two decades purportedly 'discovering' the real assassins.

He first named Memphis police officer Earl Clark of having been the shooter in the bushes across the street from the Lorraine Motel. A few years later he decided the real assassin was another Memphis police officer by the name of Frank Strausser. Incredibly, the only piece of evidence Pepper said proved his allegation was a non-itemized telephone bill.

In the decades that followed Pepper also accused the doctors attending to King after the shooting as having 'smothered him to death'.[49] Another Pepper witness turned out to be the caretaker of the Memphis Police Department's rifle range who stated he overheard a police officer say, 'Somebody was going to blow his [King's] mother's ... brains out' and said his rifle was 'special'.[50] Pepper also claimed he had found the real Raoul who purportedly manipulated Ray. He was a Portuguese immigrant whose first name was 'Raul'. Utilizing innocent comments made by the accused's daughter, Pepper alleged the government had assisted her father in covering up his role in the assassination. The innocent man had his life turned upside down by Pepper's desire to implicate him in the purported plot. The Justice Department cleared him of any involvement in the assassination.[51]

Chapter 7

Raoul

The competent liar often uses a thin 'truth line' to help keep track of what he says and to ensure that his story appears consistent to the listener.

Psychologist Robert O'Hare

[Ray's] rather impassive countenance lights up, he chuckles or something only when he's told about how he has left a false clue somewhere and the idea of FBI agents or Canadian Mounted Police chasing down alleys or false leads is the only thing that he really chuckles about, you see, this fascinates him. So he thinks of life as himself against the police. That's the game that he plays and he wants to excel at it.

William Bradford Huie

Ever since Ray had pleaded guilty to murdering Martin Luther King and been sentenced to ninety-nine years in prison he continued to claim he had been 'railroaded' into pleading guilty by his lawyer Percy Foreman. The real assassin, Ray insisted, was a person who manipulated him by the name of Raoul. During his forty years' incarceration he provided numerous conflicting descriptions of Raoul. Not a shred of credible evidence confirms any trace of Raoul or who he might have been.

From the time of his arrest Ray was busy inventing an alibi. Twenty years previously he had given police the name of 'Walter McBride' as the person who committed various offences he was charged with. 'McBride' was a fictional character.[1] Now he was ready to place the blame for the King assassination elsewhere. During his incarceration in Wandsworth Prison Ray made a number of references to his innocence and who the actual killer was. Prison officers had to make a brief report after every shift spent guarding him. 'He said the assassination had been organised by one of [King's] own lieutenants to gain control of the organisation funds,' one officer noted. Another officer wrote, 'The assassination that has taken place in the USA [was] spoken of by him in association with the Black Muslim group. He implied they could be behind the Martin Luther King shooting.'[2]

After Ray had been extradited to the United States, he continued to plead his innocence. He built a new alibi involving a mystery conspirator named 'Raoul' who purportedly manipulated him in delivering the rifle used to kill King to his Memphis rooming house on the day King was shot. Raoul then ordered Ray to leave the rooming house and 'take in a movie'. When Ray allegedly saw police in the vicinity of the rooming house on his return, he fled the scene of King's assassination.

Ray's new alibi was first placed in his mind by Arthur Hanes. A colleague of Hanes, Russell X. Thompson, told the lawyer about a mysterious visitor to his office on 10 April 1968, six days after the King shooting. He was a blonde-haired Latin man, about 35 years of age who called himself 'Tony Benevetta' or 'Tony Benevitas', Thompson said. Benevetta told Thompson his roommate killed King. There was no evidence to suggest the mystery man who called on Thompson was anything but a fantasist – the same type of individual that was always drawn to famous murder cases seeking some form of recognition and notoriety. The allegation was fully investigated by the FBI which concluded 'Tony' was not credible. However, Hanes used the story to help Ray establish an alibi.[3]

Building on Hanes' bogus Raoul story, Ray said that the mystery man named Raoul framed him for the King assassination. He said it was Raoul who gave him the money to buy the white Mustang; Raoul who told him to buy the rifle; Raoul who told him to rent a room in the boarding house; and Raoul who remained in the rooming house when Ray left shortly before the shooting.

The first detailed account of Raoul's participation in the assassination was given by Ray to author William Bradford Huie who contracted with Ray and his lawyers to write a series of articles for *Look* magazine and a follow-up book in the months before Ray's trial. In a series of letters to the author Ray said that he had merely followed directions from a man he had met in a Montreal bar following his escape from the Missouri State Penitentiary in 1967. Ray claimed he knew the blonde, Latin stranger only as 'Raoul' and said that Raoul had asked him to smuggle contraband into the United States from both Canada and Mexico. Ray told Huie that Raoul instructed him to buy a car and a rifle in Birmingham and finally to drive to Memphis and check into a sleazy rooming house facing the Lorraine Motel. When the shot was fired, according to Ray, he was parked somewhere on South Main Street. Raoul ran out of the rooming house, jumped into Ray's Mustang, covered himself with a white sheet and then exited the car eight blocks later.

Ray later said he had been lying to Huie when he related how Raoul had pulled a white sheet over his head. He excused it on the grounds he had been playing games with the author, a writer famous for his investigative articles about the Ku Klux Klan. Ray explained these inconsistencies away in his autobiography:

> Remembering Huie's obsession with the KKK, I told [my lawyer] that in the minutes after the shooting I was sitting idly in the Mustang, which was parked out front of the flophouse. Suddenly, I said, Raoul raced to the car, jumped into the back seat and pulled a bedsheet over his head, saying 'get the hell out of here fast!' Bedsheet, Klan – the joke seemed obvious to me, but I guess not everyone got it.[4]

Huie initially believed Ray and his first articles for *Look* revealed how Raoul had used Ray as a 'patsy'. However, in the intervening period between the first and final article Huie's research persuaded him that Ray had been lying about the mysterious Raoul. Later, Ray's new lawyer Percy Foreman said in a sworn deposition and under oath, 'Ray bragged about the fool he was making out of Huie. Ray told me he invented Raoul for Huie. He said there wasn't any Raoul.' Additionally, Ray's brother Jerry told George McMillan, 'That's [Raoul story] just bullshit made up for Huie.'[5]

Huie eventually became suspicious of Ray's story about Raoul and he began to see how it was inconceivable that a professional criminal like Ray would put complete trust in someone he barely knew yet never learning his surname and continuing to follow instructions without question. Flaws in Ray's story began to appear. Ray couldn't get his description of Raoul to be consistent and when Raoul purportedly told Ray to buy a rifle and check into a rooming house in Memphis Ray did so unquestionably. Huie didn't believe the paranoid and suspicious Ray would do that. Additionally, for Huie, there were no witnesses who saw the mysterious Raoul anywhere near the scene of the assassination. On the other hand, there were many witnesses who testified to seeing Ray.

During preparations for the 1969 trial, state investigators and prosecutors had addressed the possibility of whether or not Ray's alleged alibi had any substance. Ray's first alibi account placed him outside the rooming house on

South Main Street when the shooting occurred. He said he had been waiting in the Mustang for Raoul. Raoul came running down the stairs, dropped the bundle in the doorway and jumped in the back seat of his Mustang. He said the Raoul told him to stop the car a few blocks away and got out. Ray's second alibi, formulated after his 1969 trial, placed him at a petrol station some blocks from the scene when the murder of King took place.

Shelby County trial prosecutor Phil Canale said that investigators found no corroborative evidence that an accomplice had been present at the scene of the crime. Canale said:

> [In consideration that] Mr. James Earl Ray was a dupe in this thing or a fall guy or a member of a conspiracy to kill Dr Martin Luther King Jr. ... Our office has examined over five thousand printed pages of investigation work done by local police, by national police organisations and by international law-enforcement agencies. We have examined over three hundred physical bits of evidence, physical exhibits. Three men in my office, Mr. [Robert] Dwyer, Mr. [James] Beasley and Mr. John Carlisle, the chief investigator of the attorney general's office ... have travelled thousands of miles all over this country on this investigation ... and I just state to you frankly that we have no evidence that there was any conspiracy involved in this.[6]

The HSCA re-investigated the King killing in the mid-1970s. After the committee conducted an extensive investigation of Ray's activities during the pre-assassination period, they uncovered no evidence for the existence of Raoul. In all the places Ray travelled leading up to the murder – Los Angeles, California; New Orleans, Louisiana; Birmingham, Alabama; Atlanta, Georgia; and Memphis – not a single witness was found. In fact, even Ray's defence team was unable to find the mysterious Raoul or any credible witness who could identify him. The committee investigators believed that the absence of corroborative witnesses was a strong indication that Ray fabricated the Raoul story. Investigators also found witnesses from the three rooming houses, Peter Cherpes' (Birmingham), Jimmy Garner's (Atlanta) and Bessie Brewer's (Memphis), where Ray said he had met Raoul. The witnesses recalled seeing Ray but said at no time did they see a man that fitted Ray's description of Raoul or, for that matter, any other individual with Ray.[7]

For the following decades, James Earl Ray and those representing him have specifically identified as many as twenty different persons to be Raoul.

The descriptions have ranged from a blonde 'Latin French-Canadian, approximately 35 years old' to a 'red-haired French-Canadian, 35-40 years old'. Other descriptions have included a 'Latin man with sandy coloured hair' and a 'small Mexican man'.

Each time investigators have demonstrated that a specific individual named was not Raoul, another potential suspect has surfaced. The cast of those falsely accused is an assorted group, which includes a Louisiana state trooper, an employee of a company included in the Fortune 500, two CIA operatives, a government employee, an accountant, a homeless person and a cancer researcher. None of the purported suspects appear to have anything in common. They are individuals of different races and nationalities, who come from various backgrounds, parts of the country and walks of life. They do not share a common appearance or characteristic that caused them to be singled out, and none possessed most of the descriptive characteristics Ray had attributed to Raoul.[8] Accordingly, accusations related to Raoul have followed no set pattern.

Typically, an individual became a suspect merely because they had been named by someone holding some kind of animus towards the purported suspect. For example, in the late 1970s, authorities investigated whether a successful African American accountant from New Orleans, having no criminal record, was Raoul merely because Ray, who had always maintained that Raoul was Hispanic, made the accusation.

One wrongly accused individual turned out to be a deputy chief and twenty-six-year veteran of a Louisiana sheriff's department. In that case, the HSCA dismissed the charge and explicitly found that, 'Ray's allegation was merely an attempt to gain credence for his Raoul story and to raise an implication of official complicity in the assassination.'[9]

On 15 January 1999, Ray's brother John claimed that Raoul shot King and that James was falsely accused. Raoul and James were both OSS (Office of Strategic Services) agents in the late 1940s, John said, when James was in the army. John said that James confessed to the King assassination to avoid prosecution for shooting a fellow soldier in Germany.[10] However, beyond its implausibility, John's Raoul story contradicts his own brother's statements in which he insists he first met Raoul in Canada years after his military service. And there is one relevant fact that most definitely puts the lie to John's story. James Earl Ray's military career in Germany lasted from July 1946 to December 1948. The OSS was disbanded in 1945.

However, in the decades following his trial Ray was consistently inconsistent about not only his description of Raoul but also his meetings with the mysterious man on the afternoon of the assassination and his own whereabouts when Raoul planted the weapon and personal items to purportedly frame him.

Soon after Huie published his book *He Slew the Dreamer*, which concluded Raoul did not exist, Ray doubled down and began to manipulate the Raoul story, taking into consideration multiple stories spread by conspiracists. After a witness came forward to say he had witnessed Ray at a Texaco gas station at the time of the shooting he changed his original story now claiming he had indeed been at the gas station. The HSCA investigated the claim and discovered Ray's then lawyer Mark Lane had lied about the alleged gas-station witness.[11]

According to Arthur Hanes Jr, one of Ray's early lawyers:

> When we seem to be having a productive conversation, containing questions and relatively truthful answers, he opens his eyes wide, holds his head erect and is therefore pleased with himself but these good conversations ... come only when we talk of relatively unimportant activities, such as all the places Ray has been, or when he is pointing out errors, he claims he has detected in what has been written or said about him. When you ask Ray a hard question, like for a better description of Raoul ... he always hangs his head, runs his fingers through his hair, and says nothing ... then he changes the subject.[12]

Ray also 'chuckled' when caught out in a lie. Psychologists refer to this as 'duping delight'. When he was caught out in a lie by Huie he was seldom perplexed or embarrassed and simply reworked his story. He manipulated his lawyers by using information obtained by one to develop his story when he related it to another, reconstructing the 'facts' so that they appeared to be consistent with the lie.

Ray's accounts of his smuggling operations before the assassination are consistent and specific. Witnesses and documentary evidence confirm that his accounts of his travels in the nine months before the murder are, for the most part, true. However, the RCMP, FBI, US customs, US drug-enforcement investigators, local and state police forces investigated Ray's claims that he travelled with Raoul between Canada and the United States and found nothing to support his stories which would identify Raoul.[13]

Within a few years of the assassination Ray's smuggling story was contradicted by one of his brothers. Jerry Ray admitted to author George McMillan:

> The whole thing about Raoul and running drugs from Canada was bullshit. He went to Canada … [following his escape from Missouri State Penitentiary] to look the place out, how to get out of the country. The reason he broke off with that girl [a woman he had met at a holiday resort in Canada] was that he was getting serious. He really liked her. He got afraid and broke off her. That wasn't his aim in life, to stay with a woman. He wanted more than that. He wanted the Big Boy [Martin Luther King].[14]

In fact, Ray's story about the three smuggling trips he purportedly arranged with Raoul was not consistent with the modus operandi of known gunrunners or US gun laws during the 1960s. Ray claimed to have been involved in three smuggling trips organized by Raoul across the Canadian and Mexican borders to buy guns. However, Mexican gunrunners would have no need to purchase their weapons through a third party. Any type of weapon could be purchased over the counter in most Western states with no questions asked. Remington rifles could be bought in any US city or town. Why would prospective Mexican or Cuban purchasers examine a rifle in Memphis when they could have chosen a more convenient border town? It was also common knowledge that New Orleans was a centre for anti-Castro exile groups who could have easily provided illegal guns. More importantly, why would conspirators put their conspiracy at risk by using a 'patsy' in such risky ventures?

Additionally, Ray claimed that he had been set up by Raoul to be a patsy in the King killing. So why, eight months before the assassination, would Raoul use a fugitive on the run to smuggle goods across the border when, if caught, the whole plot would fall apart?

There is some evidence Ray may have gotten the idea of a partner in crime called Raoul from his days spent in Mexico. Throughout his life on the run Ray had used aliases which had a connection to some part of his life. The aliases Harvey Lowmeyer, Eric Starvo Galt, Paul Bridgeman, John Willard (adapted from his real uncle, Willard Meyer), Ramon George Sneyd, John L. Rayns, among many others, were developed from real people. It is therefore plausible Ray constructed 'Raoul' from his travels in Mexico. He often spoke of an acquaintance who was a Mexican citizen living in Campeche Bay and who ran a small-scale smuggling business. The acquaintance of Ray's spoke English well and owned a small fishing boat. He would make smuggling trips from Brownsville, Texas, into Mexico through Campeche Bay. A former Missouri State Penitentiary inmate believed Ray made trips with the man as Mexican fisherman were not checked upon entering Mexico through that port.[15]

During his four-year investigation into the King murder (1968–72) author Gerold Frank discovered how Ray had made a crucial mistake in his 'Raoul' story. During the period Ray spent in Los Angeles before the murder, he had been visiting a clinical psychologist, Dr Mark O. Freeman, to seek relief from his anxiety problems, shyness and headaches. Ray had visited Dr Freeman five times at three- to four-day intervals. He saw Dr Freeman on 14 December 1967 and left after making an appointment to see him the following Monday, 18 December.

However, Ray cancelled the appointment on the Friday morning, 15 December because on the Thursday night he had met a woman who asked him to drive her cousin Charlie Stein to New Orleans the following morning to collect her children, who had been staying with their grandmother. Frank wrote:

> If Raoul had written him [as Ray stated] days before to drive down to New Orleans on Friday 15th December, why would Ray have made an appointment to see Dr Freeman on the following Monday? He would have known then that he would be in New Orleans on Monday. This meant simply that Raoul had not written him … Friday morning, before driving with Charlie Stein to New Orleans, Ray also telephoned the National Dance Studio to say he would be out of town – additional proof that he did not know until Thursday night, and his meeting with the Steins, that he was going on the trip.[16]

According to Percy Foreman and author William Bradford Huie, Ray possessed a remarkable memory. Foreman had noticed how Ray made diagrams of places he had been to with astonishing detail. He thought it was 'close to total recall'. He made diagrams of hotels and bars setting out exact furnishings. Yet, he could not detail anything connected to his meetings with Raoul – no descriptions of barmen, waiters, hotel receptionists or anyone else who may have seen the two men together.[17]

Ray told his first lawyer Arthur Hanes that between 5 and 6pm on the day of the assassination, following his alleged meeting with Raoul in Room 5b,

Raoul told him to go to Jim's Grill downstairs to wait for him. Yet, Ray could not describe the interior of the restaurant and his diagram of the restaurant bore no resemblance to it. Hanes then described the restaurant to him. When Ray fired Hanes in favour of Percy Foreman, he described the restaurant to Foreman in exact detail. It was virtually word for word consistent with Hanes' description.[18]

According to Ray, '[Bessie Brewer] ... rented me a sleeping room. So, after I had been up there too long, Raoul had come up there, and we started talking and he said that we might be around there two or three days.'[19] However, it has never been explained how Raoul knew which room Ray rented. No one asked Brewer and it is reasonable to assume that had any roomer been asked where John Willard's room was situated it would have been reported. There was also no telephone in Room 5b and he never mentioned any telephone calls he may have made from a public telephone.

In his autobiography Ray named his landlord in Atlanta, Georgia, as a witness who had seen Raoul. 'Raoul came in [to the room in Atlanta] irritated that I was talking so long', he wrote. 'This inspired Garner [landlord] and me to finalise our deal [rent agreement] as best we could. Once that was done, Raoul led me around the block to a diner on Peachtree, where we had supper ... Around noon, Raoul showed up, evidently directed by Garner.'[20] This statement is contradicted by Garner's testimony. The landlord observed no one in Ray's company, nor did he see any indication that someone other than Ray had been in the apartment.

There were further flaws in Ray's Raoul story. Ray stated he had given the rifle to Raoul at the New Rebel Motel the night before the assassination and never saw it again. Yet, when the rifle was examined after the assassination, two latent fingerprints of value were lifted from it, both belonging to Ray. Ray was confronted, therefore, with the need to explain how Raoul, after handling the rifle, managed to remove all of his prints while leaving two of Ray's.

Each time Ray or his lawyers identified the twenty or so different persons who were 'Raoul', investigators demonstrated that the claims were false.[21] Every writer who defended Ray's Raoul story failed to find the mysterious co-conspirator. Conspiracy author Philip Melanson believed he was Jules Ricco Kimble, a convicted killer with connections to the KKK and allegedly the Mafia. Kimble's claims of some involvement in the assassination were investigated by the HSCA and were found to be without credibility. The HSCA said that Kimble was not even in Montreal at the time of Ray's visit in 1967. Kimble was called by the committee to testify and he admitted he had never met Ray. Even Philip Melanson had to confess, 'It cannot be assumed that Kimble is telling the truth or that he is lying.'[22]

The HSCA also obtained evidence from several sources who requested confidentiality that Jerry Ray believed parts of the Raoul story were untrue. Furthermore, Jerry himself admitted to the committee that he gave a false description of Raoul in a New York City radio interview in 1977 and he falsely denied that his brother ever mentioned King in their conversations during prison visits over the ten years following the assassination.[23]

Ray's lawyer Percy Foreman tried to elicit the truth about 'Raoul' from Ray when he prepared the assassin for his trial. Foreman told reporters that Ray had admitted Raoul did not exist, 'Within 40 minutes of my coming into the case he told me there was no Raoul, that Raoul was a "come on". He picked the name [from] a man he had robbed several years before in Montreal.'[24]

* * *

FBI investigators found evidence that Ray had turned up in the same places as King in the weeks prior to the assassination. Ray's 22 March 1968 trip to Selma where King was due to attend a rally in support of his Poor People's Campaign was indicative of his stalking King. As it turned out King's route was changed, and he appeared in a town near Selma. Ray drove to Selma on 22 March and registered at the Flamingo Motel. It soon became a problem for Ray and his lawyers. Ray's fabricated alibi for the King murder was predicated on disproving the stalking allegations and it became crucial to his defence. Clearly, co-conspirators like 'Raoul' would not have allowed their 'patsy' to stalk the Civil Rights leader.

Both Ray and his lawyer Mark Lane attempted to disprove these claims when the HSCA re-investigated the assassination in the 1970s. A map found in Ray's Atlanta rooming house was central to the HSCA inquiry and showed how Ray had marked the vicinity of King's home and offices in Atlanta. From the beginning, Ray had always wanted to steer the investigations away from this vital piece of evidence.

Following King's appearance in Los Angeles on 16 and 17 March, when he delivered a speech, the Civil Rights leader returned to Atlanta. At the same time King was giving his speech Ray was at a post office, 3 miles away, filling out forms requesting his mail be delivered to 'General Delivery' Atlanta, King's home town.

Ray's original story was that 'Raoul' had written to him in Los Angeles with instructions for a meeting in New Orleans. Raoul and Ray were then to travel to Atlanta together. In 1977, however, Ray told CBS' Dan Rather that he never knew he would be going to Atlanta until he arrived in Birmingham, Alabama, and there was no forwarding address. He told Rather that if the evidence proved he knew in Los Angeles that he was going to Atlanta it would be damaging to his case. For if Ray had gone directly to Atlanta, King's home town, it would prove he had lied.[25] To Ray's embarrassment, the HSCA produced the change of address card, signed by Ray.[26]

There is conclusive evidence that Ray collected the rifle from Aeromarine Supply Company in Birmingham and returned to Atlanta by the early evening of 30 March. On 1 April Ray dropped off some clothes at the Piedmont Laundry in Atlanta. Yet, Ray said that after he collected the rifle he did not return to Atlanta. Although Memphis is only a 5-hour drive from Birmingham, Ray said it took him five days to get there, taking his time and stopping off at motels on the way. The motels were thoroughly investigated and none supplied records of Ray staying in any of them. Ray claimed he left for Memphis two days before the SCLC publicly announced that King would return there for another march. The SCLC only made this decision on 30 March therefore if Ray had been directed to Memphis by Raoul as early as 30 March it would have been strong evidence of a sophisticated conspiracy by people in high places who had knowledge of King's future movements.

However, if Ray did not leave Atlanta until 1 April this would indicate he had read about the SCLC's decision in the newspapers and was strong proof he had been stalking King. Ray had told the HSCA that he did not go back to Atlanta and was very adamant about this part of his testimony. Louis Stokes, the committee's chairman, repeatedly questioned Ray to ascertain whether or not Ray was certain of his facts. Following Ray's final denial, a researcher entered the hearing room with a receipt from the Piedmont Laundry dated 1 April. Ray's lawyer Mark Lane called the receipt a forgery but the HSCA produced the original handwritten 'counter book', a ledger of each order dropped off at the laundry. Estelle Peters, the laundry's manager, testified that the documents were genuine.[27]

The HSCA, after extensive investigation, concluded that Raoul did not exist and that, 'Ray's post-assassination tale of Raoul was fabricated to conceal contacts with one or both brothers'. Ray had used the Raoul story to explain away the incontrovertible proof that he had purchased the weapon that killed King. He had to sow the seeds of doubt that he had actually pulled the trigger and therefore the Raoul story fitted nicely.

Additionally, during the period of the HSCA investigation, *TIME* magazine reported that, 'Ray began to hint that he had concocted the story about Raoul'. According to *TIME*, the first Chief Counsel for the HSCA Richard Sprague interviewed James Earl Ray three times. Sprague believed he had developed a rapport with Ray. Following the interviews Sprague concluded that Raoul 'does not and did not exist'. Sprague did report, however, that Ray insisted he had received assistance from unnamed people while he was a fugitive.[28]

* * *

In 1993 William Pepper discovered there was a witness who could purportedly confirm Raoul was a real person. A woman by the name of Glenda Grabow had contacted Jowers' lawyer, Lewis Garrison, and said she had information about who killed Martin Luther King. Grabow was a former Houston waitress who, after being hypnotized, said a customer she knew as 'Dago' claimed responsibility for orchestrating the King murder.

'Dago', Grabow said, had also allegedly confessed to assassinating President Kennedy. Grabow claimed that in the two weeks prior to President Kennedy's assassination she saw Dago receive some uniforms from Jack Ruby and was to give them to Lee Harvey Oswald. On the day President Kennedy went to Houston, before his trip to Dallas, she had observed Dago standing on the roof of a car near the presidential motorcade armed with a rifle. Grabow claimed to have spoken to Dago following the assassination of President Kennedy and he had confessed to the assassination.

Grabow's many highly dramatic claims included: she had known Jack Ruby, the man who killed Lee Harvey Oswald; she had an intimate relationship with Ruby; and she had a close relationship with former Johnson administration official Jack Valenti who she said had produced pornographic material in the 1960s. When confronted with the outrageous allegations Valenti said it was 'pure fantasy' and 'utterly false'.[29]

Raoul had supposedly told Glenda Grabow that he had also killed Martin Luther King. According to Grabow, Raoul would spend a lot of time in Houston with a relative and her association with Raoul would last over ten years until the mid-1970s. Royce Wilburn, Glenda's brother, also said he knew Raoul in Houston.

Both Jack Saltman, a British television producer, and William Pepper, working on independent investigations, located a 'Raul' in 1995. He was a retired autoworker living quietly in the north-eastern United States by the name of Raul Coelho. When Grabow and her brother Royce Wilburn were shown photos who Pepper said were of Raoul, they said they recognized him as the gunrunner they knew in Houston in the 1960s and 1970s. No one questioned how Wilburn, who had been 6 years old at the time of the assassination, was able to identify Raul.

Shown the photograph of Raul which had been obtained from immigration files, James Earl Ray also identified the retired autoworker as Raoul – which directly contradicted his earlier assertion that another passport photo he had been shown in the 1970s was Raoul. That photo looked nothing like the Portuguese immigrant Pepper named.

William S. Gibbons, the Shelby County District Attorney, sent investigators to interview Raul's family members. The picture that emerged was of a family man who had worked for the same company for thirty years, 'raised a family, had friends and lived a normal life'. The investigators discovered Raul had never been absent for long periods in 1963, 1968 or at any other time in the 1970s. Raul had no relatives in Houston and had never visited there. Investigators examined Raul's employment records, medical records, bank records and land-transfer information. They took a detailed statement from him, and interviewed family friends and acquaintances. The final report concluded, 'All this information reinforced the conclusion that "Raoul" was never involved in the assassination of Dr Martin Luther King Jr.'[30]

The allegations against 'Raul' were also investigated by Justice Department officials in 1998–2000. They looked into Raul Coelho's background from the time he arrived in the United States from Portugal in 1961. He fully cooperated with the inquiry and provided investigators with an affidavit denying any involvement in the King killing.

According to Ray he had been able to communicate well with Raoul. But Pepper's Raul had such a poor command of English during the 1960s it was impossible for him to speak anything other than basic words such as hello, goodbye etc. Raul had lived in a close Portuguese community in New York state since arriving in the United States and friends, relatives and employers who were contacted by the Justice Department investigators confirmed there was no evidence to support the allegations that he had any connection to criminal activities or government work. They also learned that Raul received formal education in the English language until 1975. The Justice Department also investigated Raul's employment records and found that Grabow's claims that Raul was in Houston during a crucial period were contradicted.[31]

In their summing up of Pepper's allegations, Justice Department investigators said:

> Our conclusion is consistent with that of an inquiry completed in 1998 by the Shelby County District Attorney General. The District Attorney General concluded that Raul was not involved in the assassination of Dr King. During that investigation, Raul voluntarily furnished finger-prints for comparison. Fingerprint analysis did not yield any matches to the latent prints lifted in 1968 from various locations relevant to the assassination, including the rooming house where Ray stayed in Atlanta, Ray's Mustang, and the Rebel Motel in Memphis, Tennessee. Based on this evidence and other investigations, the Memphis District Attorney General found no proof to connect 'Raoul' to any activity in Dallas in 1963 or Houston in the early 1970's. What proof indicates is that 'Raul' was in his home city working when the King and Kennedy assassinations occurred.[32]

William Pepper would also link another purported witness to the mysterious Raoul. Ex-FBI agent Don Wilson said he had kept evidence related to the assassination for thirty years. He claimed it 'proved' the existence of Raoul.

Wilson had been a ten-year veteran of the FBI, from 1967 to 1977, and worked in the Atlanta field office at the time of King's assassination. He had been a student in the Deep South during the time of the Civil Rights struggles of the early 1960s and believed he could further the ends of human rights by joining the FBI and helping in the struggle for equal rights. However, on the first day of training he was shocked to see only one African American in his class. Gradually, he became disillusioned with the Bureau, claiming there were racist agents on the Atlanta team. He said he agreed with ex-FBI agent Arthur Murtagh who had previously gone on record with his criticisms of the FBI. Murtagh found his workplace disturbingly racist.[33]

Wilson did not pursue his career in the FBI. He resigned and over the following twenty years he tried his hand at small business enterprises. He dissolved his most recent business in 1998, the same year he made his allegations.[34]

Wilson stated he was one of the FBI agents who descended on Ray's 1966 Mustang when it was found abandoned in an Atlanta housing project a week after the assassination.

In March 1998, Wilson made public something that said he found 'documents' in the Mustang. He said he kept the documents hidden for thirty years because he did not trust federal officials. On finding the documents Wilson thought, 'there was someone else in the car with James Earl Ray. I opened the door and the envelope fell to the ground. I put my shoe over it, and waited until the other agents were distracted, and put it in my pocket.' Wilson intended to hide the vital piece of evidence and never disclose it and that it would be something for his grandchildren.[35]

However, Wilson changed his mind when he saw the 1993 HBO/Thames television trial of James Earl Ray. He noticed that 'Raoul' was a recurrent theme and decided to contact William Pepper. When the former agent met with Ray's lawyer and Dexter King, he handed over photocopies of the documents. Initially, Wilson refused to hand the documents over to the Justice Department for examination and only did so after a search warrant had been obtained.[36]

One paper allegedly recovered by Wilson was a torn page from a 1963 Dallas phone book with a number written on it that belonged to Jack Ruby's Vegas Club. Ruby was the nightclub owner who murdered Lee Harvey Oswald, assassin of President Kennedy. He died in January 1967. The slip of paper also had the name 'Raul' written on it. The second piece of paper also had 'Raul' written on it along with some words and figures that looked like dollar amounts because they had a decimal point followed by two zeroes. One of the words was 'Canada', the place where Ray fled to following the assassination. The document, allegedly with Raoul's telephone number written on it, was conveniently torn and it was impossible to read the number. Wilson was obviously aware that if the document had shown the full number, it could be checked and verified.

Although Wilson's claims were immediately seized upon by 'The government-did-it conspiracists', the response to Wilson's allegations was not universally applauded. FBI officials immediately labelled the claims a lie. Retired FBI agent Jack T. Beverstein, who helped search Ray's abandoned car, said the claims were untrue. Retired agent Carl E. Claiborne said, 'There was no Don Wilson that I heard of.'[37]

FBI records revealed that Wilson had not been in the group of agents who had been sent to examine the abandoned Mustang. Special Agent James Joseph Dolan accompanied the vehicle when it was towed from a parking lot at Atlanta Capitol Homes public housing project to the FBI garage in downtown Atlanta. The car was examined by agents Beverstein, Claiborne, Jack B. Simpson, Richard H. Davis and Alden F. Miller. The examination lasted 5 hours and only Claiborne and Miller inspected the car's trunk and interior. Evidence that included fibres, clothing, bed linens and soil scrapings were then sent to the FBI laboratories in Washington DC. Although probationary agent Wilson did not participate in the search of the car, FBI files confirm he was involved in examining copies of money orders in the investigation to find King's assassin.

Apparently, Wilson wove his story around real evidence that had actually been discovered during the search of the car. There were indeed scraps of paper found in the abandoned car but they did not make reference to 'Raoul' or 'Jack Ruby'. In a memo dated 11 April 1968 FBI agent Frank V. Hitt stated:

> In car picked up was a piece to a top of a Kleenex box and written on it was, 'Ginger and Anita Katzwinkle, 1535 Sorrento. Galt did have an apartment there – manager out of pocket, left owing rent – they do not know him, waiting for manager to come in. Had Apt.6 Atalanta office called LA Information Opt. and the tele. no. is 4656868. This was found in trunk of car and written on it was 'at pool' – looks like may have met at pool – written on this thing OKLAHOMBE. Written above Ginger and Anita is word 'DAY' ... Galt left owing rent.[38]

In October 1968 the FBI handed over the evidence found in the Mustang to the Memphis prosecutor Phil Canale. An FBI memo dated 25 October 1968 states:

> Items From 1966 Ford Mustang, (From FBI, Atlanta) ... A piece of Kleenex box bearing letters 'At pool' on one side and names 'Ginger Day and Anita Katzwinkle, 1535 Serrano, Apt 6', on the other side ... One air release shutter in original package ... sunglasses with case ... Two pieces of cardboard from trunk ... Scraps of paper from glove compartment ... Scraps of paper from under rear seat ...[39]

Ray had relationships with two prostitutes in Los Angeles and this fact was evidently the source for the two women mentioned in the FBI memos. The FBI described Ginger Nance (Day) and Sue Harris as 'prostitutes who worked out of [Thomas] Flikaid's apartment'.[40] They denied ever seeing Ray although they had an apartment in the same block during the period when he lived in Los Angeles.[41] OKLAHOMBE was the nickname for an African American guitarist who worked at the Vegas Club frequented by the women.[42]

The Justice Department Investigators concluded that Wilson's claims of finding documents in the Mustang were not believable. They also decided that his claims to have searched Ray's apartment in Atlanta were untrue. Government records were scrutinized and showed Wilson had not been at the place where the Mustang had been found; photographs taken at the time do not show Wilson at the scene; and witnesses, both government and civilian, reported that Wilson had not participated in the recovery or the search of the vehicle. Nor was the 'door ajar', as Wilson claimed. Photographs taken at the scene of the abandoned car prove the car doors were closed and locked.[43]

Furthermore, scientific experts were asked to examine the documents. They surmised that it would have been easy to fabricate notations on them, particularly the page from an old 1963 Dallas telephone directory. The experts concluded that, 'Scientific testing established that "Raul 214-", indicating a portion of a telephone number, was written on the scrap of paper AFTER it was torn from the telephone directory. Thus, contrary to the impression the document creates, the pre-torn, whole page from the telephone directory NEVER contained the remainder of Raul's telephone number.'[44] The report thus concluded, 'The content of the writing and its position on the torn page from the Dallas telephone directory ... suggest[s] that the document was designed to create the false impression that the assassinations of President Kennedy and Dr King are connected and that James Earl Ray once had Raul's complete telephone number.'[45]

The Justice Department investigators, under the direction of Attorney General Janet Reno, did not solicit FBI assistance in their investigation, aware of allegations of FBI involvement in the murder. It is also clear that claims Justice Department officials had no interest in finding the truth about the King murder is at odds with political realities. President Clinton had high regard for the King family and was given overwhelming political support from African Americans during the 1992 and 1996 presidential elections.

For his part Ray would go on to play the Raoul game until his death in April 1998, nearly thirty years to the day since he murdered Martin Luther King. Alexander Eist, the British police officer who escorted Ray to his court appointments in London, said Ray told him, 'There's no way they can pin the murder on me [because] they can't prove I fired the gun ... I can make a half million dollars. I can raise a lot of money, write books, go on television. In parts of America, I'm a national hero.'[46]

Chapter 8

Motive

The assassin heard enough condemnation of King ... to feel that he had public support. He knew that millions hated King.

Benjamin Mays, Former President, Morehouse College

The problem is, we have trouble believing that a no-account, stumbled down bum of a convict like Ray could kill such a remarkable person like King. But he did.

Civil Rights leader, Julian Bond

We cannot deny to James Earl Ray his American heritage. The roots of his crime were seeded in our native soil and nourished within our familiar landscape. He shared our common life and he believed he shared our common ideals. Our national history, our politics, our economics, our traditions and our uniquely American social systems and social classes – these are the elements that conspired to produce his murderous act. This is an American story.

George McMillan

Well, I thought I was going to get away. I thought I'd get to Africa and serve in one of those mercenary armies and after two or three years they wouldn't send me back.

James Earl Ray

James Earl Ray was brought up in an area of Missouri that had a history of racial hatred. It was known as 'Little Dixie'. The KKK flourished there in the 1920s and 1930s. Poor families were frequently attracted to the idea that African Americans were the only people who prevented them from being 'at the bottom of the pile' and many poor whites believed the law was on the side of African Americans while they were persecuted by the law. This was one of Speedy Ray's firm beliefs.

As a young 16-year-old working at the International Shoe Company in Hartford, Illinois, Ray had befriended Henry Stumm, born in the United States of German extraction, who expressed his faith in Nazi Germany during the war years. Stumm carried a picture of Hitler around with him and hero worshipped the Nazi dictator. Co-workers told of how he would frequently give the fascist salute in the factory. Ray and his odd friend spent many hours together after work drinking in a local bar/restaurant, huddled together talking about Germany and the virtues of the Third Reich. 'Boob' Roberts, a restaurant owner, said Ray and Stumm had 'talked Hitler politics'. Eric Duncan, a shop steward, said Stumm and Ray were 'together all the time. They were bosom buddies. It looked like Ray looked up to him. He [Stumm] went around the shop calling Germany, "the fatherland".'[1]

Ray's attitude to African Americans and his relationship with Stumm was confirmed in an FBI memo, dated 24 April 1968, recording an interview with Ray's Uncle William E. Maher (named as Willard E. Maher in the memo) by FBI agents. '[Maher] stated that prior to Ray's entry into the Army he worked at a shoe tannery in Hartford, Illinois,' the agents reported, 'where he became associated with an individual who had pro-Nazi leanings; Ray became anti-Negro and anti-Jewish as a result. While in military service, Ray was stationed in Germany where his anti-Negro and anti-Jewish opinions crystallised.'[2]

The FBI MURKIN files contain numerous interviews with inmates who had spent some of their sentences with Ray but did not have contact with one another. The FBI was convinced of the veracity of their statements because agents concluded that it was impossible for this large group of inmates to conspire together to collaborate on their stories. Ex-convict Walter Rife had known Ray since he was a teenager in Quincy, Illinois. They were close friends in the 1950s and Ray and Rife were also colleagues in crime. Rife said:

> Yeah, Jimmy was a little outraged about Negroes; didn't care for them at all. There was nothing particular he had against them, nothing they had done to him. He said once they ought to be put out of the country. Once he said, 'Well, we ought to kill them, kill them all' ... He was unreasonable in his hatred for niggers. He hated to see them breathe. If you pressed it, he'd get violent in a conversation about it. He hated them! I never did know why ...[3]

Thomas Britton, fellow inmate of Ray's at Missouri State Penitentiary told the FBI that Ray had been glad when President Kennedy had been assassinated. Ray told Britton, 'That is one nigger-loving S.O.B. that got shot.' Britton described Ray as a man who hated African Americans and said that after Ray read about demonstrations organized by Martin Luther King in the newspapers, he would become angry and curse the Civil Rights leader. Britton told agents that Ray was of the opinion that President Kennedy was ruining the country by his support of the Civil Rights movement.[4]

Typical of the stories the inmates related to agents was one told by the prison barber at Missouri State Penitentiary. The barber, who cut Ray's hair for years, said Ray spoke contemptuously about African Americans, often referring to Martin Luther King as 'Martin Luther Coon' and he used the term 'nigger'.[5] Another inmate said Ray not only hated Martin Luther King but also African American activists Stokely Carmichael and H. Rap Brown.[6] Furthermore, on the back of a television set Ray had exchanged for a portable model, in Los Angeles, he had written 'Martin Luther Coon'.[7]

During the period 1969–72 Jerry Ray made numerous statements testifying to his brother James' unreasonable hatred for African Americans and one statement in particular is especially revealing. Jerry told McMillan, 'Well, I know he [James] didn't like coloured people, I know that. . . . He was unreasonable in his hatred for niggers. He hated to see them breathe. If you pressed it, he'd get violent in a conversation about it. He hated them!'[8]

Ray's attitude towards blacks is corroborated by Deputy Sheriff William DuFour, who guarded Ray following the assassin's capture and extradition to Memphis. DuFour had been one of the TACT force officers near the Lorraine Motel when King was shot. He reached Martin Luther King as the Civil Rights leader lay dying. DuFour had helped to carry King down to the ambulance, drenching himself with King's blood. DuFour would play card games and watch television with Ray during his shifts and he developed a close relationship with the accused assassin. DuFour said that Ray had pet names for people including the man he was accused of murdering. Ray often referred to Martin Luther King as 'Martin Lucifer King'.[9]

A racial incident involving Ray occurred in Los Angeles where the fugitive stayed following his sojourn in Mexico in late 1967. Bob Del Monte, a bartender at the Rabbit's Foot Club, 5623 Hollywood Boulevard, said Ray became involved in a heated discussion about race with one of the bar's female patrons Pat Goodsell. Evidently, Goodsell had spotted Ray's Mustang which had always been parked outside the club when Ray visited the establishment. The car clearly showed Alabama licence plates. Goodsell berated Ray for the way people in the state treated African Americans. Ray ended up dragging Goodsell to the bar's door saying, 'I'll drop you off in Watts and we'll see how you like it there.' Del Monte also recalled that shortly after this incident an African American patron of the Rabbit's Foot was struck on the head by a rock or brick while in the nearby parking lot. He suspected Ray threw the rock. The incident was corroborated by the testimony of another bartender, James E. Morrison.[10]

Del Monte said that Ray often spoke of his support for 1968 presidential candidate George Wallace. Morrison said he engaged Ray in a discussion about Robert Kennedy and Wallace. Morrison said that Ray became highly agitated and vocal in his support for the racist politician. In fact, Ray had offered his support for the Wallace California campaign. By 15 December 1967 Ray was so well known around Wallace headquarters in Los Angeles that campaign workers thought he was a volunteer.[11] Although conspiracists insist Del Monte later retracted his comments, the FBI agent who interviewed him, Dennis LeMaster, told the HSCA the interviews were 'accurate'.[12]

When Ray moved from Mexico to Los Angeles, he also frequented another bar, the Sultan Room, which was on the first floor of the St Francis Hotel. There he met Marie Martin and her cousin Charlie Stein. Marie was a cocktail waitress. Ray had spun her a tale of how he owned a bar in Mexico and was in Los Angeles to look for a similar type of property to buy. Marie's cousin Rita Stein had been introduced to Ray by Marie in December 1967. Marie told Ray that Rita's two little girls Kim and Cheryl lived with their grandmother in New Orleans but were about to be put in a children's home. She asked Ray if he would give Charlie a lift to New Orleans so he could collect the children. Ray agreed. However, Ray asked for one favour in return. He wanted Marie and Charlie to register for presidential candidate George Wallace in the coming California presidential primary election. In return Ray would pay all expenses for the trip. Marie and Charlie agreed.

Charlie Stein told FBI agents on 13 April 1968 that during the journey to and from New Orleans Ray 'expressed the view that if the Negro wants to be a free man, he should go to the north or west, and if the Negro wants to be a slave, he should remain in the South'. Stein confirmed that Ray not only supported George Wallace but had been involved in the California primary election campaign as a sometime campaign worker. Stein also said that Rita told him that Ray thought he was being set up for robbery and if there had been any trouble, he would have killed Charlie.[13]

Author William Bradford Huie said that after his book about Ray had been published Jerry and John told him, 'All his life Jimmy has been wild on two subjects. He's been wild against niggers and he's been wild on politics. He's wild against any politician who's for niggers, and he's wild for any politician who's against niggers. Nobody can reason with Jimmy on the two subjects of niggers and politics.'[14]

The choice of the first of Ray's many lawyers underscores the racial motive for the murder. Ray chose Arthur Hanes because the Birmingham lawyer had been involved in a famous Civil Rights murder trial in 1965. In March of that year Viola Liuzzo, a white Civil Rights worker from Detroit, had been gunned down when she was driving between Selma and Montgomery with a 19-year-old African American. Four KKK members were accused of 'violating the civil rights' of Liuzzo, the same charge made by the FBI against Ray, and the trial ended in a hung jury. Hanes had later taken over the case and won an acquittal. As a keen student of right-wing politics, Ray followed the case with interest. Ray had also read a 1956 issue of *Look* magazine which examined the Emmet Till case. In the 1950s two racists had been acquitted of that murder and afterwards they benefitted financially by selling their story.[15]

Ray's acceptance of the assistance of another lawyer, J.B. Stoner, also suggests a racial motive for the crime. Stoner worked as a lawyer in Marietta, Georgia, and became his attorney in 1969 after the 10 March 1969 guilty plea to the murder of King. He allegedly first met with Ray in late 1968 and discussed a civil suit against Time Inc. to stop pre-trial publicity. Ray retained Stoner as co-counsel in the motion for a new trial. The rabidly racist lawyer later represented John Ray and Jerry Ray in separate criminal matters in 1970.

In an editorial for his right-wing newspaper *The Thunderbolt*, Stoner wrote, 'The man who shot King was actually upholding the law of the land … He should be given the Congressional Medal and a large annual pension for life, plus a presidential pardon.'[16] In interviews, Stoner frequently referred to African Americans as 'niggers'. He derogated Martin Luther King as 'Martin Luther Coon'. From the age of 16, when he was an organizer for the Chattanooga Ku Klux Klan, Stoner frequently expressed his hatred for blacks. In 1945 he formed the 'Stoner Anti-Jewish Party' and in 1952 the Christian Anti-Jewish Party. He urged the deportation of all Jews so that their property could be confiscated and redistributed to 'Christian Americans'.

From the moment of Ray's arrest in London, he sought to represent Ray. Ray did not immediately retain him because his lawyers Arthur Hanes and later Percy Foreman wanted nothing to do with the racist lawyer believing he would tarnish the defence's case. Later, however, Ray hired Stoner.

However, it is the testimony of a British police officer, with no connections to US government institutions or state or federal organizations, that resonates most clearly when it comes to Ray's racism. Sergeant Alexander Eist had been appointed to the Flying Squad and was assigned to escort James Earl Ray between prison and the magistrates' court following Ray's arrest at Heathrow Airport. Eist related how, after hours of conversation, the accused assassin began to talk about the King assassination. Ray mentioned African Americans in a derogatory way and also said he wanted to go to Africa to kill some more 'niggers'.[17]

Although the HSCA came to believe that Ray had been motivated more by financial reward than racism, the FBI was convinced racism was the underlying factor in Ray's crime. As Assistant FBI Director Cartha DeLoach said, '[Ray's] hatred for blacks was almost pathological ... [he] had made remarks that indicated not only his willingness but his intention to inflict punishment on those who strove for racial justice. His animosity was particularly strong against King. No one who knew him well was surprised that he had committed such a crime.'[18]

Percy Foreman also believed that racism was at the core of the crime. When King's friend James Bevel offered to help with Ray's defence the assassin told Foreman, 'If we take any favours from niggers, we'll lose the support of our own people.' Ray had been referring to the millions of supporters throughout the nation who he believed would finance his defence. When Foreman consulted Ray about hiring another lawyer John J. Hooker to help with the defence Ray was grateful and agreed. That is until a prison guard told him Hooker's son got 'every nigger vote in the state running for office'. The next day Ray told Foreman, 'I don't want Hooker.' Foreman could not change Ray's mind. Ray's lawyer thought he had a deep-seated, obsessive hatred for blacks and 'had managed to conceal this hatred'.[19]

For 30 years, until his death in 1998, Ray denied he held racist views. In a 1991 talk show he told host Geraldo Rivera, 'I've never taken advantage of anybody based on their nationality or had any thoughts in that line'. Ray's estranged wife was asked by Rivera if she believed her husband. Anna Ray replied, 'No.'[20]

Ray's racist sentiments were confirmed when his papers, including 400 letters to his brothers written between 1969 and 1997, were acquired by Boston University in 2000. In none of the letters did Ray confess to the murder of Martin Luther King but in none of the letters did Ray profess his innocence either. More importantly, the letters reveal a startling lack of empathy with the Civil Rights leader. It was the central event in Ray's life yet whenever he mentioned King it was only in the context of his attempts to get a new trial. But the letters did reveal his bigotry and hatred for African Americans. Among his papers is a newspaper cutting that chronicles the rise of racist politician David Duke in Louisiana and J.B. Stoner figures prominently in the letters. Stoner's letters to Ray conclude 'With Best Racist Wishes'. In one letter Ray gave Stoner legal advice on how to escape culpability for a racist bombing. It didn't prevent the rabid racist finally being brought to justice for his crimes.[21]

* * *

William Bradford Huie believed part of Ray's motive for the crime lay in the assassin's desire to attain notoriety. Ray told Huie he expected to be on the FBI's most-wanted list when he escaped from prison. To Huie it was a 'startling' admission because, prior to 4 April 1968, Ray was the FBI's least regarded escapee. Huie believed this was a telling statement as it proved that Ray 'expected' and 'hoped' to make the list.

Ray had known Benny Edmondson when he was in the Missouri State Penitentiary. Edmondson was a high-status prisoner who had a string of convictions for robbing banks. It was clear from statements given by other inmates that Edmondson had attained celebrity criminal status in 1966 when he escaped from prison and fled to Canada. Edmondson appeared on the FBI's Ten Most-Wanted list, broadcast each week by the television programme *The FBI*. Huie said that Ray wanted to emulate Edmondson. During correspondence with the accused assassin, Huie came to believe that Ray craved attention and respect among his criminal peer group.

A former inmate at the Missouri State Penitentiary told FBI agents, three weeks after the assassination, that Ray had been a user of amphetamines, lacked the social skills required to mix with other prisoners and had 'a deep need for recognition ... he idolises notorious criminals who are the subject of widespread publicity'. The former inmate said that when he considered Ray's need for recognition together with his dislike for African Americans, it was apparent to him that Ray may have killed Martin Luther King for no monetary gain.[22]

* * *

Due to the nature of the crime the FBI looked into the possibility that a racist organization had been responsible for the murder. At the time of the killing the FBI had informants in every white supremacist group in the Deep South, including the Ku Klux Klan. A current joke was that if the Klan had a three-member cell, two of them would be FBI informants.

The Klan naturally detested Martin Luther King and would have rejoiced at his assassination. However, the HSCA examined all the FBI informant files. They investigated where the KKK or related racist organizations held their meetings, what was discussed and if any had some contact, however distant, with Ray. They found no evidence to tie the Klan to the murder of King. As one typical memo examined by the committee stated:

> In the informant's opinion, the proposition of the Klan being behind a 'bounty' or 'contract' is beyond reason. [The informant] has never heard of a 'bounty' or 'contract' for King or for anyone else. He pointed out that as much as Calvin Craig and Robert Shelton [KKK leaders] loved money that the leadership of the Klan certainly would not be behind such a proposition. He knew of no one in the Klan in Georgia wealthy enough to have put up enough money to have made the risk worthwhile in the assassination of King. In addition, he pointed out that if a Klansman or a group of Klansmen had decided to assassinate King, they would have done so for the sheer hatred of Negroes rather than for money.[23]

HSCA Chief Counsel G. Robert Blakey said no evidence had ever surfaced to change his mind about the HSCA's findings with regard to the possible involvement in the assassination of right-wing racist groups, 'There was just no evidence to connect [the KKK] to Ray,' Blakey insisted.[24]

More intriguing for the HSCA was the idea that a bounty had been put up by a group of Southern businessmen. Two days after Ray's arrest the London *Daily Telegraph* published a story about how 'a group of Southern businessmen put up a $100,000 bounty on King'.[25] According to the FBI MURKIN files numerous statements about a 'bounty' were made by serving or ex-inmates of Missouri State Penitentiary to FBI agents and reporters in the weeks and months following King's assassination.

Stuart Wexler and Larry Hancock's *Killing King – Racial Terrorists, James Earl Ray and the Plot to Assassinate Martin Luther King Jr* chronicled a dozen assassination attempts against King by white supremacist groups such as the White Knights of the Ku Klux Klan and the National State's Rights Party.[26]

Previously unreleased FBI reports gathered from Freedom of Information Act requests discovered that the White Knights made overtures to outsiders to put bounties on King of up to $100,000 at least twice. The authors present a credible argument that Ray responded to the bounty. They allege that Ray got involved with King's murder after hearing about the White Knights' bounty while in prison in 1967.

Former inmate Donald Nissen told the FBI about the $100,000 bounty that was put on King by the White Knights. Rich racists funnelled money through the Klan to pay for King's assassination and that the plan had been in the works for years. Nissen said that he learned about the bounty just before his release from Leavenworth Penitentiary in Kansas, from a fellow inmate named Leroy McManaman, who was connected to Donald Sparks, a member of the 'Dixie Mafia'.

Other FBI files connected the White Knights to National States Rights Party leader lawyer J.B. Stoner. When King was killed, several White Knights said that they attended a meeting with Stoner. Wexler and Hancock were able to show a money trail coming out of Atlanta and heading toward anyone willing to take a shot at King, but the first known offer to kill King for money came when J.B. Stoner offered to do it for $1,500 in 1958, three months after he directed the bombing of a Jewish Community Centre.

Recognizing J.B. Stoner's blatant racism and his relationship with the three Ray brothers, the HSCA decided to further investigate their possible involvement in the assassination. During the 1976–9 Congressional re-investigation, Jerry Ray attempted to lead the committee away from any suspicions that the brothers were somehow involved with Stoner. Jerry told the committee he had never known Stoner before the assassination. However, this was proven to be untrue when it was revealed that Harry Avery, the commissioner of the Tennessee Prison System in March 1969, said that Stoner had been the Ray brothers' lawyer two years before the murder of King. Avery claimed that in his official position he got to know James Earl Ray and Jerry Ray. He said that while driving Jerry to a meeting, Jerry told him that he was going to meet Stoner and that Stoner had been 'our lawyer' for two years before the assassination. Suspicion was also cast on Stoner as having foreknowledge of the assassination when he became the only lawyer not cited by James Earl Ray for the waiver of 'attorney-client' privilege during the HSCA investigation.[27]

It was also revealed by Jerry that he had confided in Stoner of his plans to help James escape:

> In fact, Stoner's the only one [who] knew about the escapes and ... [because] I would confide in him ... Whenever James would plan an escape, I would tell Stoner all about them. In fact, at one time, [James] was planning an escape, and I was supposed to pick him up out in front of that church out there close to the prison. I got a .45 calibre gun from Stoner and we taped it under the car, and I got some other stuff I had taped under the car in case the police shook it down, you know, they wouldn't find them.[28]

Stoner, who died in 2005 at age 81, was belatedly convicted in 1980 for the 1958 bombing of Bethel Baptist Church in Birmingham in which four young girls were killed and was suspected by prosecutors in as many as a dozen other racial bombings. He was investigated in connection with King's assassination – he publicly celebrated when the Civil Rights leader was shot – but was dismissed as a suspect by the FBI when agents learned he was giving a speech in Meridian, Mississippi, at the time of the murder.

Wexler and Hancock establish that J.B. Stoner never lost interest in killing King over the years ever since his 1958 King murder plot, and the conspiracies to kill King 'usually involved Stoner'. However, while establishing that racist groups and Stoner were indeed plotting to kill King the authors fall short of establishing a direct connection between James Earl Ray and Klansmen who organized the purported plot.

King assassination author Hampton Sides, however, believes Wexler and Hancock's thesis has merit. 'I've always thought Stoner was involved in the assassination,' Sides said. 'He was a real dirt ball. But so far, no one has found the smoking gun.'[29]

David Garrow believes that although Wexler and Hancock's theory is not airtight, Ray and his brothers deserved much deeper exploration than they received. 'Given Stoner's proven record of committing terroristic acts – church bombings – the Ray Family-Stoner connection should have been of the greatest possible interest to the FBI,' Garrow said. 'Stoner's hiring of Jerry Ray as a bodyguard following James' guilty plea should have raised red flags as should Stoner's becoming James Earl Ray's defence counsel, litigating an appeal. He was the only one of Ray's many lawyers for whom Ray refused to waive attorney–client privilege during the HSCA congressional probe'.[30]

Notwithstanding the absence of 'smoking gun' proof that the Ku Klux Klan planned to pay Ray a bounty, there is compelling evidence that Ray at least knew about a $50,000 bounty offered by radical right-wing groups to kill Martin Luther King. The HSCA established that two St Louis businessmen, linked to Ray through the Missouri State Penitentiary, had likely offered such a bounty.

Donald Lee Mitchell told the FBI in September 1968 that he worked with Ray in the prison kitchen and Ray told him about his plans for an escape in 1966. He asked Mitchell to help him and told him about a bounty to kill King.

> Some people [friends in St Louis] fixed it with someone in Philadelphia, for him to kill Dr King ... Ray told me not to worry about a thing. Also how did a grand sum of $50,000 sound to me? I said great, but what if we get caught? He explained we wouldn't and if we did, we would get out of it with a fixer lawyer, besides who in the South liked 'niggers'? ... [Mitchell] was to be near the building from which Ray would shoot King and after the shots were fired and attention was focused on the building, he ... was to run and create attention to get the police to chase him ... this would give Ray ample time to walk away from the building. [Mitchell] was them to tell the police that he heard shots and since he was an ex-convict, he got scared ... so he ran ...

Ray told Mitchell both of them would get $50,000 for killing King and later on they would get additional money for killing 'one of those stinking Kennedys'. Ray did not tell Mitchell who had offered the bounty.[31]

Typical of the leads which the HSCA followed up was an FBI memo reporting an FBI interview with a Missouri State Penitentiary inmate, Thomas Britton, at Reform, Alabama, dated 30 April 1968. Britton said that Ray had told him, 'One of these days if I ever get out of here, I am going to make myself a bunch of money'. The report further stated:

> When source asked how he intended doing this, Ray replied he had contacts and there are more ways of making money than robbing banks. Source then asked Ray what his plan was, to which Ray replied, 'The businessman's association has offered $100,000 for killing Martin Luther King and he's five years past his due'. The source stated he then asked

Ray what the Businessman's Association was, to which Ray replied, 'I don't know but I will find out.' The source said that Ray told him that he always worked alone and therefore limited the possibility of being caught and said, 'I have got a place picked out where I can hide', never mentioning where the place was located.[32]

Britton also said that sometime in autumn 1963 Ray had made the statement that he was going to 'get' Martin Luther King when he got out. He mentioned 'Cooley's Organisation' that would 'pay $10,000 to have King dead'.[33]

Britton said that Cooley's organization operated at the Missouri State Penitentiary and was run by the inmates. He said it was a protection and enforcer organization and he was advised to join it when he first arrived at the prison. Britton said that Cooley's organization would settle any differences or grievances within the prison and that it was a very powerful body that could arrange 'a murder'.[34]

The existence of Cooley's organization was confirmed by statements made by other inmates. A 15 May 1968 FBI memo stated:

> [Redacted] was going to escape from the 'pen' and that Ray knew 'a guy named Cooley' who could hide Ray where no one could find him. [Redacted] claimed that Ray also stated that Cooley would pay $10,000 to anyone who would kill Martin Luther King. In other conversations [redacted] recalled Ray talking about tunnelling out of the penitentiary, if he had to, and going to Liberia where Ray claimed he had a brother-in-law living, who was 'making good money'. [Redacted] recalls that at another time, in discussing the assassination of President Kennedy [redacted] stated he did not believe anyone should kill the president, to which Ray said that he, Ray, would have done it himself if he had the chance, and that Kennedy 'was nothing but a damn Catholic.' According to [redacted] Ray often expressed his hatred for Catholics and Negroes.[35]

The FBI conducted extensive interviews in order to establish if the allegations of a bounty were true. On 14 May 1968 staff at the Missouri State Penitentiary told agents that there had been twenty men by the name of Cooley in the prison over the years.[36] However, the Bureau was unable 'to ascertain any information concerning its principals or membership or the extent of its network. There are indications that this organisation exists in other prisons.'[37] In a memo to Assistant FBI Director W.C. Sullivan, dated 14 June 1968, FBI official W.A. Branigan recommended that a full investigation be made by conducting full interviews with prison staff. There is no indication the results of such interviews established conclusively that a bounty offer had been made or that James Earl Ray accepted it.

On 29 April 1968, an unnamed former Missouri State Penitentiary inmate told FBI agents that Ray's 'maximum ambition in life' was to make a 'score' of about $20–30,000 and 'hide out' in Mexico. According to the former inmate, Ray's plan was to flee to a country where it was cheap to live. Ray spoke of how he had visited Mexico on previous occasions. He liked the idea of living in Campeche near the Yucatan peninsula, a place he had visited in 1959 and where drug-smuggler friends lived. During his trips to Mexico Ray had lived frugally and budgeted his money carefully, the memo reported.[38]

Conrad 'Pete' Baetz, a former Madison County sheriff's deputy who served as an investigator for the HSCA, stated that conspirators met in a home on Arsenal Street in St Louis. The site, according to Baetz, was about 200yd from John Ray's Grapevine Tavern.[39]

During their investigation in the late 1970s HSCA investigators learned that in the 1960s career criminal Russell Byers befriended a stockbroker-turned-drug-dealer named John Kauffmann who owned the Bluff Acres Motel in Barnhart, Missouri. Kauffmann allowed Byers to store his stolen cars at the motel. In 1967 Kauffmann asked Byers if he'd like to make $50,000. They left the motel, went into a farmhouse on a hill behind the motel and met businessman John Sutherland. Sutherland wore a Confederate colonel's hat with the cavalry insignia of crossed sabres. He led them to a den decorated with Confederate flags, swords and bugles and it was there he made an offer to them to either arrange or kill King. Byers rejected the offer because he thought it was too dangerous. Sutherland was connected to the Wallace presidential campaign through a friend, Glen Shrum, a Wallace organizer who worked at the Wallace For President St Louis headquarters across the street from the Grapevine Tavern. Shrum was a patron there.[40]

The HSCA investigation found that Kauffmann had numerous links to the Missouri State Penitentiary. Kauffmann was a friend of the prison doctor Hugh Maxey, who had treated Ray at the prison. It was also believed that Kauffmann, who would later be tried for drug dealing, supplied illegal drugs to the prison through an accomplice. However, it was the 1968 Wallace presidential campaign that provided the likely conduit for the bounty offer if it existed. Sutherland helped finance the Wallace campaign and Kauffmann was actively involved as a campaign worker. The Grapevine was also patronized by Kauffmann and he made contact with St Louis criminals there.

From the evidence provided by the FBI files and the HSCA it appears likely that James Earl Ray did have specific knowledge of money having been offered by one or more groups to anyone who would kill Martin Luther King. However, there is no evidence to suggest an offer was made to Ray personally or that promises were made to deliver any money to him.[41]

Credible and substantial evidence that would confirm any 'direct' link between Ray and individuals or groups who had offered a 'bounty' has never been found. However, the strands of various witness statements gathered by government investigations and independent researchers has provided a likely 'scenario' of how Ray had been inspired by offers of a bounty on King.

Both Jerry and John Ray were in communication with their brother James both before and following his escape from Missouri State Penitentiary in April 1967. John Ray, who owned the Grapevine, knew his brother James was looking for the 'big score'.

John and Jerry were also involved in the Wallace campaign, met many campaign workers in John's bar and Wallace presidential campaign literature was distributed through the bar. Both brothers were in constant association with workers for the campaign. The Wallace staffers often frequented the Grapevine as their headquarters were in the same block. There was also some evidence that rich supporters of George Wallace may have spread the word that money would be forthcoming to anyone who killed King. Leander Perez, a New Orleans Democratic Party political boss was the key organizer of the campaign to place George Wallace on the 1968 Louisiana general election ballot as the nominee of the short-lived American Independent Party. Perez had spoken of how he might pay money for King's murder. According to George McMillan's notes he made while researching his book, 'If Ray could have got in touch with Perez he could have got money for killing King. Trouble is to get to those people – you can't just walk in.'[42]

John Sutherland participated actively in the White Citizens' Council of St Louis and began holding meetings in a building not far from the Grapevine. When the meetings finished some members would go over to the tavern and socialize with campaign workers. Some would engage John Ray in conversation. Given the nature of John and Jerry Ray's extremist politics, it is plausible that the subject of Martin Luther King had been discussed. It is also possible individuals in Kauffmann's group discussed the idea of a 'bounty'.

It is also possible that during visits John told James about his conversations at the Grapevine and that an offer of a 'bounty' had been discussed. There is no evidence that Sutherland or Kauffmann knew the offer was being relayed to James Earl Ray, but the connection is there.

The evidence to support these conclusions is convincing but impossible to establish especially as the two businessmen who purportedly made the bounty offer were deceased at the time of the Congressional hearings. The committee was therefore unable to conclusively establish the truth about the St Louis-based 'conspiracy'. In 1998 Chief Counsel for the HSCA G. Robert Blakey, commenting about the investigation, said:

> What we came up with was the possibility of a race-based conspiracy in St Louis where a $50,000 bounty had been offered on Dr King's life involving two men, Sutherland and Kauffmann. It was only a possibility; we couldn't prove it and both of them were dead before our investigation started. But we were able to trace Kauffmann to [John Ray's] Grapevine Tavern in St Louis, where he used to hold meetings of the American Party. . . . Was it possible that the $50,000 bounty was discussed in the tavern and heard by John Ray, and that John Ray then conveyed it to James Earl? Yes. Were we ever able to say definitively that John Ray was the conduit from the Kauffmann group to James Earl? No.[43]

Sutherland died in 1970, Kauffmann in 1974.

Additionally, evidence of a St Louis-based conspiracy flounders on the fact that Russell Byers stated he did not know of the existence of King in 1967. It appears to be an implausible statement as King won the Nobel Peace Prize in 1964 and frequently appeared in newspaper reports and television news programmes. It is inconceivable Byers had no knowledge of him.[44]

If a bounty was offered and taken up by the Ray brothers, it was never collected. Author George McMillan provided some evidence to support this conclusion in 1976. McMillan said that some time after Ray's capture and extradition to Memphis, Jerry Ray approached Kent Courtney, leader of a right-wing political organization in New Orleans. James had read about the conservative lawyer in a newspaper, the *American Independent*. Jerry wanted help for his brother but was unable to pay for it. Courtney had recorded the conversation with Jerry and a copy of the tape was handed over to the HSCA in the late 1970s. As McMillan argued, if James Earl Ray had been paid for killing King, the solicitation of funds would have been unnecessary.[45]

Once Ray had been arrested it would have been easy to ignore any solicitations from the brothers. Within this scenario the men who offered the bounty would only risk exposure if one of the brothers met up with them to claim the money. Once King was dead there was no reason to make the pay-off. And, as career criminals, Jerry and John lived by the criminal code of 'never rat'. Moreover, Jerry and John were in no position to challenge people who were directly tied to powerful and violent racist groups. James' life would also be placed in danger during his time in prison if their names were mentioned. As James said, 'If I inform and get out,' he once said to an interviewer in prison, 'they will solve their case. I'll go back to the Missouri penitentiary where I owe them 15 years, and I'll get murdered as an informer. So, if I inform it will work out for them, but it won't work out so well for me.'[46]

* * *

Undoubtedly, James Earl Ray knew that if he continued with his lifetime career of robbing banks it would guarantee a return to prison sooner or later. The pornography business or drug smuggling had been discussed with his brothers and seemed to offer great financial rewards. But Ray abandoned the idea, likely realizing he neither had the skills nor contacts required for those criminal enterprises. And, as a fugitive on the run, he would also risk exposure. Feeling trapped and with nowhere else to go, he decided to return to his long-held idea of the 'big score'.

Psychologically James Earl Ray wanted to become what his parents had always known – he was the child who was smarter and more resourceful than the rest. But he had chosen a life where success is not measured by conventional standards. Success to James was attaining respect from his peers, the criminal fraternity and the FBI's 'Top Ten Most Wanted'. Additionally, contrary to ideas held by some conspiracy advocates, Ray had nerves of steel, especially when he had been hyped up by amphetamines. According to his brother John, '[James has] steel nerves – he just walks in [to the bank] like it's an everyday thing, get the money, and walks out.'[47]

Stalking and then killing King would give him the status he craved and, if caught, he could enjoy the high esteem that goes with this type of crime. Believing that if he killed King in the Deep South a white jury would acquit him, Ray knew that in time he would be able to collect his reward if not as a free man then certainly through his brothers. Meanwhile, he would go ahead with his plans. He had little to lose.

Chapter 9

Brothers

The FBI's failure to probe aggressively the 1968 activities of John and Jerry Ray was its worst shortcoming in the investigation of King's murder.
Pulitzer Prize-winning King biographer David J. Garrow

A punishable conspiracy exists when at least two people form an agreement to commit a crime, and at least one of them does some act in furtherance to committing the crime.
Each person is punishable in the same manner and to the same extent as is provided for the punishment of the crime itself.
California Code – Penal Code PEN 182

I get those phone calls harassing me all the time. Some people like to harass Old Raoul.

Jerry Ray

Once Ray was in custody, HSCA Chief Counsel G. Robert Blakey said, the FBI's investigation tailed off dramatically, with only intermittent efforts to discover whether anyone else was involved. He said the Bureau had passed over a number of items indicating the possibility of a conspiracy involving all three Ray brothers including information that John and Jerry Ray had met with their brother before the assassination despite denials of such contacts; the 'probable involvement' of John Ray in the 1967 escape of James Earl Ray from the Missouri State Penitentiary, including records showing a prison visit by John on the day before Ray fled and information that Jerry Ray twice admitted knowledge of a conspiracy in the assassination.[1]

* * *

Following his release from prison in February 1960, James Earl Ray's younger brother John Larry Ray worked as a bartender, a Greyhound bus employee and greenskeeper. In 1964 and 1965, he worked for brief periods in Florida and in the Catskill Mountains of New York.

Grapevine bar worker Naomi Regazzi described John as a person who was not close to anyone because of his personality complexes caused by 'family problems' when he was a child and because he suffered from a speech impediment. She said John, in her opinion, was 'slightly more intelligent than [the youngest brother] Jerry'.[2]

Shortly after the assassination John was interviewed by FBI agents. 'What's all the excitement about? he asked them. 'He only killed a nigger. If he had killed a white man, you wouldn't be here. King should have been killed 10 years ago.'[3] At about the same time, he also told a newspaper reporter:

> If I hit a supermarket or rib a man on the street, that's a crime against a person or business. That guy King was an enemy of America. J. Edgar Hoover said so, didn't he? He called him a communist ... I rob a place and I wind up with seven to ten, and working in that hot laundry, but some nigger rapes a white woman and gets two years and works in the kitchen. Them niggers would always give the biggest pieces of meat to other niggers and would fish out a little piece for you.[4]

In January 1968 John bought the Grapevine Tavern situated in Arsenal Street in a poor neighbourhood of St Louis, a block away from George Wallace's American Independent Party (AIP) presidential headquarters. As he was a convicted felon, he was not allowed a liquor licence so he enlisted his sister Carol's help as licence holder. John used the tavern to distribute AIP literature and during the early part of 1968 he assisted in the Wallace campaign by escorting registrants to the local campaign headquarters to register to vote. The bar was also a meeting place for the White Citizens' Council and other hard-line segregationists as well as campaign staff.

Jerry Ray, the youngest brother, was divorced and had a son, Michael Eugene Ray. According to his father 'Speedy' Ray, Jerry was 'nuts and there is no telling what he will do'.[5] Naomi Regazzi said Jerry was 'a man of very low intellect and who, when he has four or five beers, desires to be in the limelight'.[6]

Jerry frequently expressed his animosity towards African Americans. He once insisted that the Bureau of Prisons had deliberately put his brother John in a cell block with African Americans, a 'black jungle', so that he would be killed. In a 1972 letter to two radio talk-show hosts Jerry Ray asserted his philosophy by making reference to 'The Nigger Beast', 'Jew Devils' and the 'Mangy Jew Devil' and Jerry's racism was confirmed by Edward Fields, secretary of the National States Rights Party, who characterized Jerry as a 'segregationist'.[7]

James Earl Ray's supporters have attempted to excuse the racist statements of the Ray brothers as typical of their social class in the mid-Western and Southern states during the 1950s and 1960s. They allege that a majority of poor white working class people frequently adopted racial expressions of resentment in the pre-Civil Rights era. However, it is evident that the Ray brothers used language more in keeping with the far-right views adopted by neo-Nazi groups than mainstream conservative thought. This became clear after J.B. Stoner offered his legal services to Ray soon after his arrest.

Jerry believed his brother James would go down in history as a great American hero alongside George Wallace. All three brothers expressed strong support for Wallace in the Alabama Governor's 1967/8 run for the presidency and embraced Wallace's vision of a racially segregated United States. James' right-wing political hopes were first ignited when Barry Goldwater ran for the presidency in 1964. Ray thought a conservative politician would bring the United States back to the 'right' in politics.[8] '[James] had it in his head,' Jerry said, 'that it would help Wallace if King wasn't around.'[9] In fact, it appears all the male members of the Ray household held similar political and racial views. Speedy Ray gave tacit support to his sons' feelings about Martin Luther King. He told author George McMillan, 'Do you realise that if Jimmy hadn't done it, King would be president today?'[10]

Both Jerry and John believed that following the election of Wallace James would be paroled within two years of his conviction.[11] James was also aware that at that time no white man had been convicted in a Southern state for killing a black man. Jerry said, '[James] believed that if he killed King in Alabama or if he killed him anywhere in the South, it would help him if he showed he was a resident of Alabama ... Of course, if he killed King in Alabama, he believed Wallace would eventually pardon him, not at first, but after a few years when things had cooled off.'[12]

A friend of the Ray family told the *St Louis Post Dispatch* that he had spent some time in a drinking session with John Ray after the assassination of King. John had visited James in the Shelby County Jail where his brother had been incarcerated following his extradition from England. The friend said John Ray waved his hand and declared, 'He [James] won't serve less than this [Ray extended three fingers] and not more than this', extending five fingers.[13]

Following his arrest for the murder of King, James had been studying the results of the 1968 presidential election. He told Percy Foreman that over 70 per cent of the voters in Shelby County (where his trial would be held) voted for Wallace and Nixon. 'I figure the jury will break down the same way,' he said, 'so I got a 70–30 chance to get out.' He added, 'I don't want to plead guilty. No white man ever got the chair in Tennessee for shooting a nigger.' He even told Foreman that if Wallace became president he would be pardoned and might even get the Medal of Honour.[14]

There were additional reasons why Ray thought he would not spend long behind bars. Jerry said his brother read a lot of law books during his time in the Missouri State Penitentiary and believed his brother could 'free himself legally before he pulls the minimum time for parole'.[15] James was convinced he could persuade a jury he was a hired killer and thus stand a better chance of being found not guilty of murder.[16]

From 1960 until James' 1967 escape John and Jerry visited their brother and the visitor's pass was used interchangeably by both men. All three brothers also communicated by letters.[17] In his conversations with McMillan, Jerry frequently intimated some role he may have played in his brother James' escape and John had visited James the day before the escape. According to a Newark FBI agent's memo, 'Jerry Ray [redacted] [said], "Just between you and me, I saw my brother right after he escaped. We had a meeting place where he would meet on my days off"…'.[18] It wasn't until years later that Jerry made a full confession of his role in helping his brother escape. He said he used coded letters to James to assist in the escape.[19]

Criminal associate Walter Rife, who had known both John and James for years, said John Ray had told him he had aided in the escape along with his brother Jerry. Close family friend Jack Gawren confirmed the Ray brothers had been in contact with James following the prison break.[20]

It wasn't until 2011 that Jerry gave a full account of how the brothers helped James escape. Jerry said his brother John had arranged to pick James up in his truck after the escape. However, Jerry said, the 'plans became confused' and John was not at the designated pickup point. James walked along railroad tracks then found a payphone to phone his brother. John returned to meet James.[21]

During the time after the brothers first met up after James' escape, Jerry said, he took a train with James to downtown Chicago. They were armed with a .38 pistol and a sawed-off baseball bat. Jerry said they went to an old, abandoned bar near South Michigan Avenue. Nearly every night, Jerry said, a local 'tough guy' by the name of 'Jess' hosted a poker game, usually attended by twelve players. Putting on ski masks, Jerry and James knocked on the door of the bar. When Jess answered the two brothers barged in. Jerry slammed his baseball down on Jess' arm disarming him of his pistol while James pointed his gun at the players. Escaping with the players' money, they divided the takings which amounted to $1,800. According to Jerry, James used his money to buy a 1962 Plymouth car which he travelled to Canada in shortly afterwards.

Additionally, an FBI memo of the time records how agents also learned that a family reunion had been held at the McArthur Hotel, St Louis, in early or mid-February 1968. The memo stated:

> Jerry Ray, John Ray and Carol and Albert Pepper apparently got together in SL in 2-68, at which time Jerry and John were both registered at the MacArthur Hotel, SL. Jerry was registered on 2 February 1968, John on 6 February 1968 and Mr and Mrs John Ray on 17 February 1968. There is no known Mrs John Ray … Albert Pepper's fellow employees advised on 20 April 1968 there was a possibility that Albert Pepper had seen subject [James Earl Ray] since his escape …[22]

In 1979, after an extensive investigation of the mysterious Raoul, the HSCA found that he did not exist. The committee concluded that 'Ray's post-assassination tale of Raoul was fabricated to conceal contacts with one or both [of his] brothers'. The HSCA also concluded that there was 'a likelihood of the involvement of one or both brothers in the assassination'. Additionally, the committee concluded the evidence was convincing that James had 'some form of contact with a brother both before and during the rifle purchase'.[23]

In 2011 Jerry Ray said that before his brother came to trial James' lawyer Percy Foreman confronted him with the Raoul story. 'Foreman told me,' Jerry said, '… if there was any substance whatsoever to Jimmy's tale of a man named Raoul then it merely was a cover name for me and I was probably involved in the King assassination – maybe even the shooter'. Jerry did not challenge Foreman's accusations but simply thought, 'King was killed on a Thursday and Thursday was my day off at the Sportsman's [Country Club]. I can see how this is taking shape … and it's not good.'[24]

The issue of brotherly collusion in the assassination of King first arose when the brothers met up in Chicago after James' escape. After John and

Jerry had helped James escape from Missouri State Penitentiary James told Jerry, 'I'm gonna kill that nigger King. That's something that's been on my mind. That's something I've been working on.' Jerry said he would help James 'where he could' but he did not want to be in on 'that job'. John, according to George McMillan, said he wanted nothing to do with killing King.[25] However, both brothers did not realize, and were ignorant of, the fact that aiding and abetting their brother in the commission of his assassination plans would inevitably ensnare them in a conspiracy. McMillan also said that Jerry had told him, in an interview dated 23 February 1975, he was in Birmingham with his brother James when the rifle was purchased and that places him at the heart of the conspiracy.[26]

In his book *The Making of an Assassin*, George McMillan provided further clear evidence that Jerry Ray knew about his brother's plans to kill King. The HSCA examined McMillan's notes and other research material and concluded the story of Jerry's foreknowledge was credible. On the morning of 4 April 1968, McMillan said, Jerry received a phone call from his brother, 'Jerry, tomorrow it will be all over. I might not see you and Jack [John] for a while. But don't worry about me. I'll be all right. Big Nigger has had it!'[27] The story told to McMillan by Jerry was confirmed by William Bradford Huie who said the assassin's brother had also related the story of the phone call to him.[28] Jerry later denied the phone call ever happened.

In its final report, the HSCA concluded that Ray's 'persistent refusal' to identify his co-conspirators would be 'most easily understood if his evidence implicated family members', and criticized the FBI for failing to check the alibis of the Ray brothers.

HSCA investigator Conrad 'Pete' Baetz contends that if there was a conspiracy it was among the Ray family. Baetz said, 'If there had been anyone else involved but his family [Ray] would have given them up in a minute. They wouldn't give up each other. And that's the only reason why "Raoul" has survived for at least 30 years.'[29]

James' wife Anna, who James married in the 1980s, believed Jerry had conspired with his brother James. Anna told of how Jerry used to drop clues as to his involvement in the assassination; during telephone conversations he would jokingly refer to himself as 'Raoul'.[30]

In 1998 William Gibbons, the Shelby County District Attorney, asked Attorney General Janet Reno to take a closer look at the Ray brothers and 'their possible involvement in this tragedy'.[31] Gibbons believed the possible involvement of the brothers was the primary unanswered question in the assassination. Former HSCA assistant Deputy Chief Counsel Michael C. Eberhardt concurred with Gibbons. Speaking about the FBI's 1968 investigation of King's murder in 2002, Eberhardt said, 'It was really quite remarkable that they didn't pursue the brothers' activity more than they did.'[32]

More damningly, the committee found evidence that Ray had contacted at least one of his brothers in the run-up to the shooting and may have even gone with them to buy the rifle he used. No less than four separate witnesses – Marie Martin, Richard Gonzalez, Tomas Lau and Donald Wood – in separate interviews with authorities shortly after the assassination provided evidence of Ray's receipt of money from, or contact with, a brother during the month preceding the rifle purchase. Wood's testimony, confirmed by the testimony of Ray's lawyer Percy Foreman, tied Jerry directly into the rifle purchase itself. There is also the testimony of a woman he met in Canada who confirmed James had been in contact with his brothers.

Their stories have verisimilitude precisely because there was no way James could have foreseen how events would unravel with regard to his Raoul story which he invented *after* the assassination.

James Earl Ray's meetings with his brothers include:

- After James broke out of prison in April 1967, John Ray said, he picked him up and drove him back to St Louis. 'We stayed all night at the Catman's in South St. Louis [referring to Jack 'Catman' Gawron, a criminal associate of the Ray brothers)'. The next day, John said they met with Joe Burnett, another criminal, at a Manchester Avenue bar, 'The reason we went there was to try and put some money into James' pocket.'[33]
- The three brothers met up at the Fairview Hotel in Chicago the day after James' escape. However, Jerry Ray disputed John's account. 'John will tell you he brought him [James Earl Ray] to St. Louis,' Jerry Ray says. 'He didn't bring him to St. Louis. He brought him to Chicago. You can check, if they still have the records. A day after he escaped, he was in Chicago that night, and I met him and John a day afterward at the Fairview Hotel on Michigan Avenue in Chicago.' However, whoever was telling the truth, the evidence is clear that both brothers assisted James in his escape from the Missouri State Penitentiary.[34]
- An FBI informant said that Jerry Ray had met his brother at least once in a pre-arranged meeting place in St Louis shortly after his escape.[35]

- Between 30 April and 13 July 1967 the brothers remained in contact. Jerry Ray admitted in 2011 he helped his brother James rob a 'gambling joint' in Chicago shortly after the escape.[36]
- The HSCA believed there was sufficient evidence to prove James participated with his brothers in robbing a bank in Alton, Illinois, on 13 July 1967, netting $27,000. An FBI investigation could not definitively tie the Rays to the robbery, though the HSCA later determined that 'substantial, albeit circumstantial' evidence existed to link the Rays. John Light, who spent thirty years on the Alton police force, said, 'Oh, yeah, that's who I think it was,' he said. 'I heard it from informants, and we knew what they had been doing.' Light also believes that James was the robber who went from counter to counter at the bank collecting the money.[37]
- Between 14 July and 21 August 1967 Ray stayed in Montreal and maintained contact with his brothers while in Canada. James told a woman he dated that he was 'working for his brother'.[38]
- On 21 August 1967 Ray returned to the United States and between then and 30 August 1967 Ray met brother Jerry in Chicago en route to Birmingham, Alabama. Ray received three payments totalling $4,500 from Jerry – proceeds from the 'gambling joint' heist and likely the Alton bank robbery. Vehicle records showed that on 25 August 1967 James Ray transferred his 1962 Plymouth motor vehicle to Jerry. This was during the period when James was making his way from Canada to Birmingham, Alabama, where he purchased the Mustang.[39]
- Between 7 October and 18 November 1967 James travelled to Mexico in the Mustang. Ray had also purchased photography equipment in the hope he could use it to film 'cheap prostitutes' in a pornography business. Giving up any hope of starting such a business, Ray travelled to Los Angeles on 19 November 1967 and established a connection to one or both brothers via telephone or mail.[40]
- On 14 or 15 December 1967 Ray cancelled an appointment with a psychologist. (Ray hoped to improve his social skills through hypnotism.) He told the psychologist he had to meet his brother in New Orleans with a view to securing employment. The HSCA said James did not identify the brother in New Orleans during his conversations with the California witnesses, but believed it was Jerry. Jerry was still employed at the Sportsman's Club in Chicago, at the time, but he admitted to the committee that he went to St Louis for Christmas that year. The HSCA stated in their report:

> St. Louis and New Orleans are only 675 miles apart, so it was at least reasonably possible for Jerry and James to have met. Further, both James and Jerry Ray conceded to the

committee that they talked by telephone during James' drive from Los Angeles to New Orleans. The committee was unable, however, to rule out the possibility that it was John Ray – then an unemployed painter living in St. Louis – who travelled to New Orleans to meet James. The committee was also unable to determine fully the purpose of the New Orleans meeting. If, in fact, it was to receive only $500, that would not seem to justify the risks Ray took in driving several thousand miles on the open highway. The committee noted that the assassination occurred 3½ months after the New Orleans trip. While the possibility of a connection between the trip and the murder of Dr. King existed, the committee uncovered no direct evidence to that effect.[41]

However, the committee was able to find a witness to testify about Jerry's meeting with his brother in New Orleans – but only under a cloak of anonymity. The witness said Jerry had told him he met James in New Orleans in the 'third week of December 1967'.[42]

- On 21 December 1967 Ray returned to Los Angeles. He told a dance instructor he had returned to the city from New Orleans after meeting his brother.[43]
- In February 1968 Jerry arranged a meeting with his brother James in New Orleans for March 1968.[44]
- Sometime between 2 March and 19 March 1968 Ray told a person at the dance school he attended he was going to meet his brother in Birmingham, Alabama. Richard Gonzales, who was a fellow student at the bartenders' school in Los Angeles told FBI agents that Ray had told him upon completion of the course that he (Ray) was going to visit a brother in Birmingham for two weeks. The FBI also interviewed Marie Martin who said that for some time before 17 March 1968 Ray had stated he need some fresh funds and was waiting for his brother to send him some money.[45]
- On 20 March 1968 Ray arrived in New Orleans and made arrangements to meet Jerry in Birmingham. Ray's route took him through Selma, Alabama, on 22 March where King was due to attend an event.[46]
- On 23 March 1968 James met Jerry in Birmingham. Both men then travelled to Atalanta where James rented an apartment.
- According to Ray's lawyer Percy Foreman, who referred to the brothers as a 'couple of morons',[47] on 29 March 1968 James and Jerry drove to Birmingham where James purchased a .243 calibre Remington rifle at the Aeromarine Supply Company. Foreman said:

I cross-examined James Earl Ray for hours and the only name that he ever mentioned other than his own at any phase or time of his preparation for the killing. ... was his brother Jerry. Jerry was with him when he bought the rifle in Birmingham, the one he did not use because it was low calibre. He took it back and traded it for a more powerful one that would be more likely to kill an individual. The smaller calibre was more suited for killing small animals. And Jerry was not with him, according to Ray's statement, when he bought the gun that killed Dr. Martin Luther King; but he was with him the day before at the same place where he bought another rifle for that purpose. ... [48]

Jerry Ray's working records were destroyed approximately six months before the committee contacted his employer, the Sportsman's Club near Chicago. Jerry's working hours at that time were 11pm to 7am. If his recollection that Thursday was his day off was correct, he could conceivably have gone to Birmingham, given advice on the initial rifle purchase on the afternoon of Friday, 29 March 1968 and returned in time to be on the job by 11pm that night.[49] Additionally, Ray lied when he said he had been inquiring about 'surplus rifles' at Aeromarine. In an affidavit, U.L. Baker, the clerk who sold the first rifle to Ray, told the committee that Ray asked only general questions about deer hunting rifles and said nothing about foreign or military surplus rifles.[50] Furthermore, Ray stated he had given the rifle to Raoul at the New Rebel Motel the night before the assassination and never saw it again. Yet, when the rifle was examined after the assassination, two latent fingerprints of value were lifted from it, both belonging to Ray. Ray was confronted, therefore, with the need to explain how Raoul, after handling the rifle, managed to remove all of his prints while leaving two of Ray's.[51]

• John Ray met with his brother James the night before the assassination in West Memphis, Arkansas, across the Mississippi River from Memphis, Tennessee.[52]

In 2002 Conrad Baetz, the HSCA investigator, said that if there was a conspiracy it was among the Ray family, 'If there had been anyone else involved but his family,' Baetz said, '[Ray] would have given them up in a minute. They wouldn't give each other up. And that's the only reason why "Raoul". has survived for at least 30 years.'[53]

* * *

There is evidence that James and his brothers knew that if a bounty could not be collected from any of the racist groups who offered money for the killing of King, they would still benefit from the publicity such a murder would generate. Following his arrest in London, Ray told his Scotland Yard police escort Alexander Eist that he would make money from the notoriety of the case. Ray said all he would be charged with was conspiracy and that he would only get 'ten to twelve years for that'.[54]

Ray's remarks to Eist were reflected in what John and Jerry Ray told William Bradford Huie and Arthur Hanes in the months after Ray had been returned to Memphis to stand trial for the assassination. According to Huie, 'We had learned early in the investigation that Ray had not been paid after the murder; later we learned that he had not expected to be paid. Not in the manner of a hired assassin.' Huie said Jerry and John had come to Memphis after the arrest of their brother expecting a 'golden rain to fall on them' in the form of donations from supporters of their brother as well as book deals and other monies paid out by the media.[55] And even if a bounty had been offered, there is no evidence it had been collected.

All five investigations into the King murder failed to provide enough incriminating evidence implicating John and Jerry Ray which could be presented to a jury and which would satisfy the stringent requirements of the US legal system. The 1977 Justice Department Task Force stated, 'We saw no credible evidence probative of the possibility that Ray and any co-conspirator were together at the scene of the assassination. . . . Of course, someone could conceivably have provided him with logistics, or even paid him to commit the crime.' The Task Force, therefore, did not rule out the possibility that others had assisted Ray in his crime but were not present during the commission of the crime.[56]

Confirming the brothers' role in the assassination had always been met with indecisiveness on the part of the Shelby County prosecutors who even-tually decided that no jury would find them guilty. Their decision came after the grand jury, which sat to hear the evidence against James and was allowed to consider whether or not the brothers participated in the assassination, did not hand down any charges.

However, if the jury had been allowed to consider the later admissions by Jerry and John Ray – proof they aided and abetted in the assassination – the outcome may have been very different. When Jerry met with his brother James in Birmingham for the purchase of the rifle it is inconceivable James would not have told him of his plans to kill King. Similarly, when James met with John the evening before the assassination, he would also not have failed to inform him of his plans. Each step of the way the brothers were providing assistance to James in the commission of his crimes. Using the simpler and broader interpretation of conspiracy – i.e. more than one person who had prior knowledge of and/or involvement in the plan for assassination – which may or may not be identical to the legal definitions for a criminal conspiracy – then there is no doubt Jerry and John were 'co-conspiracists'.

The definition of conspiracy is a combination of two or more persons committing a criminal act. Simply having knowledge of the proposed act or acquiescing to the act, or approval of the act, is insufficient to charge a person as a co-conspirator. There must be intentional participation in the agreement to commit the act. However, an implied understanding is sufficient to constitute the offence. It is not necessary that each conspirator take part in every act or that they should know the exact part to be performed by the other conspirators in the execution of the conspiracy. These stipulations, it may be argued, applied to the Ray brothers.

Jerry Ray knew of, and approved of, his brother James' plans to kill King and he assisted his brother in that enterprise. Likewise, John knew of James' plans to kill King and assisted James in executing those plans. Given these facts, it is arguable that if the brothers had been charged with complicity in the crime a guilty verdict would follow.

Furthermore, in admitting their complicity in James' escape from prison in April 1967 the brothers show their liability to prosecution. A federal law, US Code 18 USC § 752(a), makes it a federal crime for anyone to instigate the escape or help someone escape in any way from the lawful custody of a federal officer. As this is a federal crime, it carries a much harsher set of consequences than a state crime would. Additionally, it became clear to HSCA Chief Counsel G. Robert Blakey that at the very least John Ray should have been prosecuted for perjury. Blakey said, 'They [John and Jerry Ray] lied about everything that they did. John Ray, as the final report says, was a bank robber, but he denied it. He lied. We referred him to the Justice Department for perjury charges. The department declined to prosecute. Said they didn't think it was prosecutable. I can tell you; it was a prosecutable case.'[57]

Ray family members were interviewed approximately fifty times between April and June 1968. Jerry Ray was interviewed at least ten times between 19 April 1968 and 1 May 1968. John Ray was interviewed at least four times between 22 April 1968 and 4 May 1968. While Ray was a fugitive the FBI requested the Department of Justice in a memo dated 3 May 1968 to approve surveillance at the residence of Carol Pepper and the Grapevine Tavern. The Department of Justice took no action and the request was withdrawn on 11 June 1968 after Ray was captured.[58]

It is clear the FBI failed to follow up the suspicions many agents held concerning the allegations that Jerry and John had assisted their brother in the commission of the murder of King. In a mea culpa, the FBI explained to an internal investigation body that the Bureau:

> ... apparently discounted the significance of any contact between Ray and his family ... while such contact may render any actions of the family member criminally liable, it is not generally pursued absent any evidence of direct participation in the crime ... we concluded that on the basis of the information which was uncovered, the Bureau should have pursued this line of the investigation more thoroughly ... the FBI discovered that the subject of the largest manhunt in history had been aided in his fugitive status by at least one family member.[59]

Many investigators including HSCA investigator Conrad Baetz, head of the Memphis FBI office Robert Jensen and Shelby County District Attorney William Gibbons believed Jerry and John Ray assisted their brother in the plotting and planning of the assassination. Sometime in 1969 Robert Jensen crossed paths with Jerry at Nashville State Prison when Jerry visited his brother James. 'If I had anything to do with it,' Jensen told Jerry, 'you'd be in there with him.'[60]

Author William Bradford Huie, who came to know all the brothers well during the period he researched the assassination for his book *He Slew the Dreamer*, gave tantalizing hints that both brothers engaged in a conspiracy with James to kill King. Huie wrote, 'I believe that one or two men other than James Earl Ray may have had foreknowledge of this murder and that makes it a little conspiracy. But if there was a conspiracy, I now believe James Earl Ray was probably its leader, not its fool or dupe.'[61]

There was also a number of journalists who came to the conclusion that the real conspiracy revolved around James Earl Ray's relationship with his brothers. Journalist Marc Perrusquia said there was a March 1969 tape recording of Ray's brother Jerry telling the *Conservative Journal* publisher Kent Courtney 'there was definitely a conspiracy'. Courtney contacted the FBI, but the Bureau did not follow through and have Courtney wear a 'wire' to see what more Jerry Ray might say. According to historian David Garrow, 'The FBI's failure to probe aggressively the 1968 activities of John and Jerry Ray was its worst shortcoming in the investigation of King's murder'.[62]

Accordingly, many people who were involved in investigating the assassination were left wondering why the FBI did not more vigorously pursue this line of inquiry.

Once Ray had been arrested it is possible that J. Edgar Hoover had become nervous about any further questions about how the FBI operated. The Director did not want to follow a path that might lead, through unintended consequences, to revelations about the FBI's illegal domestic intelligence programme COINTELPRO, which was designed to harass and discredit domestic extremist organizations (for example, KKK, student radical anti-war groups and the terrorist organization Weathermen) as well as the Civil Rights movement. Better to leave well alone.

FBI files confirm that the agency certainly wanted to wiretap Jerry Ray. However, ever conscious of infringements on the freedoms of US citizens, the FBI knew that tapping Jerry Ray's phone meant tapping the phones of the Sportsman's Country Club, where he worked. If the FBI had done that and if that had been detected the scandal would have been enormous and would have led to a successful suit for damages against the government. The members of the country club included some of the more prominent and important people of the area. HSCA Chief Counsel Blakey said the FBI could not 'win approval for wiretaps to snoop on Ray's brothers at the time, and so, a key question lingered, without a decisive answer'.[63]

Additionally, during their investigation of Jerry Ray for his possible participation in the assassination, the FBI failed to check his alibi at the Sportsman's Country Club. Not one witness was ever interviewed by agents during the original investigation. It was also clear that several other leads such as Jerry Ray's whereabouts the day his brother James purchased the rifle in Birmingham was never adequately pursued by the Bureau. In his first meeting with the FBI Jerry said that he had not seen his brother James since 1966. Although this was disproved by the Bureau within a few days, no action was taken against him for furnishing false information to the FBI – a federal offence. Additionally, the FBI knew that Jerry had covered up his pre-assassination contacts with James.

In fact, the FBI was so remiss in following up investigations of the Ray brothers the Justice Department sharply criticized the Bureau in 1977. The FBI was also censured once more by the HSCA. It was, in the words of the HSCA, 'an astonishing lapse'.

So why didn't James Earl Ray confess to the role his brothers played in assisting him to kill King when he knew he was dying in 1998? And why didn't his brothers admit to their role in the assassination after James died?

Following King's death Jerry Ray told FBI agents his brother James would 'never talk'. It was a 'family trait', Jerry said. None of the Rays talked.[64] In fact, James was so faithful to the code of *omertà* he would even lie about the circumstances of his Missouri State Penitentiary escape to hide the fact he had been assisted by fellow inmates who worked with him in the prison bakery. The Ray brothers' whole criminal careers were centred around a hatred for authority and a belief they should never admit guilt.

And, if James had managed to have his conviction for murdering King overturned, he would still have thirteen years to serve on his previous sentence for robbery. He had nothing to lose by adhering to his protests of innocence. As Ray noted in his autobiography, 'getting caught and doing time was a cost of doing business'.[65] And Ray knew there was a well-organized effort by his defenders nationally to set him free. Admitting guilt would, at one stroke, halt those efforts.

Ray had also used his 'hired assassin/innocent patsy' story to protect himself in prison. In May 1972 Deputy Warden of Brushy Mountain State Penitentiary Rolland Cisson responded to my question about why Ray was in a cell block which held both white and black prisoners. He said that although Ray's fellow inmates had been screened to ascertain those who might be a potential threat to Ray, black prisoners believed King was killed as the result of a conspiracy, and under an unwritten 'criminal code' that made Ray's crime excusable on the grounds he did it for money and not because of any racial animosity. (Unfortunately for Ray, Cisson's words proved to be premature. In 1981, while working in the prison law library four African American inmates attacked Ray leaving him with twenty-two stab wounds.)[66]

If Ray had admitted guilt in his dying days, he would have left his brothers open to a new investigation that would inevitably follow a 'confession'. Ray loved his brothers. In fact, James was a loner except for his brothers and his sister Carol Pepper, who managed James' earnings as a prison 'merchant'. He was the older brother who was looked-up to by the remaining family members. John is on record as saying, 'James would do anything for us and we for him.'[67] He is also on record as saying, 'My record shows I would always come to the aid of my brother, unless it involved hooking up with the mob for some long-term contract or relationship.'[68]

In his plans for the assassination James did not want his brothers to take the risk of accompanying him to Memphis. He was the older brother and he was the one who was already a fugitive from justice. He wanted Jerry and John's help, but he also wanted them to avoid arrest. James' intentions were to commit the murder then meet up with his brothers later after he had organized his escape to another country. But James was clearly unaware that the assistance the brothers gave him both before and after the assassination rendered them culpable to charges of aiding and abetting in the commission of the murder of King or even charges of being co-conspirators. As we have discovered, this part of the original FBI investigation was never fully examined.

The brothers had a pact never to 'snitch' on each other and never to do anything that would bring either of them under suspicion for any criminal act. Adhering to his long-held acceptance of the 'criminal code', Ray would not give up his brothers even to the point of death. Telling the truth about the assassination would leave both brothers open to charges of murder because there is no statute of limitations to first degree murder in Tennessee. Jerry and John remained free thanks to their older brother.

James Earl Ray also knew that both brothers had made a living out of their connection to him. The money came from attending conferences about the assassination organized by groups who promoted the idea that King had been killed by the 'Deep State'. If the brothers had come clean after James' death this source of money would have dried up. Ergo, it was the 'conspiracy industry' that prevented any further 'confession'.

James Earl Ray always believed he could beat any case he was charged with even to the point of foolishly representing himself in court. He was also a life-long 'jailhouse lawyer' studying the law and assisting other inmates with their cases and holding on to the belief that one day he could have his own case overturned or find some way to bamboozle a jury if he could only win a re-trial. Ray and his lawyer William Pepper continued to fight for his release until the very end.

It is possible Ray had an overwhelming desire to rid himself of his lifelong identity as a small-time loser with a $50 bounty on his head. Ray would grasp the nettle by killing King then, if caught, take the chance of facing a Southern jury which he believed might not convict him. Alternatively, he could ensure his place in history by spreading doubt in hinting at conspiracy. According to this strategy, Ray's construct of a plausible conspiracy held out some hope for an early release from prison – yet, at the same time he would bask in the notoriety that his crime provided.

In 1996 Ray's health began to fail markedly. He was hospitalized more than fifteen times between December of that year and April 1998, thrice lapsing into nearly fatal comas. He was refused permission to travel to Pittsburgh, Pennsylvania, for a liver transplant and denied clemency to spend his final days at his brother's home or a veterans' hospital. On 23 April 1998, Ray died of kidney failure and complications from liver disease.

After James' death in 1998 both brothers spent the next two decades – fifteen years in John's case and eighteen years in Jerry's case – refusing to confess to their role in the murder of King. Clearly, they did not want to spend their remaining years alive incarcerated because they knew that there was no statute of limitations on murder. Instead, they continued their lucrative business of playing the roles of brothers to James Earl Ray and attending numerous conspiracy conferences around the nation, appearing in television documentaries and television talk shows and marketing their tall tales of an FBI conspiracy to gullible audiences. As Jerry Ray said in 2003, 'some of the things I still can't tell because the statute of limitations hasn't expired … I don't want to go to jail. I'm too old to go to jail now.'[69]

Chapter 10

Missing Truths

Rather than build a case from evidence, conspiracists deny the available evidence, maintaining that appearances deceive. Rather than admit to inconvenient facts, they dismiss them as lies, making their own theories irrefutable.

Journalist David Greenburg

The fact that Ray is still alive is one of the best arguments against the existence of any sophisticated conspiracy. If the mob, government, or anything like that had been involved, Ray would not have lived for very long after King was murdered.

House Assassinations Committee Chief Counsel G. Robert Blakey, 1997

Two figures loom over the way in which the Kings have succeeded in making themselves into national laughingstocks. The first is Pepper, Ray's lawyer, whose outlandish claims of government involvement in King's slaying have been disproven and destroyed by both ABC News' *Turning Point* and CBS News' *48 Hours*. The Memphis district attorney's report highlights 'the pervasive mention of monetary reward that key witnesses relied upon by Dr Pepper refer to in their statements'. . . . Jack E. White accurately characterizes Pepper as 'either a credulous buffoon or a con artist'. Most people who've seen Pepper's work up close would vote for the second.

Professor David J. Garrow

In the years following King's murder the idea there may have been a conspiracy was not outlandish. There were questions to be answered and facts to be ascertained when investigators, both private and governmental, began to dig deep into James Earl Ray's crime and motives. And the FBI hinted at a conspiracy when it began its investigation of the murder. When James Earl Ray was posted on the FBI's 'Top Ten Most Wanted' list the word 'conspiracy' was mentioned. However, it led to unintended consequences and laid the groundwork for the belief that King was the target of a plot organized by the FBI or even the Johnson administration.

The conspiracy theories that emerged during the 1970s always ruled out the obvious and went for the most bizarre explanations. They were amateurish in that they discounted the views of mainstream experts, and premodern in believing that there were secret powers that caused everything to happen. Primarily, such theories existed to promote extreme political or ideological agendas not the discovery of the truth. Conspiracists began to immunize themselves to rational debate and argument by believing that everything is a conspiracy and to them the idea that men and women who worked for the FBI, the CIA and the Johnson administration would conspire together to murder Martin Luther King did not seem preposterous.

In the decades that followed the initial scepticism about the government's King assassination findings saw a poisonous Internet-driven fiction concocted by extreme conspiracy believers without the faintest grounding in reality. It occurred even after government papers had been released and US courts had repeatedly rejected Ray's pleas of innocence. Missing from their scepticism was the clear evidence of Ray's racist history and his strong connections with fellow racists who had long sought the elimination of Martin Luther King.

Today, being a subscriber to the alleged 'Deep State King conspiracy' requires you to express your passionate belief in things which are patently absurd and contradict empirical evidence. Conspiracy writers contend government employees, numbering in their hundreds if not thousands, toiled together, agreeing to commit murder, giving the assassins a free pass and in the process risked destroying everything they worked for in their careers – and exposing themselves to prosecutions for the crime of accessory after the fact to murder. Pepper and his fellow purveyors of a government conspiracy to kill King draw heavily on their imaginations and sprinkle their texts with faulty inferences. And the fact that they have not been able to come up with any credible evidence to prove their allegations does not trouble them in the least.

James Earl Ray intuitively understood that not only could he 'weaponize' this type of support, but he also knew that many Americans, including African American leaders, had one thing in common – a distrust of the FBI. And it was a distrust Ray could utilize to his benefit. He also exploited the fact that domestic and foreign journalists with an anti-American bias had promoted his story that the US president and the FBI had ordered King's assassination.[1]

Ray also knew that since the mid to late 1960s public opinion was highly susceptible to conspiracy ideas. The public were inundated with various theories about the assassination of President Kennedy. Many conspiracists insisted that had Lee Harvey Oswald gone to trial he would have been acquitted. It is likely Ray learned these lessons well, knowing he could influence public opinion by promoting the government-based conspiracy idea. Additionally, conspiracists could minimize the importance of Ray's guilt and maximize the importance of a government conspiracy because Americans wanted King's death to achieve equal importance with his life. Conspiracy ideas persuaded many to recast the evidence in the case in a form that fitted more harmoniously with the idea that King was so threatening to the power establishment he had to be eliminated by powerful forces.

Most unsettling about this case has been the response of many African Americans to the official government investigations of the murder. The majority of blacks, according to polls taken over the past fifty years, have indicated a strong belief that the state may have conspired to kill King.

The conspiracy idea among African Americans is traceable to dynamics rather than the merits of the case against James Earl Ray. From the start, they believed that King was the victim of the white establishment and their distrust of the state had historical roots. African Americans had every reason to be suspicious of governments on a local, state and federal level that sought to deny them equal rights.

Proof that African American communities were susceptible to conspiracy theories came in 1991 when an anonymous leaflet appeared in the North-East of the United States warning that a soft drink had been manufactured by the KKK and contained a sterilizing agent. Although the rumour was unfounded, sales of the drink plummeted. Rumours spread about other products and they also suffered a drop in sales.[2]

Journalist Andrew Ross attempted to explain this irrational thinking by citing African American leaders who blamed every ill on racism – conspiracy theories thus become an excuse for everything that ails black people. Ross said the African American community's leaders 'have become blame-mongers with little more to offer America's besieged black community than vague references to "forces out there", like "the CIA" and "white racism"'.[3]

One of the problems with the King murder case was the revelation that J. Edgar Hoover had conspired to bring down the Civil Rights leader and some historians accepted there was sufficient reason to at least suspect the involvement of the FBI and the Memphis police. There were even some white liberals who believed that Hoover's FBI was a hindrance to the advancement of equal rights for African Americans. As historian Gerald McKnight wrote, 'One does not have to be a committed conspiracy hobbyist to harbour a rational scepticism about the official solution to the King assassination. Delving into the crevices of the FBI's campaign to destroy King as a crusader for the poor and powerless raises deep-seated doubts about the good faith efforts of the government's investigation into his murder.'[4]

President Johnson and Attorney General Ramsay Clark put the FBI under enormous pressure. They wanted the federal government involved in the investigation into King's murder. As murder was the responsibility of the state, they needed to show that a federal crime had been committed and the charge of conspiracy to deprive King of his civil rights was chosen. Therefore, the word 'conspiracy', which appeared on the FBI 'Wanted' posters, was enough for some critics of the investigation to allege the government knew more than it was revealing.

However, as historian Gerald McKnight concluded, 'there is nothing in … released documents to support, and persuasive evidence to reject, assertions that the FBI and Memphis Police Department conspired to assassinate King'.[5] Furthermore, if Hoover had planned to neutralize King by killing him, he would have first destroyed the COINTELPRO records. It is also rational to conclude that the Bureau would never conspire with organizations or individuals outside the Bureau for such a risky undertaking. After all, the FBI maintained its power by acting as a state within a state. Any knowledge of its activities by outsiders would have left the Bureau extremely vulnerable. As FBI profiler John Douglas wrote, 'anyone who's worked in the government, even in the intelligence community, will tell you that NOTHING that big or well publicised stays secret for long. The big bureaucracy is fundamentally incapable of carrying out a conspiracy and keeping it under wraps.'[6]

There were, however, additional reasons why conspiracy thinking involving the government gained traction. The revelations that the US government covered up the truth about FBI domestic spying against US citizens and other government-sanctioned undemocratic activities by the CIA gained powerful political currency in the United States. The political culture of the United States in the late 1960s and 1970s was very favourable to any theory that gave credence to government-oriented murder plots against public figures who challenged the authority of the establishment. The public was confronted with a litany of stories about the Kennedy assassination, CIA plots against foreign leaders and the scandalous reports about J. Edgar Hoover's COINTELPRO. After Watergate many Americans simply lost any faith that their government would tell them the truth.

Additionally, Hollywood became interested in promoting outlandish conspiracy theories which spoke to government malfeasance. Hollywood movie director Oliver Stone employed the rhetoric of authentic history but not its method when he made his 1991 movie *JFK*. He managed to convince millions of people that a conspiracy was responsible for the death of President Kennedy even though the movie was chock full of errors and outright fabrications.[7] Stone later said he wanted to make a movie about King's assassination. Undoubtedly his methods would have mimicked his JFK movie. He told reporters, 'Johnson was a bastard, man. The King thing may have come from the top. I think it had to. Because I don't think military people, who I believe are involved, would do something of that nature unless they had a hierarchical OK.'[8]

The idea that murder investigations are always pristine added to the arsenal of allegations by conspiracists that all was not right with the King murder investigation. The conspiracists imbued each small anomaly in the collation and collection of the evidence with suspicion, casting doubt upon the entire official explanation. However, what they failed to see was there are *always* loose ends which can never be tied up. This was true of the King assassination no less than the Kennedy assassination. Law-enforcement officials are aware of this but not always the public. The Memphis Police Department and the FBI made fewer mistakes in the King case than in a typical murder case. In most criminal investigations even routine techniques like dusting for fingerprints are frequently overlooked. Moreover, there are very real limits to investigations. If the US public demanded 100 per cent certitude in order to convict very few cases would ever come to trial. There will always be mysteries, and even after a murder is 'solved' there will be evidence that just doesn't fit.

Ray clung to the idea of a vast government-led conspiracy to keep his case alive. In Ray's mind promoting a purported conspiracy organized by the government would give him the chance of freedom and, paradoxically, also provide him with the status of 'hired assassin' or 'co-conspirator' during his time in prison if he failed to secure his freedom. Additionally, the notion of 'conspiracy' increased the sales value of his story, providing him with finances he would need to fight his case.

There were sufficient reasons why Ray knew his conspiracy case would be vigorously promoted. Following the shooting of King newspaper editorials and television news questioned how Ray was able to finance himself on the run and whether or not he had been paid to kill the Civil Rights leader.

Conspiracists were at least partially in touch with the truth when they claimed that Ray had assistance in the crime. But the help Ray received was a far cry from the elaborate and speculative claims about a sinister FBI which were made by his defenders. As we have seen, there exists a wealth of evidence which could have been used to prosecute his brothers for assisting James Earl Ray in the execution of his crime. Although it is arguable the authorities had sufficient evidence to charge them as co-conspirators, it did not happen. This lack of diligence resulted in speculation that Ray was a patsy manipulated by powerful forces.

Conspiracists omit many established facts which are indicative of Ray's guilt. Law-enforcement officials, psychologists and members of the public who came into contact with Ray have testified to his pathological hatred of African Americans and his unstable mental state. Writers like Harold Weisberg, Ray's lawyers and apologists like Mark Lane and William Pepper are typical in how they have skewered the evidence in the case by providing gullible listeners with alternative but illogical contradictions to the work of the government agencies investigating this case as well as the ground-breaking research by writers like George McMillan, Gerold Frank and William Bradford Huie. Ray's drug use and pattern of criminal behaviour, for example, was frequently overlooked by them in their quest to prove Ray was essentially normal and had no particular dislike of African Americans. During William Pepper's quixotic efforts to free Ray, he placed innocent people in the firing line and displayed no shame in accusing them of criminal acts including perjury and murder.

Another example is how many discredited 'witnesses' are still used by conspiracy writers as proof of conspiracy even though authoritative inves-tigations and the work of independent investigators disproved their claims. Conspiracy writers, for example, invariably cite the lack of Ray's fingerprints in Room 5b of the South Main Street rooming house. This allows them to conclude that Ray had never been in the room instead of considering the possibility he wiped his prints from the furniture and doors. Although Ray has never admitted to wiping Room 5b clean of prints, he did admit to wiping his prints clean in his Atlanta rooming house.[9] Harold Weisberg promoted the idea that because Ray's fingerprints were never found on the Mustang the driver could have been anyone. What Weisberg fails to inform his readers, confused by the mountains of evidence in the case, is that Ray admitted wiping the car clean of prints after he abandoned it.[10] It is therefore also logical to assume he was careful enough to wipe his prints clean in his South Main Street room.

For each and every fact about the King case conspiracists have delivered their own biased interpretation. Conspiracy authors who investigated Ray's finances, for example, concluded that Ray must have received funds from purported conspirators. They did not consider the possibility he committed robberies during his time on the run. As his brother John told FBI agents, '[James never had] any real need for money as he was always able to pick it up by ways of burglaries or robberies during his travels'.[11] In all the states Ray travelled as a fugitive the FBI carried out enquiries. There were numerous unsolved robberies of banks, stores, petrol stations and liquor stores. The FBI assassination investigation, however, did not consider robberies which had a value of less than $5,000. In 2011 the truth about James' robberies while he was a fugitive in 1967/1968 was confirmed by his brother Jerry.

Conspiracists have insisted the map found in Ray's Atlanta rooming house did not bear the markings of King's home and headquarters but instead was marked to assist Ray in searching for accommodation and restaurants. They also maintain that no fingerprints were found on the map. However, the markings did indeed contain Ray's fingerprints and clearly indicated places where King could be found. The map did not have any markings indicating other places of interest.

Another technique employed by conspiracists is to discredit witnesses who bolstered the prosecution's case against Ray. One such technique was to introduce suspicion by alleging the witnesses had ties to government agencies, particularly the CIA. Both Priscilla Johnson McMillan and her husband George McMillan, who had written books about the Kennedy and King assassinations, were accused by Mark Lane of having links to government intelligence agencies. Both authors denied the allegations and no evidence to support Lane's allegations has ever been presented.[12]

Many other individuals have also been similarly accused of having under-lying motives in establishing Ray's guilt. When Percy Foreman advised Ray to plead guilty conspiracy writers concluded that Ray's lawyer did so to benefit from the Huie book deal in which Foreman had an interest. Foreman appeared before the HSCA and, under oath, said he advised Ray to plead guilty because the prosecutor's case left him no option but to save his client from a death sentence.

William Bradford Huie was accused of having a pecuniary interest in writing about Ray's guilt. In fact, Huie's articles for *Look* magazine, which preceded his book on the King assassination, were predicated on the likeli-hood that Ray had been part of a conspiracy. The articles were based on Huie's written interviews with Ray in which the assassin repeatedly embellished his story as Huie was later to discover. The author began his investigation of the King murder at the same time he was developing his findings for the magazine articles. Huie concluded that Ray had repeatedly lied to him and he found no evidence of conspiracy involving the mysterious Raoul. In fact, Huie admitted he would have been financially better off if he had he written a book outlining Ray's innocence.

The story of how and why King was murdered was also distorted by the many 'witnesses' who can forward long after the event to claim they had proof of a government conspiracy. Many, including Jim's Grill owner Loyd Jowers, thought they could benefit financially by supporting Ray. Ray's wife Anna came to realize how 'unscrupulous hucksters' who supported her hus-band had 'milked' the conspiracy story 'for all that it's worth'.[13]

And from the 1980s William Pepper led the charge, introducing outright speculation and alleged 'facts' without producing any evidence and naming innocent people in the process. Conveniently, evidence which Pepper claimed would support his conspiracy allegations had gone missing, including the rifle he alleges was used to shoot King (at the bottom of the Mississippi River), the Memphis Police Department shooter (dead before his accusers went public), the Mafia organizer of the conspiracy (dead before his accusers allegedly found evidence of his role in the crime), photographs purportedly showing James Earl Ray did not shoot King (they have never surfaced) and members of an army sniper team ready to kill King if the police department sniper failed (never named and 'living in another country').

Five government investigations have pointed the finger of guilt at James Earl Ray. The most thorough investigation correctly concluded Ray was motivated by racism and his idea that if he killed King, he could collect a 'bounty'. However, they failed to link him directly to any of the organizations calling for King's murder. But many people in the United States have not accepted that truth. For fifty years-plus the US public has been subjected to misleading and duplicitous accounts of the King assassination yet no credible evidence to support the idea of the existence of an elaborate Deep State conspiracy has surfaced. And the conspiracists have also been unable to explain how the elaborate and extensive 'conspiracy cover-up', which necessarily had to involve hundreds if not thousands of people, was able to remain hidden.

Every decision and every action taken by James Earl Ray in the year leading up to the assassination was taken by him and he was aided and abetted along the way by his brothers. No credible evidence exists that would indicate he was used as a 'patsy' or was otherwise manipulated by Deep State conspirators. Ray researched the rifle, the ammunition and the telescopic sight. He bought the Mustang, had it serviced, rented the rooms on his journeys, made his own telephone calls, bought his own clothes and had them laundered. Ray was identified as the person who rented Room 5b of the South Main Street rooming house and he was also identified as the lodger who left the rooming house following the shooting. Ray's fingerprints proved that he owned the bundle that was dropped in the doorway of Canipe's Amusement Store shortly after the shooting. The bundle contained the rifle used to shoot King. Ray had expressed hatred for African Americans; he was responsible for robberies before and following the assassination and he also knew how to go about getting a fake passport. He picked up his passport photographs and collected his travel documents. Incontrovertible and overwhelming evidence exists to prove these facts.

Professional criminals understand the vocational hazards of their chosen 'profession'. They must be willing to submit themselves, at some stage in their careers, to long stretches in prison. They may even view the possibility of prison as a welcome respite from their stressful occupation. Indeed, life on the 'outside' was, to a man like Ray, anxiety laden and stressful. He had spoken of how he became anxious, depressed and suffered severe headaches during his time on the run. In short, Ray had nothing to lose by chancing the 'big score'.

In many ways Ray's act of murder placed him in a 'win-win' situation. As a fugitive escapee he did not or could not settle down and seek permanent employment. And without a social security number, his jobs were likely to be short term at best. He could have continued his smuggling operations out of Mexico but, as all escaped prisoners are aware, time would eventually run out. He had the option of robbing banks, but this too would likely have ended in arrest and imprisonment. Had Ray been picked up for some petty offence, he knew he would be returned to the Missouri State Penitentiary to serve out the remaining thirteen years of his sentence – plus the added time for escaping. His status in prison would remain as it had been, small and unimportant. He was also approaching 40 and he could only look forward to spending his remaining years as a nondescript inmate. But killing King would enhance his 'professional status'.

In killing King, he had a number of options that could appeal to him whichever way events turned. He could kill King and escape abroad. Later when things had settled down, he may have been able to return to the United States in the belief a future president, perhaps George Wallace, would pardon him. If events turned out differently and he was captured the return to prison would be different; he now had the prisoner status he craved. Meanwhile, he would do what he was expert at – challenge the system, deny everything and pursue his 'career' as a jailhouse lawyer. He could introduce doubt about his guilt, which was the eventual path he took, so that in the future a reduced sentence might be on offer.

From the start Ray adopted an improvisational approach to his alibi. When researchers discovered new information that purportedly supported Ray, he would change his story to accommodate the new realities. Ray changed his story about fleeing the scene of the crime when a witness purportedly came forward to say that at the time of the shooting he was at a gas station. (The story was invented by his lawyer of the time, Mark Lane.) Ray constantly changed his descriptions of the mysterious Raoul when various 'witnesses' provided their own descriptions. Ray changed his story about the stalking of King when inconvenient facts came to light.

There is no evidence that James Earl Ray met with a 'mysterious Raoul' or had any conspiratorial contact with anyone except his family following his escape from the Missouri State Penitentiary. And it would have been simply too risky for 'Raoul' and other alleged conspirators to employ an escaped convict to commit a murder of a famous public figure. It would have decisively brought all leading law-enforcement agencies into play thus endangering their purported plot.

Furthermore, as FBI, DEA and AFT agents and local police departments know too well – in the 1960s hired killers with no direct links to any criminal or extremist group could be bought for as little as $3,000. This was no sophisticated murder, as conspiracy advocates maintain. King was an easy target for any killer bent on eliminating the Civil Rights leader. He did not have an armed guard; he frequently left his home on foot; and his travel arrangements were well publicized.

If Ray had indeed been aided by co-conspirators like the CIA or FBI, they would have spirited him away and placed him in hiding as soon as the murder had been carried out and then most likely have eliminated him before he could finger 'Raoul'. They would not have allowed him to be exposed so many times during his months on the run. Conspirators would not have put themselves in jeopardy by allowing Ray the opportunity to identify fellow conspirators. And, if Ray had been an unwilling patsy, conspirators could not have been certain that Ray would have fled the scene of the crime long before the shooting. In these circumstances the whole conspiracy would have collapsed.

Because Ray had proclaimed the existence of a conspiracy during his trial it is inconceivable purported conspirators, other than his brothers, would have allowed him to remain alive during his time in prison. There were simply too many risks and they would have been exposed. If government-led killers could successfully murder the United State's greatest Civil Rights leader and then cover up the circumstances surrounding the act, they would assuredly have had little trouble in eliminating Ray.

Racist groups, on the other hand, had nothing to fear. There is no evidence that Ray or his brothers had any pre-assassination contact with the people who offered the bounty, but it is likely they believed it was genuine. There is some evidence that one of Ray's lawyers, J.B. Stoner, knew the Ray brothers *before* the assassination and may have encouraged them to seek it. It is plausible Ray may have wanted to collect whatever money was on offer through his brothers at some future date. However, there is no credible evidence that he made arrangements to collect it prior to or following the assassination and there is no credible evidence any of the brothers collected it. Neither Jerry nor John showed any evidence of having come into money in the years after the assassination. And if the bounty had been collected, it would have negated any reason for John to rob a bank in 1970 for which he was convicted.[14] If a bounty was on offer and either of the brothers attempted to collect it, they were disappointed. And because such matters were dealt with through 'cut-outs', Ray or his brothers were in no position to name them if they had indeed been double-crossed.

The evidence for James Earl Ray's motivation is clear and unequivocal. He was an avowed racist who had expressed his opinions on racial matters numerous times since he was a young man. His selection of lawyers underscored the racial motive for the crime. He told fellow inmates and his brothers he was looking for the 'big score', aware that his burglaries, bank robberies and petty crimes had amounted to little. During his time spent in the Missouri State Penitentiary Ray had associated with known racist groups, was known to harbour knowledge about a 'bounty' on King's head and evidently believed he could beat any murder case brought against him if he could kill King in the Deep South if he was caught.

However, if these were indeed Ray's plans they failed miserably. It is also plausible Ray took photographs of the crime scene as 'proof' he had murdered King – but Ray admitted he threw the camera equipment away, probably in a state of panic, as he fled Memphis after the assassination.

Additionally, Ray's life had nowhere to go. He failed in his efforts to build a pornography business and his fugitive status made it too risky to continue robbing stores and banks. Making reference to the fact that after his arrest and trial he had ended up serving time in Nashville State Prison instead of the Missouri State Penitentiary, he told his brothers, 'Hell, I'm no worse off than I was before.'[15]

It is also clear that Ray's actions were not necessarily predicated on the provision of a bounty. He knew that his crime was of such overwhelming proportions that publicity generated by the murder would never die, especially in a country like the United States which categorized famous murderers as 'celebrities'. He was fully aware that the killers of Mississippi Civil Rights leader Medgar Evers and US Civil Rights activist Viola Liuzzo had been treated leniently by Southern courts which gave him hope he would also be set free. Book deals, magazine features and television companies would always be on offer to pay for defence lawyers and financial provision for his brothers – 'golden rain' as they called it. If he had been lucky enough to escape to a foreign country, he could have sold his story. He would also have been aware that racist right-wing organizations and a large body of US public opinion were behind him.

Ray had practised deception all his life. A psychiatrist employed by the Missouri state prison system had been convinced that Ray was capable of murder. Rather than the bumbling crook he is portrayed by his defenders, Ray was cunning, crafty and manipulative. Some of his lawyers have spoken of how Ray would control them. He was an astute 'jailhouse lawyer' who had spent years learning the fine points of the law, especially with respect to appeals procedure and how the law applied to the lawyer/client relationship. He knew how to keep his hopes for freedom alive.

In the real world accusation without confirmation is worthless. However, during his trial, Ray knew he had introduced enough doubt as to stimulate future public examinations of his case. He knew the idea of 'conspiracy' would keep his case alive in the public eye and there were plenty of Deep-State conspiracy believers to fight his corner.

Had there not been a climate of conspiratorial thinking engendered by the public doubt about Lee Harvey Oswald's guilt it is unlikely the King case would have been so intensely scrutinized and the facts skewered in order to fit outlandish theories. And keeping the real truth about the assassination hidden would not have been difficult for a man like Ray. He had always been a 'loner' who never fully revealed himself to anyone – not his brothers, his family, his fellow prisoners, his acquaintances or his lawyers. All of his life he had refused to cooperate with authority, had contempt for the whole justice system, defiantly mocked the police and concocted lies for his defence. He was devoid of any moral centre; he never felt the need to 'chew the fat' with anyone or to talk about himself.

Ray had initially promoted his 'conspiracy story' as a way out of the mess he had gotten himself into. He knew he would be spending the rest of his natural life in prison therefore his only hope was to insist he had been a mere 'patsy'. It is likely that his resolve in sticking to his story would have collapsed had it not been for the support he was given by conspiracists.

It was also evident that he was able to convince himself that he had a plausible case to make. In 1959 Ray had told an arresting police officer, 'I cannot deny it and I won't admit it.'[16] During the late 1970s Mark Lane had placed in Ray's mind the difference between 'truth' and 'legal truth'. Ray could therefore persuade himself that he was really innocent because the courts had not established the full circumstances of the crime. He knew that the assistance given by his brothers established, in his own mind, a case for conspiracy but he had no intention of giving them up in his quest for freedom. This was the reason why the polygraph results were inconclusive when Ray answered questions about a conspiracy. The same polygraph examiner determined Ray had been lying when he denied killing King.

* * *

James Earl Ray's wife Anna Ray, who had been married to the convicted assassin for twelve years, recognized how her husband was an expert manipulator and capable of immense cunning. According to Anna Ray, 'As far as James' intelligence, there are many things that James is very intelligent in, very crafty in, and one of them is paperwork and getting passports ... I saw the true James.' Anna also stated that her husband was a 'racist'.[17]

Anna Sandhu had met James in 1977 when he was tried in a court of law for an escape attempt. She was a courtroom artist and they struck up a friendship, began to correspond and eventually fell in love. They were married on 13 October 1978 and the ceremony was conducted by one of Martin Luther King' friends, Revd James Lawson, a committed conspiracist.

Anna Ray frequently visited her husband in prison. Their marriage was consummated under prison guidelines and she had initially been convinced of James' innocence. However, she filed for divorce in 1990 citing 'inappropriate marital behaviour'. Anna had turned against Ray when she discovered he was an 'expert manipulator'. She had become convinced Ray had killed King and told television talk show host Geraldo Rivera:

> At first I really believed [James] was innocent ... I thought I'd be very objective about it. Even after I was married to him, I still tried to be objective. But James is very persuasive ... It was only through time passing and trial and error and finding out from various people, reading various records, paying attention to James' personality changes and then the conversation on the phone that I couldn't believe when I was hearing it, I couldn't believe my ears and I was afraid of him ... I saw the true James.

The phone conversation Anna referred to was made in 1991. According to Anna, she asked her husband for some of the money paid for the Mustang when it was sold to a collector. Anna wanted the money to pay for repairs to her own car and needed a loan of $800. Ray said he had already sent the money to his sister Carol and in any case wanted to know if she had any collateral. Anna was shocked at the change in Ray's personality. Anna told her husband that she couldn't believe he was saying such things and told him she had always stood by him in his efforts to prove his purported innocence. It was then that Ray suddenly blurted out he had killed Dr King, 'Yeah, I did it – so what?' Ray then slammed the phone down. Anna told reporters, 'Until that point, I had believed James was innocent. He just seemed like a good guy who'd been framed … We never spoke again after that. Two years later we were divorced.'[18]

Presciently, Anna said, 'James will never admit to the killing again – he'll carry his secret to the grave. He's created a mystique by recanting his original 150-page confession. He doesn't want to go down in history as the killer of Martin Luther King Jr., so he'll deny it to his death.'[19] Anna's judgement about her late husband has never wavered in the years since she first revealed her belief in her former husband's guilt. In December 2002 she telephoned Gwen Harmon, the marketing director of the National Civil Rights Museum in Memphis, which was planning to exhibit freshly unsealed evidence in the King case, including the Remington rifle that killed King. When she was asked whether her husband killed Martin Luther King Jr, Anna told Harmon, 'He did it. Oh! he did it.'[20]

Notes

Introduction

1. Salon, 'Triumphant in Death' by David J. Garrow, http://www.salon.com/news/1998/04/28news.html.
2. 'MLK, JFK, RFK, Malcolm X, Celebs and Fams, MLK Demand New Probe … Assassinations Were Conspiracies', 19 January 2019, https://www.tmz.com/2019/01/19/jfk-rfk-mlk-malcolm-x-murders-assassinations-conspiracies-reopen-trc/.
3. *Washington Post*, 'Who killed Martin Luther King Jr.? His family believes James Earl Ray was framed' by Tom Jackman, 30 March 2018, https://www.washingtonpost.com/news/retropolis/wp/2018/03/30/who-killed-martin-luther-king-jr-his-family-believes-james-earl-ray-was-framed/.
4. Ibid.
5. Ibid.
6. *Washington Post*, 'Ray Tells Dexter King He's Not Assassin' by Pat Harris, 28 March 1997, https://www.washingtonpost.com/archive/politics/1997/03/28/ray-tells-dexter-king-hes-not-assassin/df7e743b-85f6-45da-97d2-b38caa82eab9/.
7. US Justice Department, 'Justice Department to Review Certain Allegations Regarding the Killing of REV. Martin Luther King', 26 August 1998, https://www.justice.gov/archive/opa/pr/1998/August/386ag.html.
8. *Atlanta Journal and Constitution*, 'New "leads" in King case invariably go nowhere' by David Garrow, 29 March 1998, https://www.davidgarrow.com/File/DJG%201998%20AJCMLKAssass29March.pdf.
9. Oberman and Rice, Trial Attorneys, 'Conspiracy', https://www.tndui.com/criminal-defense/knoxville-felony-offense-lawyer/knoxville-conspiracy-lawyer/.
10. Although I argue throughout this book that James Earl Ray was assisted in his crime and was aided by others, thus making the assassination a 'conspiracy', I use the term 'conspiracist' and 'conspiracy theorist' to denote those people who believe the assassination of Martin Luther King was organized by the US government and one or more of its agencies, including the CIA, the FBI and the Pentagon as well as the President of the United States. Some conspiracists also argue the government enlisted the assistance of the US Mafia to murder King. Conspiracists can also be identified because they adhere to a number of characteristics: they are

speculative, relying on conjecture instead of sound logic; they are amateurish in that they require crowd-sourced explanations of laypersons speaking outside their fields of research; and they reject the idea that human error can explain many anomalies that arise in official investigations.

11. *Washington Post*, 'Who Killed Martin Luther King Jr.? His family believes James Earl Ray was framed' by Tom Jackman, 30 March 2018, https://www.washingtonpost.com/news/retropolis/wp/2018/03/30/who-killed-martin-luther-king-jr-his-family-believes-james-earl-ray-was-framed/.

Chapter 1

1. M.E. Dyson, *I May Not Get There with You – The True Martin Luther King Jr.* (Touchstone, 2000), 153.

2. *New York Times*,' Excerpts From Justice Department Report on Dr. King Assassination', 19 February 1977, https://www.nytimes.com/1977/02/19/archives/excerpts-from-justice-department-report-on-drking-assassination.html.

3. The initial twenty-six hate groups targeted for possible COINTELPRO activities were:

   Alabama States Rights Party, American Nazi Party, Association of Arkansas Klans of the Knights of the KKK Association of Georgia Klans, Association of South Carolina Klans, Knights of the KKK, Christian Knights of the KKK – Hinton WV, Council for Statehood (aka Freemen), Dixie Klans, Knights of the KKK, Inc., Fighting American Nationalists, Improved Order of the U.S. Klans, Knights of the KKK, Independent Klavern, Fountain Inn, Independent Klan Unit, St. Augustine FL, Knights of the KKK, Mississippi Knights of the KKK National Knights of the KKK, Inc., National Renaissance Party, National States Rights Party, Original Knights of the KKK, Pioneer Club, Orlando FL, United Florida KKK, United Freemen, United Klans of America, Inc., Knights of the KKK, U.S. Klans, Knights of the KKK, Inc., Viking Youth of America, White Knights of the KKK of Mississippi, White Youth Corps.

4. D.J. Garrow, *The FBI and Martin Luther King, Jr.: From 'Solo' to Memphis* (W.W. Norton and Co., 1981).

5. Paul Letersky with Gordon Dillow, *The Director – My Years Assisting J. Edgar Hoover* (Simon & Schuster 2021), 86.

6. Some writers have claimed Hoover deliberately refused to crack down on organized crime because he was being blackmailed by the Mafia for living a secret life as a homosexual and that the FBI director had been blackmailed after powerful Mafia boss Meyer Lansky, an associate of mob boss Frank Costello, obtained

photographs of the FBI boss in a compromising position with his friend and top aide Clyde Tolson. The 'proof' about Hoover's homosexuality comes from a number of witnesses who said that they had seen compromising photographs. Former members of the Mafia or Mafia associates told of how Lansky pressured the FBI director into leaving the criminal organization alone. However, acclaimed Hoover biographers Richard Hack, Richard Gid Powers and Athan Theoharis all reject the claim that Hoover was homosexual. All three authors also successfully demonstrated that no evidence exists that would prove Hoover and Tolson were sexually involved. Theoharis, in his book *J. Edgar Hoover, Sex, and Crime*, Ivan R. Dee, 1995, said that the popularization of Hoover's homosexuality was the result of 'shoddy journalism'.

7. Thomas C. Reeves, *A Question of Character* (Bloomsbury, 1991), 16.

8. *Daily Mail*, 'Sex Tapes, FBI Smears and the Double Life of an All too Human Saint' by Tom Leonard, 31 August 2013, 50/51.

9. Garrow, *The FBI and Martin Luther King, Jr.*, 374.

10. O. Revell, *A G-Man's Journal – A Legendary Career in the FBI – From the Kennedy Assassination to the Oklahoma City Bombing* (Pocket Star Books, 1998), 535.

11. *Daily Mail*, 'Sex Tapes, FBI Smears and the Double Life of an All too Human Saint' by Tom Leonard, 31 August 2013, 50/51.

12. Dyson, *I May Not Get There with You*, 198.

13. *Sunday Times*, 'FBI Tapes Reveal Martin Luther King's Affairs with 40 women' by Tony Allen-Miller, 26 May 2019, 3.

14. Ibid.

15. Ibid., 31.

16. Ibid., 3.

17. *Daily Mail*, 'Shaming of an icon' by Tom Leonard, 30 May 2019, 30/31.

18. *Sunday Times*, 'FBI Tapes Reveal Martin Luther King's Affairs with 40 women' by Tony Allen-Miller, 26 May 2019, 3.

19. *Daily Mail*, 'Shaming of an icon' by Tom Leonard, 30 May 2019, 30/31.

20. Ibid.

21. *Sunday Times*, 'FBI Tapes Reveal Martin Luther King's Affairs with 40 women' by Tony Allen-Miller, 26 May 2019, 3.

22. *Martin Luther King – Days of Hope*, BBC2 Reputations, Black Audio Films Production for BBC, Producer Lina Gopaul, 1997.

23. Ibid.

24. *Daily Mail*, 'Sex Tapes, FBI Smears and the Double Life of an All too Human Saint' by Tom Leonard, 31 August 2013, 50/51.

25. T. Branch, *Parting the Waters – America in the King years, 1954–63* (Simon & Schuster, 1988), 239.

26. R.G. Abernathy, *And the Walls Came Tumbling Down* (Harper & Row, 1989), Introduction to paperback edition, xiv.

27. *Daily Mail*, 'Sex Tapes, FBI Smears and the Double Life of an All too Human Saint' by Tom Leonard, 31 August 2013, 50/51.

28. Ibid.

29. *Martin Luther King – Days of Hope.*

30. C. Carson and P. Holloran (eds), *A Knock at Midnight – Inspiration From the Great Sermons of Martin Luther King* (Warner Books, 1998), 197–8.

31. Letersky with Dillow, *The Director*, 84.

32. Ibid., 90.

33. *Roads to Memphis*, Producer Saron Grimberg, Assistant Producers Lynsey Megrue and Stephen Ives, Executive Producer Mark Samuels, Insignia Films, Production for WGBH Educational Foundation, American Experience, 2010.

Chapter 2

1. US Congress, 1979, Report of The House Select Committee on Assassinations, US House of Representatives, Ninety-fifth Congress, Second Session, 'Investigation into the Assassination of Martin Luther King Jr. – plus evidentiary volumes I – XIII', US Government Printing Office, Washington DC, 1979, 338, https://www.archives.gov/research/jfk/select-committee-report.

2. US Department of Justice, FBI MURKIN Files, Request No. 938718 – 1 Re: James Earl Ray, 245 files on 3 CD discs received from John M. Kelso Jr, Chief, Freedom of Information – Privacy Acts Section, Office of Public and Congressional Affairs, 12 July 2001, File 34, 121.

3. Ibid.

4. Gerald (Jerry) Ray, *A Memoir of Injustice* (as told to Tamara Carter) (Trine Day, 2011), 53.

5. FBI MURKIN Files, File 104, 196 and File 44, 64.

6. Ray, *A Memoir of Injustice*, 55.

7. Ibid., 54.

8. US Congress, HSCA Hearings, Testimony of Percy Foreman, Vol. V, 208.

9. *Illinois Times*, 2 April 2008, https://stlreporter.com/tag/jerry-ray/.

10. George McMillan, *The Making of an Assassin – The Life of James Earl Ray* (Little, Brown and Co., 1976), 299.

11. Gerold Frank, *An American Death – The True Story of the Assassination of Dr Martin Luther King, Jr., and the Greatest manhunt of Our Time* (Doubleday and Co., 1972), 10.

12. Gerald McKnight, *The Last Crusade – Martin Luther King, Jr., and the Poor People's Campaign* (Westview Press, 1998), 68.

13. Ibid., 69.

14. Ibid., 68.

15. FBI MURKIN Files, File 20, 95, MEMPHIS 44-1987, 11 April 1968.

16. *The Trial of James Earl Ray*, Presenter Sheena McDonald, Ex-Producer by Roger Bolton, Director Clive Halls, Producer Jack Saltman, HBO/Thames Television, 1993.

17. H. Hampton with S. Fayer, *Voices of Freedom – An Oral History of the Civil Rights Movement From the 1950's Through the 1980's* (Vintage, 1995), 467.

18. Martin Luther King Autopsy Report, http://jfk.hood.edu/Collection/Weisberg%20Subject%20Index%20Files/A%20Disk/Autopsy%20Martin%20Luther%20King%20Jr%20Dr%20-%20J%20T%20Francisco%20Dr/Item%2001.bak.pdf. See also, Chandler A. Long, MD, Theodore N. Pappas, MD, Kevin W. Southerland, MD and Cynthia K. Shortell, MD, 'An analysis of the vascular injuries and attempted resuscitation surrounding the assassination of Martin Luther King Jr', *Journal of Vascular Surgery*, Vol. 70, Issue 5, November 2019, pp. 1652–7, https://www.jvascsurg.org/article/S0741-5214(19)31808-7/pdf.

19. FBI MURKIN Files, File 20, 22.

20. Ibid.

21. Ibid., 35.

22. Ibid., 41.

23. Ibid., 33.

24. Frank, *An American Death*, 99.

25. FBI MURKIN Files, File 20, 33.

26. Frank, *An American Death*, 99.

27. Ibid., 98.

Chapter 3

1. John Larry Ray, *Truth at Last* (with Lyndon Barsten) (The Lyons Press, 2008), 72.

2. Ibid., 75.

3. McMillan, *The Making of an Assassin*, 251.

4. Frank, *An American Death*, 189.

5. FBI MURKIN Files, File 39, 8.
6. US Congress, HSCA Hearings, Vol. V, 10.
7. Ibid.
8. FBI MURKIN Files, File 55, 154, Memo dated 13 June 1969, from Director J. Edgar Hoover to Stephen J. Pollack, Asst. Att. Gen.
9. Frank, *An American Death*, 433.
10. James Earl Ray, *Who Killed Martin Luther King? – The True Story by the Alleged Assassin* (National Press Books, 1993), 102.
11. William Bradford Huie, *He Slew the Dreamer – My Search, With James Earl Ray, For the Truth About the Murder of Martin Luther King Jr.* (Black Belt Press, 1997), 163.
12. Scotland Yard File – James Earl Ray received from Richard Sharpe, 2 January 2001. Metropolitan Police Service, Records Management Branch, Archives Branch, Wellington House, 67–73, Buckingham Gate, London, SW1E 6 BE, File CR201/77/288, statement of Jane Nassau.
13. Metropolitan Police Service, Scotland Yard File on James Earl Ray received from Richard Sharpe, 2 January 2001, statement of Ian Colvin.
14. Metropolitan Police Service, Scotland Yard file, statement of Anna Thomas.
15. Metropolitan Police Service, Scotland Yard file, statement of Phillip Birch.
16. Ibid.
17. Metropolitan Police Service, Scotland Yard File, statement of Peter Elliot.
18. Frank, *An American Death*, 209.
19. Ibid., 204.
20. FBI MURKIN Files, File 60, 114.
21. Ibid., 245.
22. *Memphis Press-Scimitar*, 'Sneyd was Name Used in Letter', 12 July 1968, 7.
23. US Congress, HSCA Hearings, Vol. IV, 18–19.
24. Ibid.
25. Ray, *Who Killed Martin Luther King?*, 223.
26. In a letter to me the Metropolitan Police confirmed that Eist retired through ill health, not on suspicion of criminal acts, on 26 February 1976. He died on 27 January 1982. Letter to the author from Richard Sharpe, Metropolitan Police Service, 2 January 2001.
27. FBI MURKIN Files, File 66, 30.
28. Frank, *An American Death*, 332.
29. Ibid.
30. Ibid.

31. Ibid.

32. C. DeLoach, *Hoover's FBI – The Inside Story by Hoover's Trusted Lieutenant* (Regnery Publishing, 1997), 234.

33. Frank, *An American Death*, 37.

34. US Congress, HSCA Hearings, Testimony of Alexander Eist, Vol. IV, 18–19.

35. Huie, *He Slew the Dreamer*, 221.

Chapter 4

1. *St Louis Post-Dispatch*, 'Ray's Biographer Talks of King Plot' by Manuel Chait, 29 December 1968, p5c.

2. *St Louis Globe Despatch*, 'Police Doubt Ray Will Return to Area', 23 April 1968, p12a.

3. Frank, *An American Death*, 175.

4. FBI MURKIN Files, File 1, 35.

5. McMillan, *The Making of an Assassin*, 96.

6. Ibid., 12.

7. Ibid., 18.

8. *St Louis Globe Dispatch*, 'Ray's Prison Record Gives Little Light', 23 April 1968.

9. FBI MURKIN Files, File 52, 93.

10. McMillan, *The Making of an Assassin*, 146.

11. *St Louis Post-Dispatch*, 13 May 1968, 3D.

12. *Chicago Sun Times*, 'Schoolboy Ray a Star Pupil – In the Art of Theft' by Burnell Heinecke, 22 April 1968, 28.

13. McMillan, *The Making of an Assassin*, 100.

14. FBI MURKIN Files, File 35, 110.

15. Ibid., File 34, 98.

16. Ibid., File 28, 233, Memo supplied to FBI by US Army Adjutant General.

17. *St Louis Post-Dispatch*, 'Ray is Put on FBI Most Wanted List', 21 April 1968, p1A.

18. McMillan, *The Making of an Assassin*, 134.

19. FBI MURKIN Files, File 34, 103.

20. Ibid., File 62, 70.

21. Ibid., File 34, 121.

22. Huie, *He Slew the Dreamer*, 201.

23. Frank, *An American Death*, 292.

24. FBI MURKIN Files, File 52, 92.

25. *Newsweek*, 'The Saga of Jimmy Ray', 20 June 1977, 35.

26. *St Louis Post-Dispatch*, 'Ray's Biographer Talks of King Plot' by Manuel Chait, 29 December 1968.

27. Huie, *He Slew the Dreamer*, 111.

28. Gerald Posner, *Killing the Dream* (Little, Brown and Co. 1998), 97.

29. Ibid., 113.

30. FBI MURKIN Files, File 62, 165.

31. McMillan, *The Making of an Assassin*, 55.

32. FBI MURKIN Files, File 30, 155.

33. Ibid., File 240, 73.

34. Ibid., File 76, 81, FBI memo from J. Edgar Hoover to the FBI Special Agent in charge of the Kansas City office dated 29 January 1969.

35. Posner, *Killing the Dream*, 375.

36. Ibid.

37. FBI MURKIN Files, File 34, 144.

38. Ibid., File 50, 54.

39. Ibid., File 34, 145.

40. Ibid., File 34, 174.

41. Ibid., File 23, 253.

42. Ibid., File 16, 141.

43. Ibid., File 32, 176.

44. Ibid., File 36, 124.

45. *Cleveland Press*, 'Jail Mate of King Suspect Gives Clue to Phony Names' by Alan Horton, 23 April 1968, pA1.

46. FBI MURKIN Files, File 15, 29.

47. Ibid., File 105, 165.

48. Ibid., File 15, 29.

49. Ibid., File 104, 196.

50. Ibid., File 44, 64.

51. Ibid., File 52, 94.

52. Flashback, 'James Earl Ray, Killer of Martin Luther King, Stayed in Earls Court in 1968' by Rob Baker, 23 April 2016, https://flashbak.com/martin-luther-kings-killer-james-earl-ray-hid-earls-court-london-59188/.

53. FBI MURKIN Files, File 66, 38.

54. Ibid., File 44, 190.

55. Frank, *An American Death*, 422.

56. Ibid., 290.

57. FBI MURKIN Files, File 52, 9.

58. Ibid., File 41, 134.

59. Ibid., File 41, 79.

60. Frank, *An American Death*, 304.

61. FBI MURKIN Files, File 41, 122.

62. Ibid., File 52, 83 and File 205, 247.

63. Posner, *Killing the Dream*, 261.

64. US Congress, HSCA Hearings, Vol. XIII, 143–51.

Chapter 5

1. Pepper even included in his book *Orders to Kill – The Truth Behind the Murder of Martin Luther King* (Carroll and Graf Publishers, 1995) a photograph of McCullough kneeling over King's body moments after the shooting. But the man in the photograph is Earl Caldwell, the *New York Times* reporter. McCullough was at the scene moments after the shooting and tried to stem the flow of blood from King's wounds with a towel.

2. US Department of Justice, Investigation of Recent Allegations Regarding the Assassination of Dr. Martin Luther King Jr., Parts 1–6 (US Government Printing Office, 2000), https://permanent.fdlp.gov/websites/usdojgov/www.usdoj.gov/crt/crim/mlk/part1.htm, Part 3, 24.

3. US Congress, HSCA Hearings, Vol. IV, 278–80.

4. Frank, *An American Death*, 347.

5. In early 1971 Jones had been sentenced to an eight-year prison term in Leavenworth Penitentiary after he was found guilty of stealing social security and other government cheques from the mail.

6. US Congress, HSCA Report, 292, https://www.archives.gov/research/jfk/select-committee-report/part-2a.html.

7. US Department of Justice, Investigation of Recent Allegations Regarding the Assassination of Dr. Martin Luther King Jr., Parts 1–6, Part 3, 11.

8. Frank, *An American Death*, 86.

9. *The Trial of James Earl Ray.*

10. Posner, *Killing the Dream*, 272.

11. Frank, *An American Death*, 13, photograph.

12. US Department of Justice, Investigation of Recent Allegations Regarding the Assassination of Dr. Martin Luther King Jr., Parts 1–6, Part 3, 8.

13. *The Trial of James Earl Ray.*

14. FBI MURKIN Files, File 99, 109.

15. Frank, *An American Death*, 86.

16. US Department of Justice, Investigation of Recent Allegations Regarding the Assassination of Dr. Martin Luther King Jr., Parts 1–6, Part 3, 12.

17. *St Louis Post-Dispatch*, 'Ray Denies He Killed Dr King', 27 June 1968, 4.

18. *St Louis Post-Dispatch*, 'Ray Denies He Killed Dr King', 27 June 1968, 4.

19. Posner, *Killing the Dream*, 288.

20. Frank, *An American Death*, 438.

21. *The Trial of James Earl Ray*.

22. FBI MURKIN Files, File 20, 31.

23. US Department of Justice, Investigation of Recent Allegations Regarding the Assassination of Dr. Martin Luther King Jr., Parts 1–6, Jowers allegations, c. Jowers' alleged concealment of the murder weapon (3). Evidence that the assassin fired from the rooming house, https://www.justice.gov/crt/iv-jowers-allegations. On 18 July 1968, a few months after the assassination Stephens had taken Walden to a local hospital in Memphis as she had hurt her foot. Because she was in such a high state of anxiety and hysteria a staff psychiatrist, Mary Slechta, was called to examine her. Schlecta believed Walden was suffering from psychotic depression and was suicidal. The psychiatrist took the decision to commit Walden. After committal, Walden began to hear voices and tried to hang herself. She was diagnosed with schizophrenia and brain damage brought on by chronic alcoholism.

24. Frank, *An American Death*, 64.

25. Ibid., 65.

26. US Congress, HSCA Hearings, Vol. IV, 268–9.

27. McKnight, *The Last Crusade*, 75.

28. US Department of Justice, Investigation of Recent Allegations Regarding the Assassination of Dr. Martin Luther King Jr., Parts 1–6, Part 3, 23.

29. US Congress, HSCA Hearings, Vol. IV, 213, 218, 223, 228, 230–1, 232.

30. M. Newton, *The King Conspiracy* (Holloway House Publishing Co., 1987), 8.

31. FBI MURKIN Files, File 71, 226.

32. Ibid., File 79, 44.

33. US Department of Justice, Investigation of Recent Allegations Regarding the Assassination of Dr. Martin Luther King Jr., Parts 1–6, Part 4, 7.

34. FBI MURKIN Files, File 71, 226.

35. Ibid., File 152, 37, Interview held on 9 May 1968 at Tallageda, Alabama.

36. Ibid., File 9, 286, Interview with FBI agents held on 13 April 1968.

37. Ibid., File 103, 204.

38. Ibid., File 66, 182.

39. Posner, *Killing the Dream*, 327.

40. Ray, *Who Killed Martin Luther King?*, 96.

41. FBI MURKIN Files, File 116, 44.

42. Ibid., File 36, 124 and File 52, 94.

43. Ray, *A Memoir of Injustice*, 57.

44. *Washington Post*, 'The King Assassination Revisited: The $7000 Question: Where Did Ray Get The Money?' by Priscilla Johnson McMillan, 2 March 1997, https://www.washingtonpost.com/archive/opinions/1997/03/02/the-king-assassination-revisited-the-7000-question-where-did-ray-get-the-money/1965cc7a-0f7d-4e8f-9304-8b3b03c9e084/.

45. DeLoach, *Hoover's FBI*, 255.

46. US Congress, HSCA Hearings, Vol. VIII, 9.

47. Posner, *Killing the Dream*, 263.

48. McMillan, *The Making of an Assassin*, 240.

49. FBI MURKIN Files, File 30, 158.

50. Ibid., File 33, 153.

51. McMillan, *The Making of an Assassin*, 239–41.

Chapter 6

1. *Daily Mail*, 'My Trial on TV Will Prove I Didn't Kill MLK', 2 April 1993, 48.

2. The idea that the government was behind the killing was debunked by an unlikely source. In 1998, following his brother's death, John Ray told the *Memphis Commercial Appeal* he wanted a six-figure sum for evidence he had about the assassination. 'Once this comes out,' he said, 'it will direct a path away from the FBI to another source'. *Associated Press*, 'Justice Department Urges James Earl Ray's Brother to Come Forward', 1 September 1998.
   The information according to John Ray 'would enhance [James Earl Ray's] guilt so much people will probably take it he's involved'. World Africa Network, 'Reno Asked to Probe Whether Brothers Involved in King Assassination', by Marc Perrusquia, 14 September 1998.

3. US Department of Justice, Investigation of Recent Allegations Regarding the Assassination of Dr. Martin Luther King Jr., Parts 1–6, https://permanent.fdlp.gov/websites/usdojgov/www.usdoj.gov/crt/crim/mlk/part1.htm.

4. FBI MURKIN Files, File 20, 124.

5. Ibid., File 20, 125.

6. US Department of Justice, Investigation of Recent Allegations Regarding the Assassination of Dr. Martin Luther King Jr., Parts 1–6, Part 2, 2, https://permanent.fdlp.gov/websites/usdojgov/www.usdoj.gov/crt/crim/mlk/part3.htm.

7. *Memphis Commercial Appeal*, 'Jowers Claims, Contradictions Find 12 Believers', 11 February 2001.

8. US Department of Justice, Investigation of Recent Allegations Regarding the Assassination of Dr. Martin Luther King Jr., Parts 1–6, Part 3, 27, https://permanent.fdlp.gov/websites/usdojgov/www.usdoj.gov/crt/crim/mlk/part3.htm.

9. Ibid., Part 2, 2, https://permanent.fdlp.gov/websites/usdojgov/www.usdoj.gov/crt/crim/mlk/part3.htm.

10. William Pepper, *An Act of State: The Execution of Martin Luther King* (Verso Books, 2003), 229. Pepper also manipulated facts to suit new realities. For example, Ray always maintained he had heard the news about the assassination via the radio in the Mustang and Pepper supported that account. The Department of Justice investigation discovered the car radio did not actually work. Accordingly, Pepper wrote in his 2003 book, 'He headed south through Mississippi to Atlanta. On the way, he heard on his car *or some other radio when he stopped* [Author's emphasis] that Dr King had been shot and they were looking for a white man in a white Mustang.'

11. Pepper even gave credence to one of the Jowers-trial witnesses, fantasist Glenda Grabow and British citizen Sid Carthew. Grabow said she knew 'Raoul' and also Lee Harvey Oswald's killer Jack Ruby. She told Pepper that Raoul had shot President Kennedy. She also maligned the character of Lyndon B. Johnson aide Jack Valenti by describing him as a pornographer. Instead of showing her the door, Pepper enlisted her as a Jowers-trial witness. Carthew was important to Pepper because the ex-British merchant seaman recalled meeting a gunrunner by the name of 'Raoul' in Montreal in 1967. During the trial and in his book, Pepper described Carthew as a 'British Nationalist' clearly aware that most Americans would believe Carthew was nothing more than a 'British patriot'. Pepper did not, however, inform his readers of Carthew's political activities in Britain. For many years the British citizen from West Yorkshire had been a committed racist and a militant member of the racist British National Party, a political organization which has established close links to neo-fascist terror groups like 'Combat 18'. As the Jowers' jury had not been informed about Carthew's past, they were unaware of the British racist's politics. (See Chapter 7.)

12. US Department of Justice, Investigation of Recent Allegations Regarding the Assassination of Dr. Martin Luther King Jr., Parts 1–6, Part 3, 14.

13. Ibid., Part 3, 10.

14. Office of the District Attorney General 30th Judicial District of Tennessee, Open Letter and Overview of Evidence Against James Earl Ray, dated 27 March 1998, 5, www.personal.bellsouth.net.

15. US Department of Justice, Investigation of Recent Allegations Regarding the Assassination of Dr. Martin Luther King Jr., Parts 1–6, Part 3, 10.

16. Office of the District Attorney General 30th Judicial District of Tennessee, Open Letter and Overview of Evidence Against James Earl Ray, dated 27 March 1998, 3–4, www.personal.bellsouth.net.

17. US Department of Justice, Investigation of Recent Allegations Regarding the Assassination of Dr. Martin Luther King Jr., Parts 1–6, Part 3, 27 and 21.

18. Office of the District Attorney General 30th Judicial District of Tennessee, Open Letter and Overview of Evidence Against James Earl Ray, dated 27 March 1998, 5, www.personal.bellsouth.net.

19. US Department of Justice, Investigation of Recent Allegations Regarding the Assassination of Dr. Martin Luther King Jr., Parts 1–6, Part 3, 17.

20. Jowers Trial Transcript, Vol. XI, 2 December 1999, Testifying: Ms. Rebecca A. Clark, ex-wife of Captain Earl Clark, Memphis Police Department (1968), https://hvp4s20gv1q2qeztnp0fzp2u-wpengine.netdna-ssl.com/wp-content/uploads/2019/05/King_Family_Trial_Transcript.pdf.

21. US Department of Justice, Investigation of Recent Allegations Regarding the Assassination of Dr. Martin Luther King Jr., Parts 1–6, Part 3, 23.

22. Ibid., Part 3, 5.

23. Ibid., Part 3, 26.

24. Frank, *An American Death*, 143.

25. FBI MURKIN Files, File 18, 84.

26. Ibid., File 18, 83.

27. US Congress, HSCA Report, 386, https://www.archives.gov/research/jfk/select-committee-report/part-2c.html#mcferren.

28. US Department of Justice, Investigation of Recent Allegations Regarding the Assassination of Dr. Martin Luther King Jr., Parts 1–6, Part 3, 19, https://permanent.fdlp.gov/websites/usdojgov/www.usdoj.gov/crt/crim/mlk/part1.htm.

29. US Department of Justice, Investigation of Recent Allegations Regarding the Assassination of Dr. Martin Luther King Jr., Parts 1–6, Part 3, 20, https://permanent.fdlp.gov/websites/usdojgov/www.usdoj.gov/crt/crim/mlk/part1.htm.

30. Ibid., Part 3, 20, https://permanent.fdlp.gov/websites/usdojgov/www.usdoj.gov/crt/crim/mlk/part1.htm.

31. Ibid., Part 3, 20, https://permanent.fdlp.gov/websites/usdojgov/www.usdoj.gov/crt/crim/mlk/part1.htm.

32. Gerald Posner, *Case Closed – Lee Harvey Oswald and the Assassination of JFK* (Warner Books, 1993), 464.

33. MLK Conspiracy Trial Transcript Vol. 12, 4, Deposition of James Earl Ray taken on March 11th and March 12th 1995 in the case of James Earl Ray v Loyd Jowers, https://hvp4s20gvlq2qeztnp0fzp2u-wpengine.netdna-ssl.com/wp-content/uploads/2019/05/King_Family_Trial_Transcript.pdf.

34. US News and World Report, 'A Curious Conspiracy' by Chitra Ragavan, 20 December 1999.

35. On 20 May 2000 Loyd Jowers died. It was reported that Jowers, age 73, who was suffering from lung cancer, died from a heart attack.

36. US News and World Report, 'A Curious Conspiracy' by Chitra Ragavan 20 December 1999.

37. *Memphis Commercial Appeal*, 'Few Expect Impact in King Ruling', 11 February 2001.

38. *Memphis Commercial Appeal*, 'Few Expect Impact in King Ruling', 11 February 2001.

39. Office of the District Attorney General 30th Judicial District of Tennessee, Open Letter and Overview of Evidence Against James Earl Ray dated 27 March 1998, www.personal.bellsouth.net.

40. *Memphis Commercial Appeal*, 'Few Expect Impact in King Ruling', 11 February 1998.

41. Office of the District Attorney general 30th Judicial District of Tennessee, Open Letter and Overview of Evidence Against James Earl Ray dated 27 March 1998, Overview of Investigation of Allegations Regarding the Assassination of Dr Martin Luther King, Jr, E. Findings of Earlier Official Investigations, https://www.justice.gov/crt/overview-investigation-allegations-regarding-assassination-dr-martin-luther-king-jr.

42. McKnight, *The Last Crusade*, 81.

43. Barry Kowalski headed the inquiry. He was a Civil Rights litigator and prosecutor who successfully prosecuted the Los Angeles police officers who beat Rodney King. He also helped investigate the wounding of famous Civil Rights leader Vernon Jordan. Kowalski was a former Marine lieutenant who served in Vietnam. Following his service, he studied for a law degree and joined the staff of anti-war presidential candidate George McGovern during the 1972 campaign. He later taught law in Washington and developed a reputation for his integrity.

He successfully prosecuted KKK members in Alabama and the neo-Nazis who shot talk-show host Alan Berg. (*Memphis Commercial Appeal*, 'Justice's Pit Bull leads MLK Probe in DC', 31 January 1999.) Kowalski also developed a reputation for aggressively prosecuting Civil Rights violations.

44. US Department of Justice, Investigation of Recent Allegations Regarding the Assassination of Dr. Martin Luther King Jr., Parts 1–6, Part 6, 2, https://permanent.fdlp.gov/websites/usdojgov/www.usdoj.gov/crt/crim/mlk/part1.htm.

45. Salon, 'What "Truth" Does James Earl Ray Have to Tell?' by Andrew Ross, www.salon.com.

46. Investigative journalist Marc Perrusquia interviewed military historians, former high-ranking Pentagon civilians and high-ranking intelligence officers. He concluded there was no evidence to support the allegations that the army watched King day to day. He did, however, believe army agents occasionally watched the Civil Rights leader at public rallies.

47. US Department of Justice, Investigation of Recent Allegations Regarding the Assassination of Dr. Martin Luther King Jr., Parts 1–6, Part 6, 7, https://permanent.fdlp.gov/websites/usdojgov/www.usdoj.gov/crt/crim/mlk/part1.htm. Pepper's worst mistake was to name a former soldier without verifying if the facts were true. As Pepper told it, the commando of the sniper team Billy Eidson was then killed off to keep the plot secret. However, not only was the military cablegram Pepper produced declared a forgery (Posner, *Killing the Dream*, 312), but Green Beret Billy R. Eidson was found to be alive and well and angry that the allegations had been made against him. He was supported by General William Yarborough, the father of the Green Berets, and his chief aide Rudi Gresham. Members of the 'team' were invited to meet Pepper during the filming of an ABC television documentary. When they refused to shake Pepper's hand Ray's lawyer became speechless.

Billy Eidson brought a $15 million lawsuit against Pepper and his publishers and received an out of court settlement and a published retraction. Carrol and Graf, famous for publishing outrageous conspiracy stories about the Kennedy assassination, said, 'Some statements by the author about Billy Ray Eidson were not accurate. Carroll and Graf regrets that Mr Eidson was identified as the leader of a military team of snipers assigned as back-up for the assassination of Dr Martin Luther King. In view of the information received since publication, Carroll and Graf no longer believes that Mr Eidson was involved in any such assassination team.' *Memphis Commercial Appeal*, 'Book Publishers Retract King Plot Allegations' by Marc Perrusquia, 22 June 1999.

48. Associated Press, 'Investigation: No Conspiracy Found in King Assassination' by Michael J. Sniffen, 10 June 2000, https://products.kitsapsun.com/archive/2000/06-10/0066_investigation__no_conspiracy_foun.html.

49. William Pepper, *The Plot to Kill King* (Skyhorse Publishing, 2016), 262.

50. Ibid., 224.

51. US Department of Justice, Investigation of Recent Allegations Regarding the Assassination of Dr. Martin Luther King Jr., Parts 1–6, Findings Regarding Raoul, https://www.justice.gov/crt/overview-investigation-allegations-regarding-assassination-dr-martin-luther-king-jr.

Chapter 7

1. Posner, *Killing the Dream*, 115.

2. *The Guardian*, 'US feared for Luther King killer in British jail' by Jamie Wilson, 21 March 2001, https://www.theguardian.com/uk/2001/mar/21/freedomofinformation.politics.

3. Pate McMichael, *Klandestine: How a Klan Lawyer and a Checkbook Journalist Helped James Earl Ray Cover Up His Crime* (Chicago Review Press, 2015), 228.

4. Ray, *Who Killed Martin Luther King?*, 126.

5. McMillan, *The Making of an Assassin*, 246.

6. *Newsweek*, 'The Assassins: Who Did It and Why?', 24 March 1969, 18.

7. US Congress, HSCA Report, 306.

8. Ibid., 303, https://www.archives.gov/research/jfk/select-committee-report/part-2a.html#alibi.

9. US Congress, HSCA Report, Findings on MLK Assassination, Ray's Alibi, https://www.archives.gov(/research/jfk/select-committee-report/part-2a.html#alibi.

10. US Department of Justice, Investigation of Recent Allegations Regarding the Assassination of Dr. Martin Luther King Jr., Parts 1–6, https://www.justice.gov/crt/overview-investigation-allegations-regarding-assassination-dr-martin-luther-king-jr.

11. US Congress, HSCA Report, Findings on MLK Assassination Ray's Alibi, 303, https://www.archives.gov/research/jfk/select-committee-report/part-2a.html#alibi.

12. Huie, *He Slew the Dreamer*, 200.

13. McMillan, *The Making of an Assassin*, 256.

14. Ibid., 257. Author's Note: Ray and his brothers were congenital liars and McMillan was aware he had to check out every one of the brothers' utterances.

15. FBI MURKIN Files, File 30, 157.

16. Frank, *An American Death*, 309.

17. Ibid., 349.

18. Ibid.

19. MLK Conspiracy Trial Transcript Vol. 12, Deposition of James Earl Ray taken on March 11th and March 12th 1995 in the case of James Earl Ray v Loyd Jowers, https://hvp4s20gvlq2qeztnp0fzp2u-wpengine.netdna-ssl.com/wp-content/uploads/2019/05/King_Family_Trial_Transcript.pdf.

20. Ray, *Who Killed Martin Luther King?*, 90.

21. US Department of Justice, Investigation of Recent Allegations Regarding the Assassination of Dr. Martin Luther King Jr., Parts 1–6, Part 5, 1.

22. Philip H. Melanson, *The Martin Luther King Assassination – New Revelations on the Conspiracy and Cover-Up 1968–1991* (Shapolsky Publishers, 1991), 177–82.

23. US Congress, HSCA Report, 357.

24. *Who Killed Martin Luther King*, BBC, 1978.

25. Dan Rather – American Journalist, Document – James Earl Ray Transcript, https://danratherjournalist.org/interviewer/cultural-figures/james-earl-ray/document-james-earl-ray-transcript.

26. US Congress, HSCA Report, 298, https://www.archives.gov/research/jfk/select-committee-report/part-2a.html.

27. US Congress, HSCA Hearings, Vol. II, 70–85.

28. *TIME*, 'Ray's Breakout', 20 June 1977, 35.

29. US Department of Justice, Investigation of Recent Allegations Regarding the Assassination of Dr. Martin Luther King Jr., Parts 1–6, Part 6. Raoul and his alleged participation in the assassination, C. The Most Recent Allegations Regarding Raoul, 1. Raoul's Alleged Participation in the Assassinations of Dr. King and President Kennedy, https://permanent.fdlp.gov/websites/usdojgov/www.usdoj.gov/crt/crim/mlk/part5.htm.

30. Office of the District Attorney General 30th Judicial District of Tennessee Report, 27 March 1998, 8.

31. US Department of Justice, Investigation of Recent Allegations Regarding the Assassination of Dr. Martin Luther King Jr., Parts 1–6, Part 6, Raoul and his alleged participation in the Assassination, C. The Most Recent Allegations Regarding Raoul, 1. Raoul's Alleged Participation in the Assassinations of Dr. King and President Kennedy. https://permanent.fdlp.gov/websites/usdojgov/www.usdoj.gov/crt/crim/mlk/part5.htm.

32. Ibid., Part 5, 6.

33. Ibid., Part 4, 2.
34. Ibid., Part 4, 2.
35. *The Guardian*, 1, 4 April 1998.
36. US Department of Justice, Investigation of Recent Allegations Regarding the Assassination of Dr. Martin Luther King Jr., Parts 1–6, Part 4, 3.
37. *Memphis Commercial Appeal*, 'Ex-Agent Didn't Search Ray Car, Records Show' by Marc Perrusquia, 25 March 1998, 4.
38. FBI MURKIN Files, File 116, 75.
39. Ibid., File 71, 221.
40. Ibid., File 103, 231.
41. Ibid., File 78, 165.
42. Ibid., File 104, 48.
43. US Department of Justice, Investigation of Recent Allegations Regarding the Assassination of Dr. Martin Luther King Jr., Parts 1–6, Part 4, 14.
44. Ibid., Part 4, 11.
45. Ibid., Part 4, 15.
46. US Congress, HSCA Hearings, Testimony of Alexander Eist, Vol. IV, 18–19.

Chapter 8

1. McMillan, *The Making of an Assassin*, 101.
2. FBI MURKIN Files, File 18, 207.
3. McMillan, *The Making of an Assassin*, 146.
4. FBI MURKIN Files, File 46, 40.
5. Frank, *An American Death*, 296.
6. FBI MURKIN Files, File 30, 155.
7. McMillan, *The Making of an Assassin*, 285.
8. Ibid., 146.
9. Frank, *An American Death*, 274.
10. US Congress, HSCA Report, MLK Exhibit F-168, FBI Interview with Bo Del Monte, 22 April 1968, Vol. IV, 122 and FBI Interview with James E. Morrison, 22 April 1968, Vol. IV, 123.
11. McMillan, *The Making of an Assassin*, 279.
12. US Congress, HSCA Report, Dennis LeMaster interviewed by the HSCA investigators, 10 March 1978, MLK Exhibit F-171, 145, http://jfk.hood.edu/Collection/Weisberg%20Subject%20Index%20Files/H%20Disk/Hardin-Ashmore%20Records%20From%20Chip%20Selby/Item%2014.pdf.
13. FBI MURKIN Files, File 9, 281.

14. Frank, *An American Death*, 358 n.

15. Ibid., 207.

16. Ibid., 220.

17. US Congress, HSCA Report, Vol. IV, 18–19.

18. DeLoach, *Hoover's FBI*, 255.

19. Frank, *An American Death*, 357–8.

20. CBS, New York, *Geraldo*, Interview with Anna Ray, Directed by Robert Hersh, Tribune Entertainment, The Investigative News Group, 1991.

21. *Atlantic Monthly*, 'Lawyers and Lizard-Heads' by Douglas Brinkley and Anne Brinkley, May 2002.

22. FBI MURKIN Files, File 26, 119.

23. Ibid., File 124, 70.

24. Salon, 'What Truth Does James Earl Ray Have to Tell?' by Andrew Ross, 3 March 1997.

25. *Daily Telegraph*, 10 June 1968.

26. Nashville Scene, 'James Earl Ray Killed Martin Luther King Jr. Here's what's wrong with Sen. Frank Nicely's resolution related to the assassination investigation' by Betsy Phillips, 25 April 2018, https://www.nashvillescene.com/news/pithinthewind/james-earl-ray-killed-martin-luther-king-jr/article_db91961d-4e87-5afc-9fbe-855c7d9ed878.html.

27. Ibid. See interview of Harry Avery, 3 December 1976, House Select Committee on Assassinations, 12 (MLK document 040007); interview of Harry Avery, June 14, 1977, House Select Committee on Assassinations, 29 (MLK document 100051); memorandum to Governor Ellington from W.E. Hopton re: interview of Avery by Hopton, 20 May 1969, 1, 4 (MLK document 200472).

28. Michael Gabriel, *James Earl Ray – The Last Days of Inmate 65477* (Cat Yoga Publishing, 2003), 362–3.

29. The Daily Beast, 'Did the Klan Kill MLK? A New Book Argues Wide Conspiracy' by R.M. Schneiderman, 13 July 2017, https://www.thedailybeast.com/did-the-klan-kill-mlk-a-new-book-argues-wide-conspiracy?ref=scroll. To their credit, Wexler and Hancock are on track when it comes to how Ray may have gotten mixed up with extremist racist groups. In fact, the book is most convincing in arguing that a Civil Rights cold case unit should investigate King's murder especially the fingerprint files. Wexler and Hancock have no doubt Samuel Holloway Bowers, the head of the White Knights Ku Klux Klan, and J.B. Stoner, the lead lawyer for the NSRP, had links to the King shooting. Stoner had links to Jerry Ray. And there is some evidence that Stoner knew the Ray brothers before the

assassination. It is therefore possible Stoner encouraged the brothers to seek a KKK bounty. However, Wexler agreed that more evidence is required.

30. Ibid.
31. US Congress, HSCA Report, 248.
32. FBI MURKIN Files, File 46, 47.
33. Ibid., File 46, 40.
34. Ibid., File 46, 50.
35. Ibid., File 46, 45.
36. Ibid., File 44, 49.
37. Ibid., File 60, 52.
38. Ibid., File 30, 155.
39. John J. Dunphy, 'Why James Earl Ray Murdered Martin Luther King, Jr', https://johnjdunphy.medium.com/why-james-earl-ray-murdered-dr-martin-luther-king-jr-d8962d84b227.
40. US Congress, HSCA Hearings, Testimony of Edward Evans, Vol. VII, 293.
41. Ibid.
42. *Memphis Commercial Appeal*, 'Prosecutor's View is Unshaken: Ray Killed King: Wanted to be "Mr Big"' by Marc Perrusquia, 22 March 1998, go.memphis.com.
43. Salon, 'What Truth Does James Earl Ray Have to Tell?' by Andrew Ross.
44. McMichael, *Klandestine*, 246.
45. McMillan, *The Making of an Assassin*, 244.
46. *New York Times*, 'James Earl Ray, 70, Killer of Dr. King, Dies in Nashville' by Lawrence Van Gelder, 24 April 1998.
47. Posner, *Killing the Dream*, 123.

Chapter 9

1. *New York Times*, 'Ray's Brothers Tied to a Possible Plot', 28 November 1978, https://www.nytimes.com/1978/11/28/archives/rays-brothers-tied-to-a-possible-plot-house-unit-says-fbi.html.
2. FBI MURKIN Files, File 62, 208.
3. US Congress, HSCA Hearings, FBI interview with John Larry Ray, 22 April 1968, Vol. VIII, 34–5.
4. Frank, *An American Death*, 364 n.
5. FBI MURKIN Files, File 62, 158.
6. Ibid., File 62, 207.
7. US Congress, HSCA MLK Exhibit F-594, https://www.archives.gov/research/jfk/select-committee-report/references-mlk.html.

8. McMillan, *The Making of an Assassin*, 205.

9. Ibid., 258.

10. Ibid., 193. During the period 1969–72 the Ray family entrusted author George McMillan to write a biography of James. However, when McMillan indicated that he was consulting a number of psychiatrists who could attest to James' mental state, the family grew increasingly antagonistic. Jerry Ray subsequently claimed that he made up stories for the author. However, as Gerald Posner discovered, the stories told by Jerry Ray to McMillan which could be proven false were only given during the period when the relationship between the family and the author had broken down, therefore Posner deduced that stories told up to 1972 were accurate and truthful which included the statements about James' racist views and his hatred for Martin Luther King. (Posner, *Killing the Dream*, 34.) Jerry's foreknowledge of his brother's plans to kill King were investigated by the HSCA. The committee's investigators found proof of its veracity by examining the notes made by George McMillan. Additionally, William Bradford Huie corroborated McMillan's claims (which he swore to in an affidavit). In an April 1977 *New Times* magazine article Jeff Cohen and David Lifton wrote of how Huie confirmed McMillan's account in a phone call to them.

11. Huie, *He Slew the Dreamer*, 217.

12. McMillan, *The Making of an Assassin*, 259.

13. *St Louis Post-Dispatch*, 'Ray's Brother Insists: "He's Not A Murderer"' by Larry Fields, 14 March 1969, 2a.

14. Frank, *An American Death*, 351.

15. Ibid.

16. Ibid., 353.

17. Additional evidence proving John Ray kept in constant contact with James and continued after James went on the run after the assassination is contained in letters sent to James when he was in London. John intended to join him there. US Congress, HSCA Hearings, Testimony of John Larry Ray, Vol. VIII, 601.

18. FBI MURKIN Files, File 59, 48.

19. Gabriel, *James Earl Ray*, 339.

20. FBI MURKIN Files, File 52, 94.

21. Ray, *A Memoir of Injustice*, 53. In his memoirs Jerry also confessed to helping James escape from Brushy Mountain Penitentiary in 'late April 1971'. During a prison visit Jerry passed two hacksaw blades to James and told him to meet him at a church near the prison following his escape. Jerry prepared for his prospective meeting up with James by arming himself with a .45 automatic pistol which he

taped to the underside of his car. The plan was for Jerry to drive his brother to the nearest train station. However, Jerry waited for 2 hours but James never turned up. He had been unable to squeeze past steam pipes during his aborted escape attempt and was caught by a prison guard. Ray, *A Memoir of Injustice*, 119–21.

22. FBI MURKIN Files, File 240, 83.
23. US Congress, HSCA Report, 358.
24. Ray, *A Memoir of Injustice*, 84.
25. McMillan, *The Making of an Assassin*, 239.
26. George McMillan Papers, Southern Historical Collection, Wilson Library, University of North Carolina at Chapel Hill, cited in Posner, *Killing the Dream*, 223.
27. McMillan, *The Making of an Assassin*, 299.
28. US Congress, HSCA Hearings, Supplemental Studies Pertaining to the Motive of James Earl Ray, Vol. XIII, 64.
29. US Congress, HSCA Report, 336.
30. CBS, New York, *Geraldo*, Interview with Anna Ray, Directed by Robert Hersh, Tribune Entertainment, The Investigative News Group, 1991.
31. World Africa Network, 'Reno Asked to Probe Whether Brothers Involved in King Assassination' by Marc Perrusquia, 14 September 1998.
32. *Memphis Commercial Appeal*, 'King Conspiracy Theories Snowballed as FBI Sat Back' by Marc Perrusquia, 4 April 2002.
33. STL Reporter, 'Mob Action', 2 April 2008, https://stlreporter.com/2021/04/09/mob-action/.
34. Ibid.
35. US Congress, HSCA Report, 116.
36. Ray, *A Memoir of Injustice*.
37. *The Telegraph*, '50 Years Later, questions Remain About Alton Native Ray's Role in MLK Murder' by Tom Emery, 4 April 2018, https://www.thetelegraph.com/news/article/50-years-later-questions-remain-about-Alton-12804606.php.
38. US Congress, HSCA Report, 351.
39. Ibid., 104.
40. Ibid., 338.
41. Ibid., 353.
42. US Congress, HSCA Hearings, Testimony of James Earl Ray, Vol. III, 203; Narration of G. Robert Blakey, Vol. VII, 315, 317.
43. US Congress, HSCA Report, 338.
44. Ibid., 353

45. Ibid., 115.
46. Ibid., 353.
47. US Congress, HSCA Hearings, Testimony of Percy Foreman, Vol. V, 208.
48. US Congress, HSCA Report, 356.
49. Ibid., 358.
50. Ibid., 351–4.
51. US Congress, HSCA Hearings, Testimony of James Earl Ray, Vol. I, 100–1 and Vol. III, 215–22; Narration of G. Robert Blakey, Vol. IV, 8, Vol. V, 219–20, 331 and Vol. VII, 316, 318; Testimony of Jerry Ray, Vol. VII, 440.
52. *Illinois Times*, 2 April 2008, https://stlreporter.com/tag/jerry-ray/.
53. *Memphis Commercial Appeal*, 'King Conspiracy Theories Snowballed as FBI Sat Back' by Marc Perrusquia, 4 April 2002.
54. US Congress, HSCA Hearings, Vol. IV, 18–19.
55. Huie, *He Slew the Dreamer*, 204.
56. *New York Times*, 'Excerpts From Justice Department Report on Dr. King Assassination', 19 February 1977, https://www.nytimes.com/1977/02/19/archives/excerpts-from-justice-department-report-on-drking-assassination.html.
57. Salon, 'What Truth Does James Earl Ray Have to Tell?' by Andrew Ross, 3 December 2000.
58. Michael Friedly and David Gallen, *Martin Luther King, Jr – The FBI File* (Carroll and Graf, 1993), 693.
59. US Department of Justice, Report of the Department of Justice, Task Force to Review the FBI Martin Luther King Jr Security and Assassination Investigations, January 11th 1977, 101, https://www.google.co.uk/books/edition/Report_of_the_Department_of_Justice_Task/EG92AAAAMAAJ?hl=en&gbpv=1&dq=US+Department+of+Justice,+Report+of+the+Department+of+Justice,+Task+Force+to+Review+the+FBI+Martin+Luther+King+-Jr.,+Security+and+Assassinations+Investigations,+January+11th+1977,&pg=PP7&printsec=frontcover.
60. *New Times*, 1 April 1977, 37.
61. John Seigenthaler, *A Search for Justice* (Aurora Publishers, 1971), 166.
62. *Atlanta Journal and Constitution*, 'New "leads" in King case invariably go nowhere' by David Garrow, 29 March 1998, https://www.davidgarrow.com/File/DJG%201998%20AJCMLKAssass29March.pdf.
63. National Public Radio, 'Despite Swirl of Conspiracy Theories, Investigators Say the MLK Case is Closed' by Carrie Johnson, 4 April 2018, https://www.npr.

org/2018/04/04/598826351/despite-swirl-of-conspiracy-theories-investigators-say-the-mlk-case-is-closed?t=1647266103326.

64. Frank, *An American Death*, 181.

65. Ray, *Who Killed Martin Luther King?*, 42.

66. In 1972, on a fact-finding trip for the Bermuda Department of Prisons, I visited Brushy Mountain Penitentiary in Petros, near Knoxville, Tennessee. The prison held approximately 350 inmates, black and white, incarcerated in a racially integrated cell-block system. Surprisingly, Ray was held in cell block C housing twenty-one other inmates, many of them African Americans. At the entrance to the prison, I was met by the deputy warden, Rolland H. Cisson, who took me to his office to discuss the institution. Later, I met Warden Lewis Tollett. During our discussion James Earl Ray passed by the windowed office and Cisson commented about their 'star prisoner'. Cisson also told me that one of Ray's friends, a man whose name I can only remember as 'Williams', was one of Cisson's prison informants. Williams told Cissons Ray had confessed to him he had killed King. (See plate section.)

67. *St Louis Post-Dispatch*, 9 June 1968, A31 and US Congress, HSCA Hearings, Testimony of John Larry Ray, Vol. VIII, 589, 600.

68. Ray, *Truth at Last*, 52.

69. Gabriel, *James Earl Ray*, 409.

Chapter 10

1. *Atlantic Monthly*, 'Lawyers and Lizard-Heads' by Douglas Brinkley and Anne Brinkley, May 2002.

2. Daniel Pipes, *Conspiracy – How the Paranoid Style Flourishes and Where it Comes From* (The Free Press, 1997), 3.

3. Salon, 'Spitting on His Father's Grave' by Andrew Ross, 4 April 1997.

4. McKnight, *The Last Crusade*, 81.

5. Ibid.

6. John Douglas, *The Anatomy of Motive* (Scribner, 1999), 249.

7. JFK Assassination, 'A Review of Patricia Lambert's *False Witness*' by W. Tracy Parnell, 2000, https://www.jfk-assassination.net/parnell/fw.htm.

8. LeBeau's LeBlog, 'Oliver Stone – Stoned Again', https://lebeauleblog.com/2017/11/08/oliver-stone-stoned-again/2/, 8 November 2017.

9. US Congress, HSCA Hearings, Vol. IX, 229.

10. Ibid., 227.

11. FBI MURKIN Files, File 62, 206.

12. Mark Lane and D. Gregory, *Murder in Memphis – The FBI and the Assassination of Martin Luther King* (Thunder's Mouth Press, 1993), 245. For information about Lane's other abuses of the evidence in numerous cases see Washington Decoded, 'Mark Lane: The Original Shyster' by Mel Ayton, https://www.washingtondecoded.com/site/2012/05/lane.html.

13. CBS New York, *Geraldo*, Interview with Anna Ray, Directed by Robert Hersh, Tribune Entertainment. The Investigative News Group, 1991.

14. *Illinois Times*, 'The Assassin's Brother' by C.D. Stelzer, 28 November 2007, https://www.illinoistimes.com/springfield/the-assassins-brother/Content?oid=11441736.

15. Frank, *An American Death*, 403.

16. Posner, *Killing the Dream*, 125.

17. CBS New York, *Geraldo*, Interview with Anna Ray, Directed by Robert Hersh, Tribune Entertainment, The Investigative News Group, 1991.

18. Ibid.

19. Ibid.

20. *The Tennessean*, 'Gun That Killed King, Other Newly Unsealed Evidence on Display' by Brad Schrade, 19 January 2003.

Select Bibliography and Sources

Government Reports and Files (United States and UK)

Circuit Court of Shelby County, Tennessee for the Thirtieth Judicial District At Memphis. Trial Transcript, Coretta Scott King, et al., Plaintiffs, Vs Case No. 97242 Loyd Jowers et al., Defendants, 8 December 1999. Excerpt of Proceedings. Vol. I – XIV, https://hvp4s20gvlq2qeztnp0fzp2u-wpengine.netdna-ssl.com/wp-content/uploads/2019/05/King_Family_Trial_Transcript.pdf

Ford, Shelandra Y., Shelby County Register of Deeds, Dr Martin Luther King Assassination Investigation, https://register.shelby.tn.us/media/mlk/

Homicide Bureau Criminal Investigation Division, Memphis Police Department, Memphis, Tennessee, July 22, 1968, Mr W.P. Huston, Chief, Criminal Investigations Division Building Supplementary Report James Earl Ray, https://www.paperlessarchives.com/FreeTitles/MPDMLKHomicide.pdf

Metropolitan Police Service, Records Management Branch, Archives Branch, Wellington House, 67–73, Buckingham Gate, London, SW1E 6BE, File CR201/77/288, Scotland Yard File on James Earl Ray received from Richard Sharpe, 2 January 2001

Office of the District Attorney General 30th Judicial District of Tennessee, Open Letter and Overview of Evidence Against James Earl Ray, dated 27 March 1998, www.personal.bellsouth.net

State of Tennessee Department of State, Tennessee State Library and Archives, Tennessee Dept. of Correction James Earl Ray Inmate Records, 1952–98, RG 341, http://www.tn.gov/tsla/history/state/recordgroups/findingaids/rg341.pdf

US Congress, 1979, Report of The House Select Committee on Assassinations, US House of Representatives, Ninety-fifth Congress, Second Session, 'Investigation into the Assassination of Martin Luther King Jr. – plus evidentiary volumes I – XIII', US Government Printing Office, Washington DC, 1979, https://www.archives.gov/research/jfk/select-committee-report

US Congress, Senate Select Committee to Study Governmental Operations with Respect to Intelligence Activities (Church Committee), Final Report, Book III, Supplementary Detailed Staff Reports on Intelligence Activities And The Rights

Of Americans, 94th Congress, 2d Session, 1976, https://www.senate.gov/about/powers-procedures/investigations/church-committee.htm

US Department of Justice, FBI MURKIN Files, Request No. 938718 – 1 Re: James Earl Ray, 245 files on 3 CD discs received from John M. Kelso Jr, Chief, Freedom of Information – Privacy Acts Section, Office of Public and Congressional Affairs, 12 July 2001

US Department of Justice, Investigation of Recent Allegations Regarding the Assassination of Dr. Martin Luther King Jr., Parts 1–6, US Government Printing Office, 2000, https://permanent.fdlp.gov/websites/usdojgov/www.usdoj.gov/crt/crim/mlk/part1.htm

US Department of Justice, Report of the Department of Justice, Task Force to Review the FBI Martin Luther King Jr., Security and Assassinations Investigations, January 11th 1977, https://www.google.co.uk/books/edition/Report_of_the_Department_of_Justice_Task/EG92AAAAMAAJ?hl=en&gbpv=1&dq=US+Department+of+Justice,+Report+of+the+Department+of+Justice,+Task+Force+to+Review+the+FBI+Martin+Luther+King+Jr.,+Security+and+Assassinations+Investigations,+January+11th+1977,&pg=PP7&printsec=frontcover

Books

Abernathy, R.G., *And the Walls Came Tumbling Down*, Harper & Row, 1989

Baden, M. with Adler Hennessee, Judith, *Unnatural Death*, Sphere Books Ltd, 1989

Baird, R.M. and Rosenbaum, S.E. (eds), *Hatred, Bigotry and Prejudice – Definitions, Causes and Solutions*, 2nd edn, Prometheus, 1999

Blair, C., *The Strange Case of James Earl Ray*, Bantam Books, 1969

Bleiweiss, R.M. (ed.), *Marching to Freedom – The Life of Martin Luther King*, The New American Library (A Signet Book), 1968

Blumenthal, S. (ed.), *Government by Gunplay*, New American Library, 1976

Branch, T., *Pillar of Fire, America in the King Years 1963–65*, Simon & Schuster (Touchstone), 1998

——, *Parting the Waters: America in the King Years, 1954–63*, Simon & Schuster, 1988

Cagan, S. with Dray, P., *We are Not Afraid – The Story of Goodman, Schwerner, and Chaney and the Civil Rights Campaign for Mississippi*, Bantam Books, 1988

Carson, C. (ed.), *The Autobiography of Martin Luther King Jr.*, Abacus, 1998

Carson, C. and Holloran, P. (eds), *A Knock at Midnight – Inspiration From the Great Sermons of Martin Luther King*, Warner Books, 1998

DeLaughter, B., *Never Too Late – A Prosecutor's Story of the Justice in the Medgar Evers Case*, Scribner, 2001

DeLoach, C., *Hoover's FBI – The Inside Story by Hoover's Trusted Lieutenant*, Regnery Publishing, 1997

Demaris, O., *The Director, An Oral Biography of J. Edgar Hoover*, Harper's Magazine Press, 1975

Douglas, John, *The Anatomy of Motive*, Scribner, 1999

Dyson, M.E., *I May Not Get There with You – The True Martin Luther King Jr.*, Touchstone, 2000

Frank, Gerold, *An American Death – The True Story of the Assassination of Dr Martin Luther King, Jr., and the Greatest Manhunt of Our Time*, Doubleday and Co., 1972

Friedly, Michael and Gallen, David, *Martin Luther King, Jr – The FBI File*, Carroll and Graf, 1993

Gabriel, Michael, *James Earl Ray – The Last Days of Inmate 65477*, Cat Yoga Publishing, 2003

Garrow, David J., *Bearing the Cross – Martin Luther King and the Southern Christian Leadership Conference*, Vintage, 1993

——, *The FBI and Martin Luther King, Jr.: From 'Solo' to Memphis*, W.W. Norton and Co., 1981

Gentry, C., *J. Edgar Hoover – The Man and the Secrets*, W.W. Norton and Co., 1991

Hampton, H. with Fayer, S., *Voices of Freedom – An Oral History of the Civil Rights Movement From the 1950's Through the 1980's*, Vintage, 1995

Huie, William Bradford, *He Slew the Dreamer – My Search, With James Earl Ray, For the Truth About the Murder of Martin Luther King Jr.*, Black Belt Press, 1997

Kesler, R., *The FBI – Inside the World's Most Powerful Law Enforcement Agency*, Corgi Books, 1994

Lane, Mark with Gregory, D., *Murder in Memphis – The FBI and the Assassination of Martin Luther King*, Thunder's Mouth Press, 1993

Lesher, S., *George Wallace – American Populist*, Addison-Wesley Publishing Co., 1994

Letersky, Paul with Dillow, Gordon, *The Director – My Years Assisting J. Edgar Hoover*, Simon & Schuster, 2021

McKnight, Gerald, *The Last Crusade – Martin Luther King, Jr., and the Poor People's Campaign*, Westview Press, 1998

McMichael, Pate, *Klandestine: How a Klan Lawyer and a Checkbook Journalist Helped James Earl Ray Cover Up His Crime*, Chicago Review Press, 2015

McMillan, George, *The Making of an Assassin – The Life of James Earl Ray*, Little, Brown and Co., 1976

Melanson, Philip H., *The Martin Luther King Assassination – New Revelations on the Conspiracy and Cover-Up 1968–1991*, Shapolsky Publishers, 1991

Newton, M., *The King Conspiracy*, Holloway House Publishing Co., 1987

O'Reilly, K., *Racial Matters – The FBI's Secret File on Black America, 1960–1972*, The Free Press 1989

Pepper, William, *The Plot to Kill King*, Skyhorse Publishing, 2016

——, *An Act of State: The Execution of Martin Luther King*, Verso Books, 2003

——, *Vindication*, excerpts from the book (Chapter 9), The King Centre, theking-center.org, 2001

——, *Orders to Kill – The Truth Behind the Murder of Martin Luther King*, Carroll and Graf Publishers, 1995

Pipes, Daniel, *Conspiracy – How the Paranoid Style Flourishes and Where it Comes From*, The Free Press, 1997

Posner, Gerald, *Killing the Dream*, Little, Brown and Co., 1998

——, *Case Closed – Lee Harvey Oswald and the Assassination of JFK*, Warner Books, 1993

Ray, Gerald (Jerry), A *Memoir of Injustice* (as told to Tamara Carter), Trine Day, 2011

Ray, James Earl, *Who Killed Martin Luther King? – The True Story by the Alleged Assassin*, National Press Books, 1993

——, *Tennessee Waltz – The Making of a Political Prisoner*, St Andrew's Press, 1987

Ray, John Larry, *Truth at Last* (with Lyndon Barsten), The Lyons Press, 2008

Revell, O., *A G-Man's Journal – A Legendary Career in the FBI – From the Kennedy Assassination to the Oklahoma City Bombing*, Pocket Star Books, 1998

Seigenthaler, John, *A Search for Justice*, Aurora Publishers, 1971

Sides, Hampton, *Hellhound on His Trail, The Stalking of Martin Luther King and the International Manhunt for His Assassin*, Penguin Books, 2011

Theoharis, A., *J. Edgar Hoover, Sex and Crime*, Ivan R. Dee, 1995

—— (ed.), *From the Secret Files of J. Edgar Hoover*, Ivan R. Dee, 1993

Theoharis, A. with Cox, J.S., *The Boss – J. Edgar Hoover and the Great American Inquisition*, Harrop, 1988

Wexler, Stuart and Hancock, Larry, *Killing King – Racial Terrorists, James Earl Ray and the Plot to Assassinate Martin Luther King Jr*, Counterpoint, 2018

Articles

Long, Chandler A., MD, Pappas, Theodore N., MD, Southerland, Kevin W., MD and Shortell, Cynthia K., MD, 'An analysis of the vascular injuries and attempted resuscitation surrounding the assassination of Martin Luther King Jr', *Journal of Vascular Surgery*, Vol. 70, Issue 5, November 2019, pp. 1652–7, https://www.jvascsurg.org/article/S0741-5214(19)31808-7/pdf

MLK Conspiracy Trial Transcript Vol. 12, Deposition of James Earl Ray taken on March 11th and March 12th 1995 in the case of James Earl Ray v Loyd Jowers, https://hvp4s20gv1q2qeztnp0fzp2u-wpengine.netdna-ssl.com/wp-content/uploads/2019/05/King_Family_Trial_Transcript.pdf

Television Documentaries

CBS New York, Geraldo Interview with Anna Ray, Director Robert Hersh, Tribune Entertainment, The Investigative News Group, 1991

Martin Luther King – Days of Hope, BBC2 Reputations, Black Audio Films Production for BBC, Producer Lina Gopaul, 1997

Oprah, 'Martin Luther King', Kingworld, Harpo Productions Inc., 2002

Orders to Kill, Executive Producer Stephen Phelps, Producer and Director Tony Stark, Channel 4/Just Television Production, December 1999

Roads to Memphis, Producer Saron Grimberg, Assistant Producers Lynsey Megrue and Stephen Ives, Executive Producer Mark Samuels, Insignia Films, Production for WGBH Educational Foundation, American Experience, 2010

The Secret Files of J. Edgar Hoover, Castle Vision, 1989

The Trial of James Earl Ray, Presenter Sheena McDonald, Ex-Producer Roger Bolton, Director Clive Halls, Producer Jack Saltman, HBO/Thames Television, 1993

Who Killed Martin Luther King?, BBC, 1993

Who Killed Martin Luther King?, BBC, 1978